Sweatshop

Sweatshop

THE HISTORY OF AN AMERICAN IDEA

WITHDRAWN

LAURA HAPKE

RUTGERS UNIVERSITY PRESS
New Brunswick, New Jersey, and London

LIBRARY OF CONGRESS CATALOGING-IN-PUBLICATION DATA

Hapke, Laura.
    Sweatshop : the history of an American idea / Laura Hapke.
        p.   cm.
    Includes bibliographical references and index.
    ISBN 0-8135-3466-6 (hardcover : alk. paper) — ISBN 0-8135-3467-4 (pbk. :
alk. paper)
    1. Sweatshops—United States—History.   I. Title.
    HD2339.U6H37   2004
    331.25—dc22   2004000296

A British Cataloging-in-Publication record for this book is available
from the British Library.

Copyright © 2004 by Laura Hapke

Manufactured in the United States of America

CONTENTS

Acknowledgments

In my research on the American sweatshop, many individuals provided generous assistance. I had the privilege of interviewing members of Local 23–25 of the Union of Needletrades, Industrial and Textile Employees (UNITE): Miriam Baratz, Roosevelt Alexander, and their group of long-time colleagues at the New York City headquarters. Lisa Morancie, director of retiree programs at UNITE, provided important information on the workings of garment unionism in the 1990s, as did Lynda Whittaker and Mayra Mendoza at UNITE's New York City Apparel Project/ Worker's Justice Center. Patrizia Sione of the Kheel Center for Labor Management at Cornell University was patient and thorough in answering long-distance archival questions. In New York City, Michelle Fanelli, Elisabeth Birnbaum, and their staff at the Pace University Library were similarly attentive. Mark Rosenzweig of the Reference Center for Marxist Studies was a fount of information on the leftist needle trades. I am grateful as well to Rachel Bernstein of the Wagner Archives at New York University for Chinatown ILGWU photographs and Web site labor art. Tamiment Library at NYU was also instrumental in providing me with materials on garment workers' socialism.

In the course of researching the art of the sweatshop, I had the privilege of speaking with the filmmaker David Riker and of corresponding with the artist Sue Coe. They provided me with biographical material and insights that I could not have otherwise found. The Social Realist painter Eugene Salamin shared with me his recollections of organizing in the textile trades and the difficulties of shop-floor activism—and painting—in the period of the House Un-American Activities Committee. Roger Keeran at the Harry Van Arsdale School of Labor Studies has had a lengthy friendship with Salamin and speaks eloquently of him. The prominent artists Bernard and Honey Kassoy filled me in on New Deal– and Cold War–period subjects. Esther Cohen at the Bread and Roses arts project of UNITE was generous with her time. I was further informed by reminiscences about their garment-trades parents by Walter Srebnick, Antonia Garcia-Rodriguez, and Roger Salerno.

Jon Bloom of the Workers' Defense League gave me vital information on workers' rights in the new millennium; I am grateful too to the labor scholars who responded to my queries on the H-labor Listserv, among them Eileen Boris, Dan Bender, and Norman Markowitz, who provided bibliographical leads on the United States sweatshop and shared their conclusions about this unique American institution with me.

ABBREVIATIONS

ACW(U)	Amalgamated Clothing Workers (Union)
AFL	American Federation of Labor
CFA	California Fashion Association
CIO	Congress of Industrial Organizations
DOL	Department of Labor
EW	United Electrical Workers
FAP	Federal Artists' Project
HUAC	House Un-American Activities Committee
ILG(WU)	International Ladies' Garment (Workers Union)
ILR	Industrial and Labor Relations School, Cornell University
INS	Immigration and Naturalization Service
OED	*Oxford English Dictionary*
PWAP	Public Works of Art Project
UAW	United Auto Workers
UHT	United Hebrew Trades
UNITE	Union of Needletrades, Industrial and Textile Employees
USAS	United Students Against Sweatshops
USW	United Steelworkers of America
WPA	Works Progress (later Work Projects) Administration
WRC	Worker Rights Consortium

Sweatshop

CHAPTER 1

Narrating the Shop

"The aims of the imagination are not the aims of history."
—Cynthia Ozick, quoted in Sarah Boxer,
"Giving Memory Its Due in an Age of License,"
New York Times (1998)

THE SWEATSHOP IS as American as apple pie. But what has it meant to the American imagination? Scholars, of course, have long told the story of sweated labor. Of late, excellent work by Andrew Ross, Edna Bonacich and Richard Applebaum, and others has clarified our understanding of the sweatshop from its antebellum origins to the era of cyberspace.[1] My concern here, though, is the language, verbal and pictorial, in which the sweatshop is imagined and its stories told. A century and a half of writings on the shop, punctuated by graphic art, does more than narrate or define. Even in the writings of authors who seek "scientific" definitions, language itself undermines, refashions, challenges, and sometimes contradicts the official goals of policy makers, advocates, and workers themselves. For this multitude of storytellers, the invented is submerged in the real sweatshop. I use the word "story" here in the broadest sense. It is an imaginative construction, yes, but one that relies on the rhetoric, helps organize the knowledge, and is the repository of its culture's (or subculture's) beliefs and myths, assumptions, and prejudices.

Though such imaginings inevitably build on the troubling actuality, finding this real sweatshop is a difficult enterprise. The sweatshop has taken many different forms over the century and a half it has existed in the United States, yet it remains an exploitative urban workplace associated with the garment trades and still synonymous with the lowest and most degrading kind of American employment. There is no agreement on how many American sweatshops there are, where in this country they are actually located, how extensive they are, or what exactly constitutes one. The year 2000 Department of Labor (DOL) definition is correspondingly vague: "a place of employment that violate[s] two or more federal or state labor laws governing minimum wage and overtime, child labor, industrial homework occupational safety and health, workers' compensation or industry registration." Nongovernmental reform groups, though working loosely with that definition, broaden it further to include other working conditions that would not constitute DOL violations (such as working for abusive supervisors and not being able to take unpaid sick leave or vacation).[2] Unions themselves tacitly widen the scope outside the garment trades: the new UNITE, the onetime International Ladies' Garment Workers Union (ILGWU) antisweatshop watchdog of garment-trades socialism, not only is now a "Union of Needletrades, Industrial and Textile Employees" but also has satellite locals well outside of those trades. And a recent privately funded study that surveys Chicago's garment industry, still a principal sweatshop venue, showed that it was actually quite small compared to bicoastal ones, and argued that the new definition of sweatshop must be expanded to restaurants, domestic services, and light industry.[3]

Andrew Ross, whose groundbreaking anthology *No Sweat: Fashion, Free Trade, and the Rights of Garment Workers* limits itself to the clothing trades, writes that there is a "tendency to see sweatshops, however defined, as an especially abhorrent species of labor, and therefore in a moral class of their own. . . . People are more inclined to accept or tolerate the existence of labor conditions that cover the legal standards, but only barely. Sweatshops are seen to be morally and politically apart from the lawful low-wage sector, which is condoned as a result."[4] This moral and political distinction reinforces the perception of the sweatshop as a general description of exploitative labor conditions rather than as a "subpar outfit, as defined by existing laws in whatever country the owner chooses to operate."[5]

However broadly it is defined—for it comes in all shapes and sizes—the sweatshop retains its late-nineteenth-century association with the seamstress and the tailor. Candy wrapping, cigarmaking, and assembling artificial flowers were among a host of occupations inevitably bundled into sweated work, but the always pejorative label "sweatshop" remained synonymous with the Singer sewing machine, the hard-driving clothing-floor subcontractor, the ingenuous immigrant good with the needle, the piecework system. In fact, as Andrew Ross's subtitle ("Fashion, Free Trade, and the Rights of Garment Workers") indicates, the garment industry is a useful prism through which we can look at both the sweatshops of the past and the reemerging ones of today staffed by the newest waves of legal and illegal immigrants of the late 1960s and early 1970s from China, Korea, Southeast Asia, Mexico, the Dominican Republic, and Central and South America.[6] These workers join those earlier arrivals whose jobs were created by the growth of U.S.-based international garment production. As such, these new immigrants form the basis for a discussion of the changing nature of the workplace and of the American working class itself.

Any analysis of the impact of today's sweatshops, however, is incomplete without a look at Americans' historical response to the sweatshop. Have we viewed it as a social wrong? As a symbol? As an embarrassing reminder of immigrants? As a situation that ethnics, especially today's illegal immigrants, "deserve"?

Antonio Gramsci defined ideology as "a distorted vision of what is in fact the historical truth of a particular situation."[7] Nowhere have ideological battles about the shop and the events that affected them been more powerful than in New York City. New York is, of course, central to the American imagination of manual work in many crucial ways. The city was, among other things, a locus of middle-class reform campaigns against the "immoral" working poor, the "unwashed" tenement ethnic, and the propriety of women's paid work outside the home. Workers themselves saw the city as a mecca for self-transformation, especially economic, or alternatively as a place whose radical political ferment could transform and be transformed by the lived experience of class.

As a city in which all of these notions of class and gender mobility and stratification continue to be played out, New York provided the garment trade with a quintessential ideological battleground in its formative years. By the end of the nineteenth century, when the sweatshop was so pervasive as to be institutionalized, sweated labor venues in New York, from apartment size to factory loft, numbered in the thousands. Most were clandestine, closed to knowledge and inspection. Organizers with United Hebrew Trades (UHT) tried to persuade sweatshop workers not to choose competitive individualism over working-class solidarity. They

were faced, however, with a recurrent problem in clothing trades militance: the early strikes and walkouts were short-lived victories over shop
conditions more than drives for social justice. Nevertheless, with the
founding of the International Ladies' Garment Workers Union in 1900
and the Amalgamated Clothing Workers (ACW) in 1914, sweatshop in-
surgency began to gain members and bargaining power in the larger
struggle for industrial democracy.[8]

Chicago and Rochester were also prominent sweatshop cities in the
late nineteenth and early twentieth centuries, but New York City was by
default the premier sweatshop venue because it not only lacked mass-
production facilities but also had none of the heavily male industrial
unions that carried on interethnic battles in the cities to the west. Beth
Wenger makes the point that one garment-work hub, New York's Lower
East Side, was never "the Old World transplanted." Instead, in its heyday,
"the East Side reflected the social, economic, and cultural life of Jews
adapting to the American environment, not recreating the European
world."[9] Many of New York City's sweated laborers—East European,
Mediterranean, Asian—represented to the dominant culture the discourses
of otherness that the vested interests of the Gilded Age and Progressive
era had sought to transform into an "American" culture.[10] In the Depression era, New York's centrality to garment trade and sweatshop labor remained, despite limited New Deal collective bargaining gains. As late as
1948, the ILGWU cited peak membership, much of it in New York City.
The decades of postwar affluence and waning union clout saw reloca-
tions of the trade to right-to-work states and, as the 1960s began, increased manufacturing in Third World countries well removed from U.S.
minimum wage and unionism alike.

In the nation itself, waves of Third World immigrants in the 1980s
shored up old sweatshops and created new ones. By the 1980s, California
was fast becoming the largest garment manufacturing center and sweated labor hub in the United States.[11] Poorly organized, the apparel factories, often
staffed with undocumented Latina and Asian immigrants (mostly women),
easily fell beneath already poorly enforced National Labor Relations
Board/Department of Labor standards for pay and working conditions.

Periodic raids of sweatshops on both coasts continued to scandalize
and then be forgotten by the American public. By the late 1990s, Los
Angeles had eclipsed New York City as a garment manufacturing center,

but familiar terms such as "Chinatown sweatshop" continued to connote New York's Asian labor site. When the immensely popular television show *Law and Order* addressed the sweatshop as another indigenous urban problem, the subcontractors who even murdered in the name of sweatshop profits were fused in the show's typically hard-boiled fashion with the avarice of New York lawbreakers.

Whether limited to the industrial Northeast or expanded to other American and Third World cities, the term "sweatshop" periodically resurfaces and then disappears from the popular imagination. This association is not limited to the apparel trades: from the food-processing industry to the data-processing office floor, the worker is no stranger to the merciless speedup, the drastic pay cuts, the unhealthy environment, and the lawless boss. Yet garment trades exploitation has historically been both synonymous with the sweatshop and a barometer for exposés of shop-floor squalor, for antisweatshop movements, for management justifications, and for recurrent (and current, to judge by the furor generated by a 1997 Smithsonian exhibit) national debates.

Charting the idea of the sweatshop to the citizens of the United States is an important act of historical reconstruction. The core of my book is a study of the many representations of the sweatshop: prolabor, entrepreneurial, mass-cultural, social documentary, literary, and artistic. Necessarily, I am also interested in the battle to wrest representational control of the sweatshop narrative. Who would write the "song of the shop"? Who would paint or photograph it? Which were the more authentic narratives? What tropes, convictions, and fugues emerge consistently over time and across discourses? Does today's reiterated claim that sweatshops raise the standard of living in the Third World, combining global expediency with compassion, form a new narrative? Or is it simply the old story retold?

The sweatshop story has had highly visible narrators of many political stripes, and the book will consider three of the most numerous: reformers (surveyors and unionists), artists (painters and photographers), and managers (of cultural institutions and corporations). Satirizing the language of managers, the new student antisweatshop movement will provide a kind of antimanagerial postscript. These three groups in particular have addressed the "spectacle" of the shop for 150 years.[12] They are the narrators who have remembered and reinvented the sweatshop, or salvaged and sentimentalized it. On another level, elucidating the sweatshop as what Leon Stein famously called "a state of mind" contributes an alternative discourse to the study of resistance literature as well as to the "managerial narrative" that blames the victim. Taken together, these theme-specific pro- and antilabor texts (and those with divided loyalties) add a dimension to the study of the marginalized American worker.[13]

My contention is that those who have represented the sweatshop in narratives have done so as part of a larger American ideological battle between labor and managerial-corporate elements. Thus the shop was often presented not as a hopeless endpoint of exploitation for unskilled immigrants but rather as a transitional phase in the upward mobility, however "cramped," that awaited them as assimilated Americans. Whether such social fluidity was termed the "peculiar conditions of American life," the myth of the classless society, or American exceptionalism, the long-lived debate on it between these narrators framed the ways of mapping the shop.[14] Largely according to the "Americanness" of their views of working- and underclass immigrants, these narrators engaged in or rebutted militance, were apologists for sweatshop life as a "stage" in upward mobility, and aestheticized or expressed revulsion at "dirty" tenement-house ethnicity. Thus the sweatshop is an integral part of a nativist tide that ebbs and flows. From the late nineteenth century to our "global village" time, it has reflected a variety of ethnic, gender, and class prejudices. That this agenda exists alongside the sanitizing gentrification of labor-historical sites like Pennsylvania coal mines (now theme parks) and Lower East Side tenement houses (now museums) only validates it further.

As clothing-trades shops were the earliest and remain the most enduring symbols of sweated labor, my study is somewhat modest in scope, selective rather than exhaustive. I apply to sweatshop surveys Michel Foucault's notion of omniscient social surveillance.[15] This dominant social model is one in which agents of the state, physicians, social engineers, philanthropists, and others made sense of the shop in the "taxonomic" nineteenth century and the "social hygienic" early twentieth century. However many variants on perspectives of the sweatshop there were, at base was the conviction that assimilation would trade sweatshop debasement for social mobility. I then turn to those social protest painters and photographers who from the late nineteenth century to our time have produced an alternative approach that criticizes the assumption that sweatshops are a phase in the immigrant ascension tale. These visual storytellers, many from proletarian origins, made art of the shop, forging an aesthetics from the alleged ugliness of lower-depths subjects. The final section returns to sweatshop "outsiders," this time the managerial narrators—publicist creators of corporate Web sites and the like. I consider how the megabusiness "spin" on sweatshops repudiates the various reformist narratives of the past but recycles the cherished American idea of self-transformation through competitive individualism. Now the Third World sweatshop is nothing less than a vocational path.

Part 1 of the book, "The Sweatshop Surveyed" (chapters 2 and 3), covers sweatshops from their heyday to their supposed demise, 1840 to 1940. It establishes why it has been so difficult to conceptualize a tradition, however fragmentary, of sweatshop ascension and debasement narratives. Chapter 2 considers how a wide range of surveyors, their scope ranging from the antebellum Lowell mills to the "classic" turn-of-the-century tenement space, used the troubling idea of the destroyed domestic space to define the metropolitan sweatshop, particularly on New York's Lower East Side. Though the trope of the sweated worker's weakened body dominated the discourse, gender was at odds with class: Men's livelihoods, if not their very lives, were at risk of the sickness nicknamed the tailor's disease, consumption. Women's impaired vocational health was not framed in this way. Rather, theirs was dangerous eroticism or imperiled childbearing caused by the shop.

Garment workers brought to the New World an ethnic labor consciousness, whether that of an Italian anarchist or socialist or of a Jewish Bundist. In the contentious history of garment unionism, gender battles and beliefs were sometimes subordinated to working-class solidarity. Looking back over a half century of sweatshop representations, the second chapter traces mid- to late-nineteenth-century attempts to demystify the increasingly militant sweatshop for an audience without access to the "spectacle" of immigrant poverty. The shop found its vernacular voice in the 1890s, although the gender politics of the shop were such that in the writings of the best-known, and thus male, sweatshop bards, men's militant or weakened bodies were the chief subjects. When they spoke for women's struggles, they replicated the era's "separate sphere" ideology: a sweatshop was never woman's proper domestic space. Although there were many women reformers who deplored the imperiled sweatshop girl, the trope of rescue through marriage made little room for the feminine mass strike.

The chapter closes with the ways in which masculine sweatshop poets and novelists either diverged from or bought into the prevailing reformist notions of sweated workers as dirty ethnics. Again the gender difference was profound: men polluted or were polluted by tuberculosis germs, women by reproductive diseases. At odds on whether the sweatshop girl's shop-floor experience made her sterile, lustful, or both, there was no doubt that the dirt of the shop was symbolic as well as real. For both women and men at the sewing table, however, the shop housed multiple and contradictory meanings. By century's end it was as much a facilitator of assimilation as an epitome of exploitation.[16]

The third chapter addresses the chief sweatshop irony of the Progressive era: these shops were by then thought to be an anachronism. By acknowledging this curious survivor, the new industrial experts had to admit and wrestle with its longevity. Despite the enlightened reform measures and knowledge cornucopia generated by the "social engineers" of the Progressive movement, 1911 saw New York's worst industrial tragedy. Progressives had paid particular attention to the sweatshop as a woman-fueled site; in spite of this attention, the Triangle shirt factory fire took the lives of 140 immigrant girls and women.

The spate of strikes in the 1910s led by immigrant male clothing workers used the non-Progressive rhetoric of "taking down the shop," but that did not mean the sweatshop had become the bully pulpit of garment trade unionism. For one thing, men's voices dominated the discourse of unionism, while women, the unheralded sweatshop majority, continued to be overlooked by male unionists as spokespeople for the sweatshop experience. Not surprisingly, such gendered neglect extends to artistic representations of the shop. Early in our culture, a sweatshop school of imaginative art had claimed the prisonlike space of the garret and sub-basement. But because the sweatshop was a woman-filled space, a landscape of feminine oppression, those works have never been elevated to canonical status. Seeking rhetorics, conversations, subtexts, and iconic images, I consider the many Italian and Jewish memoirists, novelists, and reformers who wrote themselves into and out of the shop.

Alessandro Portelli, in his groundbreaking work on working-class oral history, has pointed out that what people remember is not so much a distorted version of historical truth as what that truth meant to them.[17] What do we choose to remember? How did sweatshop women in some sense create themselves? Françoise Basch, for instance, considers Theresa Malkiel's novelistic *Diary of a Shirtwaist Striker* (1911) crucially important in the era's narratives of female working-class life. How did such books in some way help to understand and even generate what Basch terms "female industrial fighters on the front line"?[18]

Chapter 3 of part 1 considers the "advances" in social scientific documentation in the 1920s and during the Great Depression, which were both officially postsweatshop eras. A wide range of sources maps the site. They range from the social-scientific 1910 Pittsburgh Survey tours of garment basements and factories, to female versus male unionists' appropriations of the lessons of Triangle, to the talkies of early Yiddish cinema. Whether the interpreter believed the sweatshop was a preindustrial dinosaur or looked back on it with recent loathing, its supposed obsolescence was never sure.

Knowledge building in this last decade of the sweatshop panopticon is above all methodical, prompting one former sweatshop girl, Anzia Yezierska, to give her 1932 novel about the late 1920s John Dewey study of Polish workers in Philadelphia the satirical title *All I Could Never Be*. Indeed, Yezierska's battle with Progressives (she became a case history in their files as an unfit working mother) mirrored the dueling visions of sweatshop life held by the social hygiene "experts" and by those who sweated in the shops. But as ethnic assimilation became a compelling theme for otherwise contending surveyors, the anachronistic "ethnic spectacle" of the shop continued to challenge cherished American myths of upward mobility.

Part 2, "Sweatshop Aesthetics," draws on the antithetical images of exploitation and sanctification that have pervaded the painting and photography of the sweated shop from the late nineteenth century to the golden age of worker art, the Great Depression. In the vastly different Works Progress Administration (WPA) canvases of Ben Shahn, William Gropper, George Biddle, and Moses Soyer, the sweatshop was truly transformed into art. Yet its antecedents were venerable, for sweatshop portraiture was grounded in a European studio tradition of sweating and sweated working-class subjects. (See, for instance, the industrial laborers, gleaners, and laundresses of Millet and Degas.) The fourth chapter thus probes how American artists working in the figural mode of painting departed from or harnessed the more "academic" art of the past. Influences aside, I argue that these WPA artists, many from proletarian backgrounds, did not remember the shop so much as they created it. Whether it was the proletarian slave site of Gropper, the feminized private space of Soyer, or the patriotic shop of Shahn and Biddle, these men's visual narratives of the sweatshop expressed the anxieties of their own time.

Women's body language is particularly important in 1930s sweatshop paintings. Whether lumpenproletarians, angelic martyrs, or eroticized working-class women, these seamstresses continued to symbolize the gendered nature of sweatshop representation that had characterized so many earlier observers of sweated labor.

The fifth chapter brings the visual study of sweated saints and slaves to our postindustrial time. Michael Denning in his superb study of Depression-era radical culture has found that tumultuous period marked by "the combination of a cultural politics and an aesthetic ideology."[19] Artists depicting the American sweatshop in the New Deal years and certainly in the Cold War ones did not, however, always share either political or artistic struggle. It may well be the function of the revolutionary artist to discover new pictorial modes as well as new uses for the old style. I consider the restoration of the subject in the beautiful sweatshop of Ralph Fasanella's paintings and drawings, the dystopian sweatopolis of artist Sue Coe, and the heroic shop of filmmaker David Riker. If they agree on little else, they are unified in representing the sweatshop as a labor icon in a fragmentary tradition of socially concerned artists.[20] For this generation of sweatshop artists, the question is not whether but how to modernize the subject in the name of conscience.[21]

Part 3, "Spinning the Shop," applies the question of who authenticates the sweatshop narrative to cultural, corporate, and watchdog institutions themselves. A highly controversial 1997 Smithsonian Institution exhibit, "Between a Rock and a Hard Place: A History of Sweatshops, 1820 to the Present" has been one of the most public examinations of sweatshop history.[22] It attempted the impossible: an acknowledgment of the long-lived history of the shop that somehow gave voice to labor and management alike. Instead it aroused universal criticism: unions found it biased against labor, and management disliked the recital of a long string of sweatshop tragedies, from the New York Triangle factory fire to the El Monte, California, sweatshop raided by the Immigration and Naturalization Service (INS) in 1995. Given the conditions in both, it seemed that in the worst of the shops little had changed in a century. How did the museum, intense media coverage, and successful lobbying by the apparel interests each in its own way use the show to rewrite the actual shop, as had so often happened in the history of the sweatshop idea?

The Smithsonian exhibit also contained carefully phrased self-advertisements for Kathie Lee Gifford, K-Mart, and other name-recognition clothing manufacturers that claim they follow a "workplace code of conduct" that obviates union or government inspection. Yet the apparel industry applauded itself far more effectively outside the Smithsonian Institution.

Chapter 7 discusses the ways in which American business has battled to recast the sweatshop past as a crucial part of its public relations campaigns for the allegedly enlightened approach of companies like Gap, Nike, and Liz Claiborne—all megaliths dependent on "offshore" labor. I examine ways in which escaping or abolishing the sweatshop has become a symbol of what sociologists call the "industrial sublime."[23] Dusting off old arguments about the sweatshop as an avenue of immigrant (or in this case, Third World) upward mobility, business interests have reshaped what is known as the "sweatshop quandary," or the theory of "sustainable development," into a defense of modern sweatshops as a venue for competitive individualism and self-transformation. In a parallel development, name-brand manufacturers from Guess to Gap purvey high-cost versions of blue-collar clothing as the last word in fashion. Whether insensitive to or subtly capitalizing on the irony, these "working-class chic" costumes are often the product of exploited tailoring, both offshore and in the United States. The discussion thus charts how, disrupting union discourse about the mistreatment of newly arrived immigrants and the union-busting campaigns of corporate America, the "industrial sublime" is successfully disseminated by corporations with batteries of lawyers and spin doctors.[24]

The final chapter finds that in the ideological history of the sweatshop everything old is new again. The social engineers and radical trade unionists of the early to mid-1900s could not, of course, reach cyberspace. The Web and its manifold sites have been crucial in expanding protest through grassroots activism, electronic or otherwise. As Students Against Sweatshops rally, march, and boycott, they continue the culture's century-and-a-half debate on the Americanism of the sweatshop. But it remains difficult to assess the ephemeral effect of service learning, sweatshop semesters, and community involvement for college credit.

If crusaders against the shop are to reach masses of people through stories of worker mistreatment and exploitation, they may wish to take into account that the shop has been a form of entertainment from George Lippard's lurid wronged seamstress tales to the *Law and Order* episode mentioned above. Exposés of sweatshops, however, no longer seem to shock. The time thus seems ripe, unfortunately, for sweatshop nostalgia. It is not impossible that a sweatshop will be recreated in much the same spirit as a cut-rate Colonial Williamsburg—a breach of taste committed in a tasteless time.

Reimagining the industrial and postindustrial sweatshop may indeed become bizarre contributions to cultural retrieval in the era of what the historian Mike Wallace, in reference to the Disney-sponsored Civil War battlefield replica, calls "Mickey Mouse history."[25] At a soon-to-be-venerable site in Monterey, California, there will be erected a sanitized set of the "Cannery Row" houses that supposedly inspired the Steinbeck title. Efforts to preserve the famously strike-torn Homestead space and that of Bethlehem Steel (which closed in 1998), however, have traded a vague nostalgia for a clear sense of the arduous labor once characterizing these sites. "We seem, as a nation, to lose our industrial places with much equanimity," observes a Pittsburgh steel mill history.[26] The New York City tenement house that is now the Orchard Street Museum makes a point of emphasizing the fond memories of the families who lived there. And the Ellis Island Museum of Immigration makes similarly rosy-hued use of immigrant ephemera. With renovated labor sites becoming such contested ideological terrain—a "commodified cultural product," to use Wenger's expression for the Lower East Side[27]—the Register of Historic Places elevates the ethnic subjects to almost mythical status and thus blocks off ways of knowing the shop historically. As ethnic suffering transmogrified into the successful struggle of immigrants to achieve a better life for their children and grandchildren, even the sweatshop may be reborn as "packaged, safe, and colorfully exotic."[28]

One publisher with whom I spoke about this project asked whether the sweatshop could have an intellectual history. This book helps answer that question, but only to raise new ones about the extensive symbolic and political weight this site has carried. In pursuing key types of narrative, *Sweatshop* lays the conceptual groundwork for other studies. There is certainly room for more exhaustive histories or those that go into greater depth. A rich periodical and reform literature from the antebellum era to the present offers multiple metaphors and presentations. Other scholars may examine the cyberworld of online exhibits, posted daily by sweatshop opponents and economic defenders. Finally, my discussions of what might be called the sweatshop lobby, which focus on corporate responses to the 1995 El Monte, Cailfornia, sweatshop raid and, over garment industry objections, its inclusion in a 1998 Smithsonian exhibit, may help inspire follow-up studies of manufacturers who continue to use sweated labor at home and abroad.

OVER THE PAST two centuries, metropolitan work cultures have evolved, and sweated workers have strengthened movements of resistance. It is still difficult, however, to conceptualize a sweatshop narrative tradition. Each hyphenated American group employed in the shop has engaged, upon escape, in a willful forgetting. In spite of the lived sweatshop legacy born of waves of mass migration, Americans express surprise at its continual rediscovery, whether in an illegal Long Island City loft, an offshore Nike plant, or the Honduran factories supplying the sweated products of cultural icon Kathie Lee Gifford, who famously promoted her clothing line in a disinformation campaign.

UNITE, the former ILGWU, publishes a consumer guide pointing out that "the care tag tells you how to treat the garment but not how the worker who made it was treated."[29] The best way to honor the sweatshop is not to idealize or sanitize, but to remember and acknowledge. Nor should we slight the eloquence and passion, individual and collective, unleashed at this site of oppression. The work of the cultural historian is to understand the contradictions inherent in the sweatshop's relationship, now a century and a half old, to the official myths of classlessness, guaranteed assimilation, and certain self-transformation. To that end I dedicate this book.

PART ONE

 *The Sweatshop
Surveyed*

CHAPTER 2

A Shop Is Not a Home

DIRT, ETHNICITY, AND THE SWEATSHOP

Lack of air, smell of lamps used by pressers, and
stench of filth made this a most horrible hole.
—Corinne Brown, in 1891, quoted in Katherine Kish
Sklar, *Florence Kelley and the Nation's Work* (1995)

WHEN THE PHOTOJOURNALIST Jacob Riis wrote, in narrating the Lower East Side sweatshop, that the "'homes' in these pictures are, truly, nothing but factories," he was wrestling with an issue that had long defined American sweatshop discourse. From antebellum times to the beginnings of Progressivism, observers of the oppressive environment of home industry pointed to it as a destroyer of the domestic space. By 1892, the subcontracting system at the heart of this exploitative labor site, routinely associated with the garment trade, was under serious scrutiny in Congress and had become the subject of a host of reform venues.[1] It was in the century's last decade that "sweatshop" joined, and eventually replaced, the earlier terms "sweated labor," "sweating system," and "system of subcontract" in the turn-of-the-century "discovery of poverty."

Well before the Industrial Revolution the word "sweater" had entered the language to describe "one who works hard, a toiler; a tailor who worked overtime at home for an employer." That large pool of textile workers came to the city in the wake of the Industrial Revolution and became part of "the sweating system," inspiring watershed works like Friedrich Engels's 1844 *Condition of the Working Class in England* and, five years later, Charles Kingsley's discussions of sweated labor in industrial production.[2]

A host of nineteenth-century articles discussed such solitary outwork and domestic manufacture, and the *Oxford English Dictionary*

(*OED*), "the [dictionary] most devoted to a single word," documents the shift in discourse.[3] By the early nineteenth century, the term "sweating" had become an umbrella for a quota system of subcontract in which the employer demanded outwork (or home piecework) while operating a centralized place of production, however primitive. In this proto-factory workspace, exploited labor either dropped off piecework or toiled along-side the well-paid artisan who also worked there. In further delimiting this space, the meticulous *OED* offered the definition that would have so many implications in the century and a half to come. As one of many subcategories of "sweat," it positions the new term: "Sweat-shop orig. U.S., a workshop in a dwelling-house, in which work is done under the sweating system (or, by extension, under any system of subcontract); also, *fig.* and *attrib.*" The dual British assumption is that sweatshops were in-digenously American and that the term was recognized as a descriptor before the Civil War. Controversy is embedded, however, in even such a brief formulation.[4] Contrary to the *OED*'s implied linkage of the "American" term with the Industrial Revolution, the explicit labeling of a poor dwelling or house as a sweatshop did not come into common parlance until well after the Civil War. Furthermore, the *OED*'s illusive term "dwelling-house" might be, variously, the tenement apartment "housing" the workers, whether or not it was used for living as well as working; an early factory with a master tailor and seamstresses of varied skills; or some ad hoc combination.

What can be accepted is that before there was an American name for it, the sweatshop from its inception was both a kind of workshop charac-terized by the "lowest paid, most degrading of American employment" and a symbolic labor environment for sweated labor conditions.[5] By the 1890s those conditions had changed very little since antebellum times. Why then such cultural diffidence about using the term "sweatshop"? How and when was the term for it employed?

Answers to such questions reside in tracing the connections between home and work from antebellum times through the classic sweatshop era of the turn of the twentieth century. We need to understand as well the complex moral and cultural implications of a place that functioned as both shelter and work site. The shift in the sweatshop from domestic to shop floor and later factory work space reveals how the prototypical sweatshop replaced the disrupted domesticity of early industrial piecework. In a wider sense, scrutiny of why it took so long to find and name the sweatshop can illuminate attendant cultural anxieties about ethnicity, class, and gender, especially notions of ethnic "purity" and "pollution."

BEFORE THERE WAS A NAME FOR IT:
SWEATED TAILORING BEFORE THE SHOP

In its construction of the sweatshop, the *OED* in fact delineates the antebellum American "sewing workshop." In abbreviated form, it was simply "the shop," but the meaning of that term would change radically with the rise of the Jewish labor movement late in the century. The massive British dictionary also assumes that a sewing shop was necessarily a sweated labor venue. Americans complicated and often feminized that idea. There arose a dichotomy between the "sweated workers," especially the poor and increasingly ethnic garret outwork population of indigent solo tailors, and the skilled male tailors and "lady seamstresses" who worked both "inside" and "outside" the shop. Native-born Protestants in a field whose lower rungs were neither, these people's skills—and in the women's case, their virtue—were considered beyond cultural reproach.[6]

Nineteenth-century representations of domestic outwork were not monolithic, but there were some dominant strands: Outwork was deemed appropriate employment for supposedly underworked antebellum women if the home itself did not furnish sufficient purpose. Underneath the myth was the grimmer reality for these women (even more than for somewhat better-paid men). The historian of antebellum women's labor, Jeanne Boydston, points out that by 1850, New York City's craft workers were put out of work as their skills were superseded by machines, and they were left to menial home labor. Especially in the large cities were they "among the most vulnerable of early industrial wage earners."[7]

Overriding this reality of homework, the discourse on women's sewing work soon accommodated the shift from domestic outwork to textile factory looms; the ideology of True Womanhood at the Loom arose to serve the profit-driven management at Lowell, Massachusetts, and the early mill villages. Lowell mill workers were not domestic outworkers but factory hands. They were among the earliest textile operatives, spinning yarn and weaving cloth, in contrast to those in home workshops and workrooms of the antebellum women's clothing trades. But at Lowell as well, a distaff industry depended on the groups of

Yankee daughters who endured industrial pollution and overwork, prayed in church in their few leisure hours, and went home to the board-inghouse dormitory under the watchful eye of a matron hired by the company. Extending working-class domesticity to the factory or work-room had its hazards, however: the moral implications of being in unpro-tected space, the dangerous ideas of economic self-sufficiency, and the ever-present threat of seduction and pregnancy. These labor historians explore how a Yankee female workforce, characterized as the daughters of native-born, yeoman farmers, legitimized, even as it saw the demise of, a manufacturing force that was never left alone and always protected.[8]

Lowell's managerial narrative, which touted its morally regulated group housing and state-of-the-art factory floor and was skillfully dis-seminated by that highly profitable enterprise, was at the opposite end of the spectrum from the pale but pretty solo seamstresses who sang "The Song of the Shirt," the title of a widely circulated 1843 poem by the Briton Thomas Hood.[9]

> With fingers weary and worn
> With eyelids heavy and red
> A Woman sat, in unwomanly rags,
> Plying her needle and thread—
> Stitch! Stitch! Stitch!
> In poverty, hunger, and dirt,
> And still with the voice of dolorous pitch
> She sang the "Song of the Shirt!"

Its easily memorized lyrics poeticized the childlike vulnerability of a de-fenseless garret woman, white-faced and hollow-eyed but still attractive. Why the poem caused, in the women's historian Christine Stansell's words, a "sentimental sensation on both sides of the Atlantic," is no longer clear.[10] Pulp novelists like T. S. Arthur caught the public mood it generated throughout the 1840s in *The Seamstress: A Tale of the Times* (1843). Perhaps the Hood poem's appeal lay in the catchy lament for her "sewing at once, with a double thread, / A Shroud as well as a shirt." She reaffirmed her purity with every stitch she took. Thus, though such women were icons of sewing slavery, they also countered the imagery of the seamstresses who took to streetwalking to provide for themselves.[11] In any case, these waiflike English-speaking unfortunates were among the first sweatshop dwellers. The attics and basement rooms where they subsisted were also sites of endless freelance labor. Thirty years later, popular magazines continued to play on the poem. One cover can speak for all: *Every Saturday*'s October 29, 1870, issue featured a pretty, sad-eyed seamstress seated near her attic candle, shedding tears while sewing a shroudlike garment.

Wraithlike white men sang the song of the shirt, too: Cornelius Mathews's novel *The Career of Puffer Hopkins* (1842) features a scene between a master tailor and his wretched skilled employee, Fob, exiled to outwork in his garret. The piece was unusual in the period for its focus on the tenement home of a bachelor with no band of clinging children or invalid seamstress wife. It conforms to the city novel's emphasis on the extreme differences between the employer and employee classes. Having arrived to pick up some finished work, the master exhorts Fob to sew until he dies ("overwork yourself, Fob") and guarantees him a handsome burial.[12]

George Lippard, the eccentric founder of the secretive labor organization the Brotherhood of America, was another well-known period writer who used fiction to call attention to the wrongs suffered by both male and female clothing workers. Active in early guildlike industrial organizations, he addressed in most of his writings the self-employed craftsman reduced to beggary by de-skilling. Departing in his unfinished novel *The Nazarene* (1846) from his emphasis on artisans, however, he links the antebellum slave quarters with a kind of early industrial servitude. "The factory," he comments, "is a slave 'house,'" one too horrible to visit. Establishing the shop as a closed-off horror, he continues: "You may be sure, that for one mile round this slave-house, the very air is tainted with misery."[13]

Lippard's devoted readers expected this "mammoth factory" to leave verisimilitude behind. His version of a Lowell enterprise is a combination of city state and torture chamber. Audiences savored his hyperbolic prose and sadistic depictions of this "immense structure, filled with innumerable looms, and thundering with the roar of the Steam Engine." There, Lippard explained with more imagination than accuracy, the textile worker and the sweatshop tailor somehow worked in tandem. What struck his narrator was the labor symbolism: Under the lash of capitalism, every worker gives his body up to help "coin our thousands, our tens of thousands of bright, round, solid, beautiful dollars."[14]

Lippard well knew that such rabble-rousing socialism needed a
Gothic overlay. But he also took care to play on the fears of his white audience, which included working people, of what the nativist elements in
the labor movement called "nigger work." Even as he acknowledged labor
exploitation, Lippard retained the distancing language of observers. More
outside than in, he did not elaborate. In his fantasy, the sweatshop was no
more than a set of props. The real melodrama took place elsewhere.

What was firmly ensconced instead in the cultural vocabulary of exploited labor was the home as the site of the "outside system." Images
had yet to coalesce around a permanently exploited sewing class at labor
in a dwelling not intended as or suitable for a clothing-trades workshop.
Ultimately, though, physical locale mattered less than the stark fact of
underpaid outwork. Hence the vagueness in defining an antebellum
sewing space that was a combined prison, home, and workplace. That
form of light industry had yet to be consolidated under the term "sweatshop." The venue was less crucial than the narrative of such downward
mobility, for the sewing-slave convention, at least for the major players,
most often involved a fall from affluence or gentility. (Presumably Lippard's "slaves," on the other hand, had been born in abject poverty.)

A corollary assumption, which was later to be enlarged in the dominant sweatshop narratives of the late nineteenth century, was that the
garment worker's home had been disrupted or preempted by the very
necessity to labor there.[15] The reformer and women's novelist Elizabeth
Stuart Phelps, in an 1869 address, voiced a common worry. Sewing
women were so used up by their piecework travels from contractor to
home and back that they had made no proper home for themselves.[16]
Even worse, they were periodically ejected from their meager rooms because, paid so sporadically, they could not pay the rent. Phelps was harking back here on one level to the antebellum preoccupation with
workers, particularly women workers, uprooted by poverty. On the other
hand, she anticipated the sweated worker (with or without sewing machine) who was herself a portable shop.[17]

Attempting more rigorous assessments than the trope of the "Song
of the Shirt," others did attempt to study such abodes, among other
workplaces, in Dr. John Griscom's *Sanitary Condition of the Laboring Population of New York* (1845). But a taxonomy of workers' bodies did little to
penetrate the continuing cultural and linguistic vagueness about where

the site was located, who dwelled and worked there, and what kind of labor they did.

HOME ALONE: UPDATING THE "SONG OF THE SHIRT"

The "Song of the Shirt" was a fixture of British sweatshop discourse from the 1840s, and there were some American versions of the trope of poor, native-born women sewing in solitary, shabby quarters by their would-be rescuers, Matthew Carey and others. But by the post–Civil War era, there was an added resonance to the poignance of this indigenous type. As factory conditions worsened, the first wave of mill women, Lowell's Yankee daughters, left the vast millworks with dowries for their New England farm marriages.

In the decades to come, Lowell's Yankee daughters went home to sew with their native-born peers. Ariel Cummings's Lowell novel, *The Factory Girls* (1847), set in that factory's large workspaces, had early on established the marital transit of these New England-born loom tenders who would presumably simply transfer their skills to a family setting. Their genteel counterparts in New England's sewing workrooms were similarly idealized by the cherished American imaginer of young womanhood, Louisa May Alcott. Her novel *Work* depicted happy gossiping women in a Boston workroom.[18]

Alcott's sewing workroom, often at the back of a lady seamstress's shop, retained the connotations of (if not the cultural admiration for) ladylike behavior.[19] Her novel entirely bypassed the suffering urban seamstresses isolated in a rooming house attic who telegraphed the fate of genteel girls deracinated by the Civil War. Such young women could neither afford the luxury of returning home nor work alongside the rough-hewn Irish women who now accounted for two-thirds of Lowell's factory work force.

The fiction of Cummings and Alcott clearly belied a multicultural truth. As early as the 1850s, according to the urban historian Christine Stansell, an ethnically diverse army of outworkers, mainly women (men, a more skilled population, worked "inside" the shop), worked in what she finds is a proliferation of family shops and sweatshops.[20] Yet the label "sweatshop" seems retrospectively applied rather than faithful to period rhetoric. Moreover, the site itself is contradictory terrain. Although she

argues that some families found sweatshops safer (morally?) than factories, she also quotes a story that Irish girls prostituted themselves, presumably as streetwalkers, on Sundays because weeklong seamstress work
in these shops did not pay.

The anecdote about Irish girls, whose reputation for chastity was
never high in period writings, has another implication. Unseemly ethnics, who were not averse to selling themselves, were beginning to replace the genteel seamstress, for whom, in popular urban dime novels,
prostitution was a fate worse than death. The urban garment trades increasingly relied on the cheap labor of immigrants who had migrated
en masse from the Old World in the postbellum decades, and the ethnic home disappeared into the sweated work space usurped for shop
purposes—the "sweaters' den" in which women ethnics labored.[21] As the
immigrants continued to arrive and the discourse evolved, many surveyors of the 1870s and 1880s still blurred the "den" of the sweaters' den
with the homes of the sweated. But even as they extended the discussion
of factory spaces, they glossed over the question of whose "home" the
work occurred in. These ambiguities would be incorporated into the
classic sweatshop of the late nineteenth century.

As the next decades inherited the ambiguity, the sweatshop became
a spectacle in and of itself. With the official discovery of poverty, the social hygienist's era was ripe for horror stories attendant on the "further
proletarianization of the sweatshop" in the decade to come.[22] The gendered, sexually segregated nature of shopwork increasingly assumed social and political importance. Thus, in expanding the study of the shop,
the discourse of the next decades would greatly complicate its meaning.

MAKING SENSE OF THE SHOP:
HOW THE ETHNIC HALF WORKS

By the 1890s, the tenement house had become all but synonymous
with the foreign-born, whether in a backyards section of a company
town or the "Jewtown" of a metropolis such as New York City, to use the
photgrapher and reporter Jacob Riis's phrase.[23] Whatever the ethnics' vi-
cissitudes at the lowest end of the job (or criminality) market, their tenement stasis was not perceived as stability, fostering habits of cleanliness
and order, but instead as cause for perennial criticism of the intem-
perance and immorality, infection and crime pervading their terrain. As

waves of new immigrants arrived, they occupied an underclass habitat perceived, in the words of Riis's 1890 watershed text, as the place where the other half lives. The slum revision of the American work ethic required that urban immigrants live in the mire, close to the job supply on docks, in warehouses and factories, and on business streets, crowding in an unprecedented density in American cities. By 1890, to cite a prime example, New York City's thirty-five thousand tenements contained an overwhelming number of the total population of a million and a half.[24] To influential cultural commentators like Riis, Jewish, Slavic, and Italian strategies for survival had little in common with the craft-based self-reliance still invoked by Gompers or the strike-torn industrial unions in their negotiations and confrontations with corporate expansionism.[25]

In their unfamiliar customs, unsanitary lifestyles, and frequent association with criminality, immigrants occupied the urban terrain in ways that pointed to the cultural crisis of the acculturation experience.[26] In actuality, the city, particularly New York City, altered the new foreign laborers more than they altered it, by inexorably incorporating them into their adopted society.[27] It is risky to generalize about the social fluidity of laborers, tailors, and peddlers. Nevertheless, New York's numerous Jews and Italians began the 1880s at the bottom of the social order and by the 1890s had moved in significant numbers out of manual labor or into jobs with some hope for improvement in the long run.[28] The many investigators who studied them, however, as well as other newcomers, were poised between stereotyping and inquiry. They christened some groups of foreign toilers the "well-paid working poor," the odd phrase suggesting the typical period confusions about ethnicity and economic struggle.[29] And possibly in an oblique reference to workplaces of ethnic versus native-born clothing workers, statisticians such as those at the Illinois Bureau of Labor Statistics even found that "the better class" of the "so-called sweating shops" could provide a hospitable environment, "though the baser sort present most objectionable features."[30]

Looking past such linguistic confusion, the historian Eileen Boris finds that "sweating," "sweating system," and "sweatshop" were used simultaneously by the late 1880s and 1890s. A piece in the liberal-minded *Outlook* magazine of 1895, "The Evils of the Sweat-Shop," was one of numerous pieces to confirm its existence and urge its eradication.[31] Many period commentators still used the old jargon. They spoke of "small rooms in tenement houses with revolting conditions," or of "workshops." "Tenement-house manufacture" thus meant home work or "outwork" under unfavorable conditions and for low pay, in other words, "sweated," supplying "inside shops" that received their work and finished it in a factory setting. But the venerable terms "sweating" and "sweating system" were now joined by the growing and soon predominant use of the word "sweatshop."[32]

In the late nineteenth century, would-be social reformers discovered poverty in the cities and mounted a massive attempt to create social order among "statistical persons," to borrow a phrase from the historian-critic Mark Seltzer in *Bodies and Machines,* and to impose surveillance on them. They often found that the sweatshops proved particularly impenetrable sites of poverty.[33] They were as clandestine as a stale beer dive or flophouse, and as well often lacked the public access on which these other establishments depended. Indeed, sweating's increasing illegality made those whom sweated employees called "cockroach contractors" anxious to conceal their place of operation. Moreover, given the uncertain taxonomy of past decades, observers never knew when they visited a given building whether they would find a domicile, a workplace, or a hybrid.[34]

Inquiries of the period, besides adhering to the old "inside work" and "outwork" categories, also distinguished between tenement and factory industry—specifically, between a sweatshop or tenement dwelling and a factory or loft space. Yet they discovered that neither size nor locale could be definitive, nor even level of skill or rate of pay. A sweatshop could be a large factory or a bedroom in a poor subcontractor's home.[35] Carroll Wright, the first U.S. labor commissioner, avoided employing the term at all. He confidently located the dressmakers, seamstresses, tailors, tailoresses, shirt-, collar-, and cuffmakers, and sewing machine operators of his slum classification reports to Congress. But he preferred to position them as workers in "manufacturing and mechanical industries," no matter how low their pay.[36] He thus avoided the "outwork" issue entirely.

Florence Kelley was one of the foremost campaigners against the sweatshop. She was the executive secretary of the National Consumers' League, a devoted New York–based crusader who also hunted down hundreds of Chicago shops for the Illinois Bureau of Labor Statistics. Writing in 1895 of the abuses in the "shops" or "sweaters" of Chicago's

Nineteenth Ward, she noted: "There is not in the whole ward a clothing-shop in any building erected for the purpose. . . . Under a clause of the law which prohibits the use of any bedroom or kitchen for the manufacture of garments by any person outside of the immediate family living therein, the inspectors are waging war. . . . The law is loosely drawn, the difficulties are many, and progress is slow toward an entire separation of shop and dwelling. Nor will such separation ever be complete until all manufacture in any tenement house is prohibited by law."[37]

Only decades after this oppressive labor space was born did American culture christen it the sweatshop. Now Riis's alarming photographs and essays, in which workers' sweaty bodies and communal dirt were sites of contagion as much as the shop itself, made it possible for anyone from sanitary inspectors to middle-class curiosity seekers to probe the relation of sweaty ethnic shop workers to the garments and cleanliness of the mainstream.

The Ethnography of Dirt: The Classic Sweatshop

As part of the larger reform effort attendant on the late-nineteenth-century discovery of poverty, muckraking the sweatshop coincided with an expanded movement in public health and urban reform to uncover, unearth, and clean up the social structures causing these conditions.[38] The images of the photographer's light and the policeman's lantern shining into the urban blackness recur often in the tenement literature of the decade.[39] Images of dirt and darkness inform this investigative shift from "individual surveillance to consideration of environmental and social causes of poverty."[40] Increasingly, government authorities "turned to regulatory measures: paving, draining, ventilating, and disinfecting public space."[41]

This is not to deny the strides in public health achieved by the Sanitary Control Board and allied organizations and the effectiveness of their antitubercular campaigns. It is rather to assert that in uncovering literal filth, particularly among the largest population of garment workers—East European Jews and their first-generation children—these public health agents stigmatized not only the sweated space, which often doubled as a worker's home or as a boarding house, but also the workers themselves. Indeed, commentators often dwell more on the sweat than on the shop, with what historian Alain Corbin calls "olfactory vigilance."[42] Whereas mid-century iconography had focused on the wraith-like bodies and yellowed faces of the underclass Walking Dead, now it was workers' bodies, assumed to be unclean and grotesque, that offended the middle-class observers who toured, surveyed, and investigated the urban landscape for municipal and religious authorities. One historian of the public bath movement, in pointing out that by 1897 almost two-thirds of New York City's public bath houses were Jewish, notes that the linkage of Jewish garment workers with poor personal and home cleanliness was more controversial than it appeared.[43]

Historian Alan Kraut's medical epistemology of the perceived ethnic menace to health, particularly from the tubercular Jewish tailor, points out how widespread was the assumption that sinister and unsanitary ethnics carried disease along with their dirt. Beneath the surface compassion, middle-class authors were convinced that "a man cannot truly respect himself who is dirty."[44] Florence Kelley was appalled at ethnic labor's seeming indifference to infestation. After some verbal shudders at sour smells, greasy bodies, and grimy work clothes, she avers: "The whole dwelling was crawling with vermin, and the capes were not free from it."[45] Kelley, it should be remembered, was a crusader for consumer change and advocated boycotts of sweated goods, as did many period reformers. But along with her horror of clothing that crawled with vermin seemed to be the equal repugnance toward unsanitary ethnics carrying disease into the very mainstream of cape-wearing society.[46]

It is no accident that the implicit nativism and anti-Semitism of the hygiene campaign was given force by the concomitant shift from drawing to photographs, the invention of artificial lighting, and even the proliferation of glass windows, all of which revealed the dirty bodies of the "submerged tenth" and their children. Before the 1890s, even noted academic artists like Kenyon Cox had smoothed out poverty's rougher edges in illustrations.[47] Riis's ethnic vignettes in his *Scribner's* pieces—the genesis of *How the Other Half Lives*—as well as in the first book-length version, were also accompanied by drawings. These visual companions of Riis's melodramatic and sentimental prose made the scene far less forbidding. Joining child laborers and gnarled seamstresses, figures of desperadoes and destitute mothers are nevertheless rounded and healthy, and one is caught up in the narrative of the drawing as a piece of exotic slumming whose shock value has been sanitized for entertainment.

But the cumbersome cameras that penetrated the dark corners of late-nineteenth-century cellars and attics were beginning to document a special kind of visual field. Slums were already perceived in less enlightened quarters as human zoos. Because the poor were so often at home doing piecework, the clarity of these documentary photographs set off nativist fears. Riis had been on the cutting edge in his photographs of sweatshops and other tenement spaces and streets as early as 1888 in a series of lantern-slide lectures on "New York City's Slum Life."[48] Only in the 1890s, a new era in which metropolitan dailies hired staff cameramen, did Riis publish his own surveillance photography, and not until 1900 did *How the Other Half Lives* feature photos rather than illustrations.[49]

Sweatshop photography issued from Riis's work as a police reporter as well as from his tours with his amanuensis Roger S. Tracy, a sanitary inspector.[50] The Riis sweatshop photos are extraordinary on a number of counts.[51] But one of the most salient is the sense they convey of people who have been reduced by, and become a part of, their squalid surroundings. It is not difficult to see the elision of person and place that, in essence, blames the victim. Riis's picture of humanity reduced by the very inability to get clean reinforced the day's medical nostrum: "In proportion as the body is kept cleanly, are the moral faculties elevated, and the tendency to commit crimes diminished."[52]

Just as there was no unitary view on the sources of tenement blight, even such medical certitude on the effects of sweatshop dirt did not lead to consensus on what it meant or on who caused it. The socialist garment trades unionists in New York City and other large clothing centers such as Chicago and Rochester sought to achieve solidarity among workers to accomplish a variety of reforms, including a powerful lobby with municipal and state government to abolish sweatshops and clean up the slums. But workers' activity was driven by their own anger at the worsening conditions rather than by anger on behalf of those suffering from them. The veteran clothing trades organizer and Jewish Socialist David Dubinsky recalled years later the ILGWU's early fights with the older craft unions in which the stigma of the "great unwashed" was a

taunt about the ethnic workforce.[53] Thus, the rhetoric of the early political battles that created unions among the many sweated trades on, for
example, New York's Lower East Side emphasized that immigrants were
not constitutionally different from native-born workers, or more prone
to disease because of hereditary flaws.

Moreover, the purveyors of the sweating system were no longer depicted as the unseen hands or shadowy figures of Lippard's day. Now "it
took only a small capital investment to turn a tenement dwelling or a
rented loft space into a workshop. Purchasing or renting sewing machines or, cheaper still, hiring workers who furnished their own machines, 'outside' contractors arranged with the 'inside' manufacturing
firms or factories to produce a line of garments."[54] Remarked Florence
Kelley of this arrangement: "Any demand of the inside hands for increased wages or shortened hours is promptly met by transfer of work
from the inside shop to a sweater."[55]

The *Jewish Daily Forward* editor Abraham Cahan, a key advocate of
the clothing trades community, sought to change the cultural conversation about sweatshops as ethnic "housing." In his essays and stories,
sweated sites were seething with ambition, not bugs. Cahan attempts to
lift the smirch of the sweatshop by suggesting that this workplace is a
roving, expanding, and thoroughly transitional phenomenon. His ethnics
are on the move, their moveable workplace filled not with germ-ridden
menace but with feisty entrepreneurship.[56]

Contractors, former sweated laborers themselves, were routinely depicted as unsavory, if not "avaricious."[57] In such portraits, they pose an
ideological as well as a social hygiene problem. The "endless workroom" that provides profits for the sweater could also ignite the spark in
the sweated to become sweaters themselves as soon as they could. Even
the formation of unions in response to the deplorable conditions pales
by comparison to the fact that poverty "in nine cases out of ten 'has' a silver lining in the shape of a margin in the bank." Using stereotypes of
dirt, stinginess, shrewdness, and "the natural talent of [Jews] for commercial speculation and investment," Riis and others admit that ambition and
a family's "united efforts" could well prove their economic salvation.[58]

Masculine economic salvation, that is. In late Victorian culture,
which was still committed to the feminine separate sphere and the argument that women worked for "pin money" or until marriage, garment

women's very presence was yoked with an unseemly sensuality. Ethnic women were particularly at risk. Women experienced the shop differently from men, even when they shared the experience of a place where the "boss did not care two cents for the factory laws," as the author of "Sweatshop Girl Tailors" observed in 1897.[59] Despite opposition from male co-workers, a women's culture of everyday resistance—including "men's tactics" such as strikes, boycotts, and work slowdowns—challenged assumptions that they were temporary workers, unorganized and ill-suited to political behavior.[60] Much revisionist research has found a culture of sweatshop women's resistance, from reading dime novels to lodging complaints, as early as the century's turn.[61] Although controversy remains on the definition of self-empowerment, feminist historians have now documented how real-life women created areas of self-expression and offered covert challenges to the shop's gender hierarchy. Yet in the masculine sweatshop narrative, any collaboration that questioned the exploitative work remained the province of the man, whether pale-faced operator or not. His female counterpart is always figured as passing through en route to marriage. As such she serves to inspire a male trade unionism that will protect her rather than guarantee her an equal wage.

In much period writing on sweatshop disease, men, debilitated by tuberculosis, saw women's lives and livelihoods imperiled by sweatshop conditions. In this gendered view of bodily weakness, they were all future mothers.[62] Their bodies susceptible to taxing work, they risked injury to their childbearing functions. The very unsanitary nature of the sweatshop led one contributor to the usually liberal-minded *Forum* to conclude that women who sewed there were endangering their "maternal functions." Azel Ames, a doctor whose ideas from 1875 still held sway at the turn of the century, warned women that "labor requiring great celerity of manipulation" could produce sterility or other reproductive problems.[63] And another kind of illness, one with far more cultural opprobrium, preempted motherhood entirely.

With these contradictory but linked threats to women's health, the sewing shop floor was a dangerous landscape of moral hazards. Feminine workplace identity, observes the historian Daniel Bender, very much depended on women's sexual behavior.[64] The young ethnic women who entered sweated work outside the home for lack of other opportunities complicated the rhetoric of the dirty toiler. Cultural fantasy gave an illicit allure to what were more likely uncomfortable and humiliating women's work spaces; commentators noted that sweating sweatshop girls sometimes worked half-undressed in a room with sweatshop men.[65]

From the working-girl's advocate Clare de Graffenreid's fact-filled 1893 essay, "The Condition of Wage-Earning Women," to the prurient passages of less enlightened male tenement novelists, the discussion of unceasing, mechanized sweatshop toil took on a seductive dimension.[66] The very "bad air … wet cloth … human bodies" pressed together in the shop, the lull of the "hot, stifling room ten hours a day," supposedly worked like an intoxicant.[67] Stephen Crane's widely read *Maggie: A Girl of the Streets* (1893) substituted his title character's pathos for her eroticism, but acknowledged the hothouse atmosphere of the New York City collar factory where Maggie worked before her fall to the street. Many were the other male-generated stories of the likes of Minnie Kelcey and Rose Baruch, who scorned the overtures of the tailors and bosses only to be courted by flashier and less scrupulous men in dance halls and saloons.[68]

A parallel feminine narrative was slower to arise. Genteel women novelists had penned cautionary tales about the seamstress as a target of upper-class seduction for decades. In Victorian America, most female authors, though, were reluctant to imagine any sewing girl's workplace or afterhours life. Women surveyors of seamstresses' budgets and more innocent pleasures did form a pre-Progressive genre of sorts, but not one joined by working-class women writing about the sweatshop life.[69]

Imaginary forays into the seamstress's domestic space, however pinched and shabby, revealed a long-lived cultural squeamishness that had informed both men's and women's portraits of white working women from antebellum times to the 1890s. Comments on the workrooms of these "distressed gentlewomen" employees rarely included asides about the sweat of bodies in close quarters. In fact, the dominant imagery of pre-ethnic workers was of the shivering, white-faced seamstress (an oblique reference to her hard-kept virtue?), not the overheated one. With the rise, however, of what Hutchins Hapgood termed "the sweatshop woman," this working woman's very "dirt" is eroticized as she becomes the sweatshop innocent who succumbs, or else she becomes the suspect ethnic who is variously pleasure-loving, misbehaving, or tragically harassed.[70] The period saw many comparisons between prostitutes and bad drains, the loose woman and the fetid sewer.[71]

Jacob Riis was curiously representative in finding one way only to cleanse women of their sweatshop dirt. In fact, Riis, like his colleagues, brought a more hostile ambivalence to his observations of sweatshop girl tailors than he did, say, to his "Jewtown" observations. Fictional seamstresses now experience martyred, sullied, or hard-kept innocence. The social and settlement worker Helen Campbell's Rose Haggerty is sanctified by the sweatshop. In "Cohen's Figure," by the tenement storyteller J. W. Sullivan, Ernestine Beaulefoy jumps out a window rather than work with a lecherous owner; and Riis's Rose Baruch falls down an airshaft as punishment for acting as a "charity girl," the period term for women who gave sexual favors in return for dinners and gifts.[72] In these readings, the sweatshop house is no home because it is a bordello.

By the century's last decade, the sweatshop was a prime cultural site in which sympathy for the woman forced to sew there fit uneasily at best with the conviction that women were wrong to abandon home for the perilous world of paid labor. Just as immorality clung to the stage actress and entertainer, so it made sewing women actors in their own melodrama of endangered virtue. To the many who theatrically saw the sweatshop woman as "at the mercy of employers," there was no last-minute rescue.[73]

As a theater of sullied bodies and unclean (female) behavior, the sweatshop had many stories to tell the horrified and fascinated bourgeois audiences of the late nineteenth century. Certainly the era's more sober analyses returned to the injustice of sweated immigrants who sought only purposive work and an escape from proletarian subjection. But the very discourse that deplored the regimentation of the sweatshop body, imprisoned by the sewing table, was disturbed by the odor of sweat. Such an unwashed environment, so different from the well-regulated middle-class home, was proof that the smirch of the shop and the ethnic who sewed there were one.

THE SWEATSHOP AND ITS DISCONTENTS: VOICING THE SHOP

Turn-of-the-century inspectors, amateur and professional, looked through classed and gendered lenses and saw but did not see sweatshops. Anecdotal evidence suggests that workers themselves were surprised at being told where they worked. Some immigrants used the word "sweatshop" interchangeably with "the shops" or "the garment shops."[74] Others labored there for years without hearing the word itself.[75] Young seamstresses posed proudly with the forelady in another sweatshop.[76] And in a ghost-written *Independent* interview with a clothing worker in 1902, "factory" and "sweatshop" are used interchangeably. Divided in her attitude, the narrator decries the conditions even as she says that she is able to save money.[77] Although her comment suggests a practicality about other job options, it also suggests the kind of belief in the American success ethic that prompted the *Independent* interviewer to single her out in the first place.

Until the rise of literary interest in the "bottom depths," understandably little emphasis was placed on the voices of the people who worked there. The attempts of fiction writers as diverse as Stephen Crane and J. W. Sullivan to put their oratory in the mouths of sewing-machine men, and, less often, women, did little to balance a cultured and stilted late-Victorian narrative voice with the workers' own enraged complaints. Although the works of "Anglo" novelists, social scientists, and reformers did not coalesce into one generic narrative pattern, there was a pervasive insistence on foreign labor's disease and dirt. In "Not Yet: The Day Dreams of Ivan Grigorovich" (1895), the popular local color novelist and journalist J. W. Sullivan offers a rare outsider's vignette of a Russian Jew whom the sweatshop drove to lunacy. But the focus is on the suicidal tailor and his cruel coworkers rather than the sweatshop milieu in which they are all encased. In contrast, in the ethnic counter-narrative that arose by the 1890s, the very air that is breathed, so socially and physically impure, inspires a lyrical though pained insistence on being stifled.

Several factors, including the rise of ethnic authors, combined by the 1890s to allow the predominantly male ethnic laboring voice to claim narrative authority. The resulting stories, poems, and sketches, often in Yiddish and written largely for fellow workers, reflected the common experience and provided a catharsis of sorts. Translated for American readers, the poems broke through the literary landscapes of sweatshop life produced by newsmen and novelists. The rebuttal in this literature of "scientific," journalistic, and social scientific presumptions about sweated labor space was neither aimed at nor did it reach the community of social engineers who had developed their reformist expertise. Instead, the sweatshop that began to voice itself personalized the narrative site in so doing. Like the works of mainstream observers, this literature recognizes the sweated ethnic workspace as a hybrid slum home and factory at the margins of American assimilation. But it does not foreground the stigmatization inherent in the shop experience. In the participant-observer's view, the sweatshop is a living environment, not the literary landscape of hell produced by mainstream observers. Abraham Cahan, a Russian-Jewish immigrant and onetime cigar worker, was a sweatshop success story. His novella *Yekl* displeased community leaders when it appeared in 1896 with its unflattering depictions. Nonetheless, on the strength of his advocacy of Jewish Socialist causes, Cahan went on to edit the *Jewish Daily Forward,* the largest Yiddish-language paper in the nation. Throughout the 1890s and beyond, he was a cultural leader and moral authority in New York's Lower East Side ghetto.[78]

Cahan's tailors in *Yekl* are at a cultural crossroads. His fictional Jewish garment-trades workers respond heartily to assimilation, biculturalism, and the lure of new moralities and popular entertainments. Through them Cahan critiqued the new cultural practices that informed real-life Jewish ambition. In so doing, however, he reshaped the discourse of the "odd ethnic" in ways that none of his contemporaries could have imagined. All of Cahan's garment-shop characters are hard workers, and Yekl is no exception. In a rejection of tragic toilers, Yekl is determined to become a real "Yankee" by learning English, saving money, and generally moving up. Again, his aspirations are emblematic of enterprise. Many Jews traded a sewing machine or pushcart for a clothing shop or real estate holdings.

Like his sweatshop coworkers, Yekl, renaming himself Jake, turns the Lower East Side into a school. He improves his English while attending boxing matches or following betting scores. English is spoken even at the dancing academy where he seeks a more American wife, and he hums popular songs at the machine. In describing Professor Joe Peltner's dance academy, Cahan adds, significantly, that the sweatshop workers learning the new dances look more like they are working than playing. Like the ambitious, diamond-hard Mamie Fein, whom Jake, though married, is courting, he is enticed by clothing and amusement and bent on enjoyment as well as ascension, but Jake also has entrepreneurial ambitions that, with Mamie's savings, he will realize.

Cahan's sweatshop is evolutionary, an ethnic rite of passage. The way in which the workers colonize the shop, infusing it with their own work culture, suggests Cahan's understanding of the transformative power of workers in even the most oppressive conditions.[79]

Another artistically rendered space is the eternal sweatshop of a revered Yiddish poet without Cahan's command of English or links to the American literary elite. Author of *Songs from the Ghetto,* a Yiddish-language chapbook, Morris Rosenfeld led Yiddish poets in the discourse of horror and the language of dirt.[80] But the injustice experienced by their figures is so horrific that the space depicted is more psychic than literal. The so-called dirt includes, for instance, the blood coughed up by consumptive workers. Reclaiming an oppressive space as their habitat, the responses of the figures in these works range from making their own space out of their very alienation in the sweated shop to becoming fatally ill or psychotic in it. Locked out of the embourgeoisement possible for Cahan's vital, pushing figures, the workers who read and were poeticized in *Songs from the Ghetto* felt their machines had "damagingly inscribed a place in the Jewish soul." In Rosenfeld's lyrics, the bondage to the machine is the most important relationship of his life—a hellish substitute for home. The poet enters the mind of the enslaved operator who hears only the call of the timeclock and the sewing machine. A fevered, hallucinatory guide to a schizophrenogenic environment, Rosenfeld's work elides Poe and the "Song of the Shirt."

In entering the space of the shop, Rosenfeld was concerned with the worker's personal relationship, both slavelike and resentful, to his or her machine. He personifies the machine in various ways. Sometimes it is the voice of the clock: "It calls me machine/And says to me sew!" At other times it is a companion in arms, a comrade in the sorrow of the garment toiler. Rosenfeld is an important artist because he recasts what was often called the "tailor's disease," consumption, in an aggressive threnody.[81] Poems like "The Pale Operator" use the alarming image of the sewing machine wheel stained with blood from the coughing of "lungers" made ill by the shop. A mixed message of lament for the dead workers is delivered by those who, perhaps themselves soon to die, nevertheless bear angry witness. The stained machine becomes a sweatshop monument, a marker where a breadwinner lost life's battle.[82] Given so many disturbing images in this vision, the rage beneath the seeming passivity takes on a life of its own.

The sweatshop setting is central to Rosenfeld's poetry of contradictions. The busy shop, heavy irons, and blood-sucking work are more than a grotesque slum sideshow or fetid worksite. Rather, the reiterated image of the death camp is in a dialectical relationship with the substantial labor wrung from pale operators. These two tropes collide: "Months fly, and years pass away, and the pale-faced one still bends over his work and struggles with the unfeeling machine. . . . I stand and look at his face: his face is besmutted and covered with sweat. . . . And the tears fall in succession from daybreak until fall of night, and water the clothes, and enter into the seams."[83] This masculine anomaly, ever more feeble, whose every thought is death-inflected, is as absorbed in as he is enfeebled by his work. Endlessly sewing or standing at the iron, standing and pressing, he is at the same time always taking his emotional pulse. The sweatshop becomes a kind of cruel beloved with whom he is obsessed. It is as least as necessary to his attempt to form an oppositional identity that, rather than rebel, he looks to dying as the only exit from the shop.

Songs from the Ghetto argues for a psychic divide between the sexes. Emotive strength exhausted on the cruel shop, the pale operator sees women as only the orphaned girl seeking work ("Whither?: To a Girl"), the skin-and-bones mother selling candles on Hester Street ("The Candle-Seller"), or the faithful wife and mother unable to console her tailor husband at day's end ("My Boy"). Women are thus defined by what they are not: neither objects of desire nor effective helpmeets, neither contributors to the family wage nor matriarchal mainstays.

Cahan, Rosenfeld, and colleagues like the socialist author Edward King, whose hyperbolic novel *Joseph Zalmonah* (1890) featured a feverish but resolute cadre of cloakmakers, were not palliating sweatshop horrors. They were seeking to understand them through an insider's ethnography that acknowledged the authority of the sufferer. There were some difficulties balancing gender and class. Whether, as in Cahan's world, women were the organizing presences, or, as in Rosenfeld, the backgrounded relatives of sweatshop tailors, they defined themselves through the helpmeet role. In the next decade, sweatshop women would claim narrative authority in reminiscences, memoirs, and spirited accounts of the female militancy that erupted in the Shirtwaist Strike of 1909. But as the "Song of the Shirt" became that of the "Pale Operator," the late-nineteenth-century sweatshop gave the stage to men.

It is within that gender shift that we should understand labor historian Steven Fraser's comment on the interactive nature of that workplace: "Relationships at work, for example, might be familial, communal, or utterly impersonal, depending on where one looked."[84] For the male voices that shaped the discourse on sweatshop customs and gender relations, men's struggles were to separate the tailor's occupation from the subcontractor's shabby home-and-work site. Women's strivings were to escape the shop for a real domesticity of their own. As new voices as divergent as those of the Protestant women philanthropists and firebrand Yiddish women organizers entered the conversation, they would labor mightily in the new century to disconnect the sweatshop from the home.

LOOKING BACK OVER a half century's worth of sweatshop representations, one finds a concerted attempt to demystify the sweatshop for an audience that had no way of seeing the "spectacle" of Lower East Side poverty. This brief survey of the discourse on substandard garment-trades workrooms in the mid to late nineteenth century demonstrates its lack of clarity about whether the literature was offering a view of a system, a workroom, or a home, as reflected in the elusiveness of the term used to describe it. The century ended with an answer: these workrooms were all three. The term "sweatshop," however, provided no clarity but rather gave rise to a hydra-headed phenomenon that was at once familial and industrial. Whether the site it provided for doing piecework was a factory, workroom, shop, or working home, the sweatshop moved over the course of more than fifty years from prop to stage setting.

As the sweatshop became a protagonist in its own right, surveyors sharpened the debasement narratives with which the sweaty ethnic work was increasingly associated. To be sure, the sordid surroundings of the ill-paid needle workers were a reproach to the many advocates of American self-transformation who visited or imagined the shop. Yet the sweatshops also validated the view that the poor manufactured their own misery in the same filthy nests where they produced garments for the affluent. As sweated laborers crowded the cities, housing themselves in deference to, and often in the same rooms as, their jobs, "the crucial stress on apartness" embodied by sweated work only increased.[85]

The sweatshop's moral and cultural implications would only expand with the new century's wider ethnic aspirations. A number of those one-time coworkers who now controlled the clothing factory floor (or their

first-generation sons) were as likely to become entrepreneurs as to remain "cockroach contractors." As a parallel event, with the rise of the
social hygiene movement, campaigns to sanitize the city's home workplaces and the ethnics who lived to work in them proliferated. Sadly,
despite legislative efforts to abolish the system, sweatshop operators successfully dodged the law, and in 1911 there were still thirteen thousand
home-work tenements functioning in New York alone.[86]

Nor should it be forgotten that this separation or merging of home
and paid labor was profoundly gendered. In the next two decades,
women increasingly provided sociological analyses and created fictive
worlds to account for the sweatshop's sexual politics. But even as women
sought and sometimes found male unionist support to define and protest
the sexualization of the garment shop, they became its most dramatic
victims. The next century would see the sweatshop not only as a home
to horror but, in New York's Triangle shirtwaist factory fire of 1911, a
venue for complete disaster.

CHAPTER 3

Surviving Sites

SWEATSHOPS IN THE PROGRESSIVE ERA AND BEYOND

"There are so many of us for one job that it matters little if 146 of us are burned to death."

—Rose Schneiderman, quoted in Meredith Tax,
"Conditions of Working Women in the Late
Nineteenth and Early Twentieth Centuries" (1970)

"[That] vigorous relic of an earlier industrial system—the sweat-shop."

—Annie Marion MacLean, "The Sweat-Shop in
Summer," *American Journal of Sociology* (1903)

THE SWEATSHOP DISCOURSE had provided late-nineteenth-century reformers with a narrative structure that linked economic exploitation, moral outrage, fear of germs, social control, and modern social science. In the new century, as sweatshop containment strategies played a minor part in a wider social survey movement, the very term itself seemed to fall out of reform language. The American sweatshop seemed to have disappeared, almost as if its demise paralleled the assimilation of cheap ethnic labor into an American workplace that no longer registered their distinctive presence.

The nineteenth century had early recognized that industry could be damaging without being sweated. Work accidents had been routinely noted and classified in classic nineteenth-century surveys; Labor Commissioner Carroll Wright, among others, led the way.[1] With the coming of the twentieth century, the focus was firmly on factory floors rather than diminutive garment shops with sweated "inside" or home labor. There was a tacit but widespread acceptance of workplace neglect that the few well publicized "model" tenements and "transmigrations" of

sweatshops into model workplaces did little to assuage, at least for organized labor.

As Daniel Bender points out, the labor movement "sought to move the
industry from sweatshops to model shops, understood as shops that had cor-
rected all of articulated problems of sweatshops . . . [and] were clear, spacious,
and located in industrial buildings, not cramped tenement apartments."[2]
Some manufacturers even deliberately contrasted the old sweatshop paradigm with their up-to-date "model" factories. Between 1898 and 1918,
company photographers utilized the photojournalistic art to "prove" the difference between "old-style" sweatshops and the new factories.[3] One enlightened employer, in supposed disgust at the excesses of sweated industry,
founded an actual colony for his employees in New Orange, New Jersey.[4]

This supposed escape for "toilers of the tenements" to a New Jersey
workers' town, however, did little to palliate the environmental evils of
the metropolitan textile and clothing trades. Outside garment-trades organizing, social scientists deplored the human cost of industry and found
the oldtime sweatshop industrially indefensible. The historian Eileen
Boris adds the home-work perspective, commenting: "Precisely because
it appeared as the invasion of the factory into the home, reformers spoke
of 'the wreck of the home' and continued to view industrial homework
as a sweatshop menace."[5]

Yet all of these new professionals—sociologist-surveyors of company
workforce, mill town, native-born and "foreign" labor—struggled to understand the reasons for the survival of the classic shop, whether in the
sweater's or the pieceworker's own flat. As they continued the last century's conflation of marginalized ethnic and substandard sweatshop, they
revealed still widespread anxieties about Jewish, Italian, and East European assimilation.

Before examining the ideology and language of the shop that resulted
from their studies, it would be well to summarize the sources of the new
rhetoric. We turn briefly to the early-twentieth-century social engineering movement in general and the Pittsburgh Survey in particular.

SOCIAL ENGINEERS, THE PITTSBURGH
SURVEY, AND THE RESISTANT SHOP

The survey movement in many ways attempted a social scientific version of the artist who expresses and the god who understands.

Viewing cities from Syracuse to Detroit as laboratories of social problems, the surveyors set out to replace the previous century's limited in-
ventories of and moralizing conclusions about how the other half lived
with detailed knowledge-building about ethnic communities of skilled
and unskilled workers. They balanced this mammoth ethnographic research task with a parallel inquiry into industrywide conditions in major
manufacturing centers of the nation, with particular emphasis on the
Midwest and Northeast. Although they often claimed to withhold judg-
ment about the studied subjects of Atlanta and Birmingham, Milwaukee
and Detroit, they customarily interrupted statistical tables on occupational descriptors, wage differentials, workplace hazards, gender, ethnic,
and racial workforce breakdowns, and the like. Inserted were passages
about community values and behaviors, marked by a reliance on anecdotal evidence. Suggestions for reform, in keeping with their informa-
tion-gathering mission, were minimized. But the repeated assertion that
they applied a thoroughly scientific method was optimistic at best. Surveyors often gave employers great latitude or expressed nativist or racist
views. Thus factors such as the seasonal nature of many garment jobs, the
incidence of illness among the workers with the lowest skills, and the incidence of workplace discrimination or sexual harassment were often at-
tributed to the immigrant's failure to assimilate. In a similar vein,
surveyors, the majority from privileged or middle-class backgrounds, at-
tributed ethnic accidents with heavy equipment in the coal mine or the
foundry to an ignorance of the newest technology.[6]

As the most visible reformers of the early twentieth century, those
broadly labeled Progressives were at least as interested in the force and
power of the new technology to "engineer society" as they were with
what the Pittsburgh Survey director Paul U. Kellogg termed "the question of the relation of industry to health."[7]

In recasting the factory as a social-scientific laboratory, Progressives
faced new problems of interpretation, nowhere perhaps more clearly
than in the six-volume Pittsburgh Survey conducted by professional social workers for the Russell Sage Foundation. Of the avalanche of such
titles, the Pittsburgh Survey was the quintessential product of the new
scrutiny. As such, it embodied the religion of expertise preached everywhere from the settlement house to the city planning commission to the
platform committee of the Socialist Party—and in the key muckraking,

Socialist, and antilabor fiction of the day. Funded by corporate philanthropists, the Pittsburgh Survey was the first extensive study of a major industrial city.[8] It was in all ways intended "to connect the reformist purpose with all the newest methods of scientific inquiry, and [to list] and coordinat[e] a variety of methodologies and academic disciplines in the quest for the totality of the social fact."[9] A massive research enterprise, between 1907 and 1914 it produced six volumes with 525 photographs, drawings, and charts. Compared to the highly selective ghetto and sweatshop sorties of the previous century, its scope was vast. The six volumes—prominent among them *The Steel Workers* (1911) by John A. Fitch and *Wage-Earning Pittsburgh* (1914), edited by Kellogg—scrutinized that city's industrial relations, workplace loss of life or limb and legal redress, blue-collar stratification in the mill, the panorama of urban women's jobs, and the lives of their domestic counterparts in the mill towns.

Although other cities, featured in other studies, were less devoted to heavy industry and were associated instead with "light" manufacturing such as the needle trades, the survey is a touchstone for understanding the period discourse on sweatshops for a number of reasons. For one thing, Kellogg's authorial group prided itself on distinguishing between modern and less up-to-date shops in an enormous range of trades. For another, given massive influxes of Slavic and East European subgroups, Pittsburgh was home to a wider variety of ethnic seamstresses and homeworkers than New York City. That these women were often married to or seeking husbands in the steel industry (rather than, as in New York, socializing with tailors or contractors) also provided surveyors with an alternative gendered way of contrasting the factory. Nor, in the context of its New York City counterparts, did the survey trade breadth for depth. It even devoted a substantial section of Elizabeth Butler's *Women and the Trades: Pittsburgh, 1907–1908* (1909) to tenement work at home.

This is not, of course, to imply that the Pittsburgh Survey was alone in its extended attention to home work. The 1912 New York Factory Investigating Commission, for example, was attentive to manufacturing in tenements and deplored the practice. Yet even before the publication of the Pittsburgh Survey, the outmoded technology of the home-factory sweatshop, combined with its tenement size, had largely relegated it to the background. Social investigators who found the equivalent of sweated conditions in factories refrained from using the term. However dismal the working experience, they called these large clothing sites (as well as many cigar-making venues) "factories" and nothing else.[10] As in nineteenth-century discussions of the shop, however, contradictions abounded. In his memoirs the celebrated Socialist reformer Morris Hillquit positioned the sweatshop in the late 1880s and 1890s even as he opined that not until the 1910 rise of the International Ladies' Garment Workers Union (ILGWU) did "taking down the shop" become a reality.[11]

By 1900, numerous clothing factories boasted mechanically driven machines capable of delivering many times the number of stitches that could be produced with foot-powered machines.[12] Within this context, rather than crusade mightily for eradication of home work, prominent trade union leaders who deplored the sweatshop in theory suggested that action had already been taken to render it obsolete. Such optimists pointed to technological advances in the garment trades or, as one garment unionist put it, the "modern equipped shop, operated directly by the firms."[13] ILGWU (and later Amalgamated Clothing Workers [ACW]) leaders saw manufacturers moving to increase profits and replace the three to twenty operators working in the old-fashioned sweated shops. Roughly between the beginning of the new century and heightened garment trades reform of the 1910s in Pittsburgh's sister city, Chicago, as well as in the garment hub, New York City, the unionist dictum that sweatshops were labor dinosaurs in the twentieth century overshadowed public acknowledgment of their existence.

By 1911 some of the same New York City Progressives who were making contributions to the Pittsburgh Survey had conducted surveys of their own, some under the aegis of the Russell Sage Foundation, and knew full well that home work lingered in tenement flats. (The ubiquitous Florence Kelley, a veteran sweatshop inspector in New York City and Chicago in the 1890s, even contributed to *Wage-Earning Pittsburgh*.) Their interpretations of what they saw, however, seemed to differ from non–Pittsburgh Survey authors. But to illustrate their commitment to social hygiene in the slums, they employed a narration of pastness that deliberately juxtaposed "home-work" tenements with the more professionalized sites.[14] Even Elizabeth Butler, who preceded her Pittsburgh investigations with a study of New Jersey's sweated work as the secretary of that state's Consumer's League, declared, "In Hudson county, there are probably not many sweatshops . . . for the sweatshop proper is bound to become more and more a negligible quantity." But "much sweated work" will be done in homes, she said, because modernized plants in Hudson County simply will not manufacture goods that could be finished either more cheaply or more expertly "outside."[15]

Invoking then-current associations of that city with America both as a land of business optimism and ever-increasing factory blight, the survey confidently asserted, "for Pittsburgh read the United States."[16] In the surveyors' broad sweep, "Pittsburgh became a symbol of larger urban industrial problems, and the "industrial class" (a term often employed by the American Federation of Labor [AFL]) stood for society as a whole.[17] With its preponderance of heavy industry, Pittsburgh was hardly a sewing trades magnet in the manner of large cities like New York and smaller ones such as Rochester and Troy. Still the language used by Pittsburgh social workers not only explained in passing that industrial city's sweated trades but applied the new rhetoric to New York itself. Joshua Freeman points out that in the century's early decades, the New York metropolitan region also had its share of large-scale manufacturing, from oil refineries to candy factories. But especially as a garment center, New York was correctly envisioned as a vast landscape of buying and selling. By 1910 the city's annual output of about $250,000 and the labor of 37,000 to 47,000 workers, depending on the season, were producing $40 million in profits.[18]

Nativism strengthened this emphasis on modern industrial output. The social survey movement had a decided bias toward white skilled workers in the heavy industrial trades. (For these and other reasons, modern labor historians minimize the Pittsburgh volumes, seeing them as the efforts of apologists for industry.) Pittsburgh industry was, to steel-town analyst John Fitch, an American one.[19] The sweaty ethnic, if not the ethnic sweatshop per se, was represented as alien to an "American" landscape. Within this framework, slowness and ignorance were the marks of technological incompetence. Another volume in the survey (complete with Lewis Hine photos), *Work Accidents and the Law* (1910), distinguishes between an unthinking, careless "Italian who took his rest against the company's rolling stock" and a presumably English-speaking "brakeman ... struck ... by a piece of overhanging ... construction."[20] More than one observer found Slavic workers "fools" for losing their balance when they handled dangerous machines.[21] Compounding this ethnic "ignorance" was a lack of familiarity with the English language. As if their retention of native customs would endanger the Americanness of the worksite, the foreign-born were urged to adjust.

The Progressives' survey movement set the tone for the next three decades when it implicitly associated ethnic assimilation with the "vanishing" sweatshop. But the continuity of sweated labor, especially in the Lower East Side loft clothing factories, gave the lie to these assertions.

This chapter considers the wide range of ways in which period observers made representational or narrative use of these surviving sites as resistant to technological change rather than as venues of substandard conditions. Between the 1910s and 1940, these observers, both in and out of the garment trade, both prolabor and antilabor, used reportage, narrative, and fiction to visit discursively this out-of-date workscape. By the time sweated jobs marked their return in the desperations of the Depression, the sweatshop had accumulated complex and contradictory meanings as a site of oppression, a reminder of an exploited labor past, and a curious witness to bygone ideals.

In a more important way, though, from policymakers to Lower East Side authors, the era employed the disappeared versus surviving shop to help launch an ethnography of urban Jewish and Italian clothing trades labor. How would this new discourse fit into a larger inquiry into working-class modernity and acquire gendered dimension?

READING SWEATSHOPS
FOR THE PROGRESSIVE ERA

The years from 1909 to 1919 were particularly critical in the governmental census of "acceptable" industrial sites. In the spirit of statistical thoroughness that pervaded social surveys, whether private or governmental, the census reports carefully elaborated the minutiae of their inquiries. One typical sample, as noted in the *Census of Manufactures, 1914*, produced by the Department of Commerce, painstakingly pointed out that "suspenders, garters, and elastic woven goods" were first shown separately in the 1909 census and that more data on each manufacturing concern were in preparation.[22]

What was not quantified in these reports was the widespread conviction that the ethnic workforce in the Northeast and selected Midwest garment trades, though still Yiddish or Italian in origin, was ripe for

Americanization. Using this assimilation lens, the social worker Louise Odencrantz remarked of a New York City garment factory fueled by an Italian immigrant and her daughters: "Her work place is the means by which she may come to look upon herself not alone as an Italian, but as a part of the big American labor force."[23] Written in 1919 and based on research conducted in 1912 and 1913, Odencrantz's lengthy report was funded by the Russell Sage Foundation, which also underwrote the Pittsburgh Survey. Another New York City author, Mary Van Kleeck, also worked under the Russell Sage aegis to investigate Italian women's home work as artificial-flower makers, which had been an ongoing concern since Riis's time. In *The Artificial Flower Makers* (1913), Van Kleeck deplored the continuation of this sweated home labor, which she fit into a narration of pastness.[24] In this worldview, home work was not a primitive and outmoded system but an outgrowth of manufacturing (in)efficiency. Thus both Odencrantz and Van Kleeck positioned this ethnic worksite in the larger surroundings of industry itself.

Odencrantz comments trenchantly on the industrial vastness of which this garment work is a small part, her writing often dominated by descriptions of the vast, labor-intensive clothing trades. Blurring the reformist focus, she reveals a kind of admiration for the lofts converted to crowded workrooms. Viewed from outside, gray buildings are places "where men's clothing is made by the wholesale, hats turned out by the gross, and flowers and feathers pasted, branched, and packed for shipment to the farthest corners of the country."[25] By the end of the passage the main message emerges: speed, vastness, and progress are the hallmark of those who can stand the strain and survive, not of the weaklings who drop out of history.

In reading the sweatshop through the lens of progress and ambition, these observers could be said to have taken their cue, again, from the Pittsburgh Survey. Elizabeth Butler, in *Women and the Trades: Pittsburgh, 1907–1908* (1909), admonishes: "No girl who is *incapable of concentration* can stay in a garment factory. No girl who is so *unambitious* as not to care whether she drives her piece wages up to $6.00 a week can hold her place at the machine. Others *whose needs sharpen their ambition are waiting for her place*. There are young girls here, but they are not irresponsible."[26] Butler's narrative of speed replaced that of the sweated women's work experience in her survey volume, which devotes a large section to the

garment trades. *Women and the Trades* analyzes in detail the garment factories of the men's and women's clothing industries, including the glove
and millinery trades. It provides a veritable taxonomy of garment workrooms, categorized by the use of artificial light, the arrangement of windows, the cleanliness of the surroundings, and the safety of the machines
(104). In charts and commentary, Butler is anxious to establish the number of male and female employees in pants factories and their weekly
wages; she is principally concerned, however, with female occupations,
from single-needle operators to vest makers to examiners (117). But in
the welter of detail about industrial production, her report lacks a sense
of living workers performing these tasks.[27]

Like the veteran investigator Annie MacLean of Chicago, an *American
Journal of Sociology* author, Butler initially minimizes the importance of
sweated labor.[28] She perceives the actual site, though "within the city limits of Pittsburgh," as "a hundred miles away" because it is located in outwork tenements (133). There she finds that foreign home laborers are
"pale, tired girls who would not break into the old ways of their life by a
new routine." Like women in stogy shops, candy factories, and laundries,
her figures are not objects of compassion despite their grim case histories.
The tubercular risks they endured, for instance, simply place them in a
category with the disreputable, the unemployed, and the drunken poor.
Aside from these throwbacks, Butler prefaces her discussion of "outwork"
by alleging that only the "occasional" workroom "degenerated" to the
sweatshop level (102). Left ambiguous is the question of who is responsible for such degeneration: employer, employee, or both.

These assertions prove problematic, however, when Butler tries to
limit sweatshops to outwork. She attempts to define the "contract shops"
in Pittsburgh as not technically sweated because they were located in
buildings rather than homes (128). Yet she returns to the sweatshop idea
when she points out that these shops were staffed by Italian and Jewish
workers who worked in unclean surroundings and were ignorant of and
unequipped for "the standards of industrial work" in garment factories
(129)—just like those pale ethnic girls at the Pittsburgh city limits who
stayed at home and sewed. Rather than wrestle with further distinctions
about whether ambition and speed rather than conditions and location
primarily separated women's work in the shop, she invokes the stereotype of the sweatshop as an institution of the industrial Northeast, im-

plicitly New York City.[29] In this, she uses the distinction between New York's low wages and Pittsburgh's supposedly better ones to shore up the idea that sweated laborers, out of step with machines, had to conform to industrial routine to be released from bondage (127–128, 378).

Mark Seltzer in *Bodies and Machines* has argued that in sweated and nonsweated industries, management joined government in a statistical reading of workers' bodies that made no numerical provision in the data for collective action or shop floor militance. The association of industrial anachronism with Mediterranean, Slavic, and Eastern European workers was so pervasive, in fact, that one coal industry analyst argued that as the "immigrant is the feeder of the sweatshop and one of the chief causes of the long hours prevailing there, so the foreigner is the chief factor in the retention of the long hours in the coal mines." Out of step with the machine, then, ethnics represented a vestigial workforce of sorts harking back to sweatshop days.[30]

At the height of this Progressive-era "social engineering," the 1911 Triangle shirtwaist factory fire, the worst tragedy of the city, reminded Americans of the durability of the very sweatshop that had been minimized by their disgust at ethnic resistance to complete Americanization. How then did the predominantly reform discourse on sweated labor, first in the face of and later in the wake of the Triangle fire, square its view of ethnic-connected work accidents with the unpleasant reminder of the sweatshop in the midst of industrial modernism?

THE "NEWER TYPE OF SWEATSHOP" AND THE TRIANGLE FIRE

The Pittsburgh surveyors declared confidently that "sweated workers are a clog in the upward progress of labor in general," and would soon be forced out or go on public assistance.[31] But trade unionism was not recommended in that city's fairly circumscribed garment trades. In New York City, with a large number of sites and a proliferation of faster sewing machines, the metropolitan shop floor took the lead in speed of production. The growing clothing trades unions seized the initiative and struck, picketed, boycotted, and produced labor actions with terms like "The Great Uprising of the 20,000" in 1909–1910. In that famous job protest (of which more below), young immigrant seamstresses made common cause with tailors and even the American Federation of Labor's

elite craftsmen to forge a general strike. Women not only had the support
of many like the Pittsburgh Survey photographer Lewis Hine, who contributed photos of their oppressive sites to *McClure's* magazine, but also
of an impressive reform coalition including social engineers, women
trade unionists, the socialist and garment unions' labor press. The first
mass women's strike even received approval from the conservative AFL.[32]

But that was not the whole story. The gains in solidarity and respect
as a result of the first successful large "women's strike" were short-lived.
For years, the AFL and other labor entities well knew that the unskilled
ethnic sweatshop had either gone underground or resurfaced as a larger
business situated just outside New York City's Lower East Side and other
tenement districts. The notoriously sweated Triangle Shirtwaist Company, located in a large nearby loft building, had over one hundred employees. This "new" urban clothing factory found larger quarters in loft
buildings than had been available in old-fashioned tenements or converted tenements.[33] As the sweatshop became larger and more state-of-
the-art, rather than less unjust, the eyes of America were diverted from
Great Uprisings and clothing strikes. By 1911, the year of the Triangle
fire, Pittsburgh Survey author Crystal Eastman had contributed mightily
to the discussion of industrial negligence—employer versus employee—
in coal, steel, and other male-dominated industries. Dr. Alice Hamilton
had by this time also begun publishing working papers in medical journals on industrial toxins.[34] Both authors analyzed the most labor-
intensive jobs against the background of Pittsburgh's or New York City's
soft-goods and needle-trades industries. Others fueled the argument of
ILGWU organizers that a greed-driven management profited by pushing
clothing workers to produce faster and thereby exposed them to hazards.

In New York City, Frances Perkins, who would later be the principal
investigator of the Triangle fire, toured factories similar to those in the
unskilled ethnic garment trades. The owners of such places, which employed mainly women, typically informed Perkins that when young
women workers were maimed by machinery, the young women themselves were at fault.[35]

Perkins's investigation revealed that the fire exits to the Triangle loft
factory, where fire hazards abounded, had all been locked and that most
of the workers burned to death, either incinerated on site or as they leapt
or fell to the pavement below. The conditions for work, for escape, and

for rescue at the street level were grossly substandard: oily rags in the loft space, blocked-off exits, and a dearth of safety nets or rescue equipment. The Triangle fire of March 25, 1911, in which 146 perished—126 of them Jewish and Italian seamstresses—was a horrendous human bonfire. In the eyewitness account of a young *Milwaukee Journal* reporter, "The first ten thud-deaths shocked me. I looked—saw that there were scores of girls at the windows. The flames from the flood below were up beating in their faces. . . . Behind them I saw many screaming heads. They fell almost together. . . . Then the flames burst out the windows on the floor below them, and curled up into their faces."[36]

The tragic magnitude of the event was too much for the Pittsburgh Survey's powers of description. Such mammoth worksite mismanagement could not be categorized as a "throwback." Nor was the fire attributable to an "accident," gross negligence, or industrial "disease." The horrific details of what happened to the fire's ethnic victims, described as resembling bales of cloth as they jumped to their deaths, was in all ways at odds with the calm tones and suggestions for gradual change associated with the Pittsburgh Survey.[37] Triangle turned assumptions about efficiency and modernization into reproaches.

The irony was that the Triangle Shirtwaist Company's production process was considered state-of-the-art. The company had banished foot power in favor of an electrically powered motor built into each machine.[38] The Washington Place Brown Building loft was a "modern" factory that seemed in fact to have solved the problems in industrial engineering identified by Butler and other Progressives.[39] As in the Pittsburgh Survey, New York's tabulators, in quasi-scientific deference to the large numbers employed at the Triangle facility, labeled this kind of place an industrial establishment.[40] At Triangle and other factories there was timeclocked labor, to be sure. Yet pieceworkers toiled there rather than in their own homes or in those of subcontractors; in essence they did sweated work in the midst of the salaried. The text that accompanies the statistical table of job classifications comments on the scientific management of the work floor and garment production. What it does not mention, however, is that in the Triangle factory, as in similar establishments, efficiency measures included old-time sweatshop ploys: for instance, conversation among women workers sitting next to each other was prohibited.[41] That skilled cutters and tailors, almost all of them men, were not so regulated at Triangle and elsewhere did not testify to enlightened industrial relations but rather reinforced the relegation of unskilled workers to a kind of sweatshop within a factory.

The larger truth was that Triangle's size and power in the industry had enabled it to resist sanitation and safety reforms. One of only a handful of firms that had not settled with the ILGWU after the 1909 Uprising, it remained a non-union shop in 1911. Its ability to pay prevailing union wages, import strike breakers and thugs, and contract out gave it the strength to beat the union in 1909–1910. To ensure a non-union shop, the owners kept a very close eye on their workers, most of whom were young immigrant girls; it was common practice for overseers to search them when they left work and to lock them in the shop during work hours.

In some of the most "modern" features lay the very dangers that claimed so many lives: for maximum productivity, Triangle utilized every available square inch. In these cramped conditions, workers performed their jobs on top of one another.[42] As a vast economic enterprise, the building had passed inspection and was up to date according to the insufficient laws then prevailing. Because the building was allegedly fireproof, many of the workers were toiling in a building whose upper stories were higher than firefighters could reach in a fire. Indeed, often forgotten in accounts of the Triangle fire is that the New York City fire chief himself had for years been urging girls to refuse to work in such shops. Male officialdom, however, had little understanding of female economic need. As Rose Cohen, one sweatshop veteran, remembered, there was very little choice: such places paid immigrants far better than department stores did.

If the Triangle fire was to municipal authorities and more enlightened businesspeople a disastrous example of the extremes of industrial negligence, in the socialist labor press it became a call to action on behalf of all garment workers. The *New York Call,* for instance, revived old associations of "shop" with "sweatshop" to affirm that every garment workers' shop in ethnic New York City—every clothing factory—was a Triangle Shirtwaist Company tragedy waiting to happen.[43] The socialist forum was animated by anger. Mixing labor and Old Testament imagery, the *Call* headlines exhorted workers to claim their rightful place in society. The bard of sweatshop anguish, Morris Rosenfeld, echoed this message in the *Jewish Daily Forward*. One poem, written as a hyperbolic dirge—his signature style—warned that "hell's fire engulfs these slave stalls / And Mammon devours our sons and daughters." But in a sober article on the fire for the same journal, Rosenfeld called Triangle simply "the newer type of sweatshop."[44]

Taken together, Rosenfeld's alternative descriptions of the Triangle fire signaled a return to the late-nineteenth-century language of the sweatshop, with a crucial difference. Even as it was portrayed as a sweated workers' tragedy, the 1911 conflagration became a seminal event for worker self-activity. Workers pointed to the fire as incendiary evidence of a repressive economic and political system. Rather than serving as a reminder of the persistence of inequity in the garment trades—a throwback to the old "cockroach contractors"—the fire signified the "conditions that make life unbearable," in the rousing phrase of one memorial speech.[45] At the funerals and in meeting after meeting near the site of the fire, outrage strengthened the newly formed ILGWU, which would soon become pivotal in the Jewish labor movement.[46]

It was a male ILGWU, however, that publicly appropriated the image.[47] Male unionists immediately used the bully pulpit provided to the ILGWU to forge alliances with influential reformers and push through the Protocols of Peace in 1913 in Chicago. Under these agreements, which from the beginning were honored waveringly in various garment centers in the United States, in the name of raising the industry as a whole, employers signed on to respecting the legal rights of employees. In effect, what Supreme Court Justice Louis D. Brandeis termed "the powers created under this agreement" amounted to "a government to control the relation between employer and employee." The resulting boards of grievances and arbitration standards were part of a management acceptance of unions.[48] In some ways the Protocols of Peace strengthened the union movement in its quest for industrial democracy and enabled it to substitute imagery of empowerment for that of the sweated laborscape.

In 1914, a year after he helped put the Chicago protocols in place, Amalgamated Clothing Workers (ACW) leader Sidney Hillman moved his base of operations from Chicago to New York City.[49] The protocols that Hillman had helped to forge garnered the praise of Pittsburgh Survey leader Paul Kellogg.[50] Yet Kellogg's imprimatur signaled something else as well. In the years to follow, the commissions that were formed by allying professional reformers and unionists in the mold of the protocols excluded workers and used instead the language of Progressive reform. Some anti-strike moderates opposed some of the most forward-looking reforms in the years after the Triangle disaster, in part because skilled cutters, as they had done before the fire, continued to make decent wages at Triangle.[51]

Male unionists honored the Triangle women as they did the other seamstresses whom they viewed as fated by necessity to go out to work. These leaders publicly lamented the young girls sacrificed to the shop and the seamstress mother devoted to the family wage. But they did not include female breadwinners in executive councils or grant them much voice on the shop floor. Among the rank and file there was resentment of any women who managed to get ahead.[52] As the garment trades historian Susan Glenn concludes, the "unwritten laws that kept women out of certain jobs were in part a product of the status anxieties of immigrant men."[53] The pay scales of the Jewish women who were members of the rebel women's subunit of ILGWU local 25, run by the blacklisted garment shop organizer Clara Lemlich and the Italian women members of the "bread and roses" dressmakers' local 89, were not raised appreciably by any of the Protocols of Peace and remained largely unaffected by union initiatives.[54] Lamented Walter Lippmann in a 1915 article, "The Campaign against Sweating," a full four years after Triangle, "We know that thousands of women are below the line which the most moderate estimate can call a living wage."[55]

Antiunion employers in New York–based industries such as white goods and kimonos recruited newly arrived girls. Although they were far from "unorganizable," as male unionists claimed, such young women were unused to or unaware of the efforts of working-class women activists. The former capmaker Pauline Newman, for instance, had worked for years in her girlhood at the Triangle Company and went on to play a prominent—if gender-proscribed—role in the ILGWU. Both she and the organizer Rose Schneiderman lost friends in the Triangle fire, and their public pronouncements urged women workers to honor Triangle by reinvigorating a fighting spirit.[56] The National Women's Trade Union League, with which both women were allied, dated the rhetoric of agency to the Triangle fire itself: "The women who jumped from the tenth story of the Ashe Building," wrote Elizabeth Dutcher, an officer of the Ladies' Waist and Dressmakers' Union, in 1912, "were self-reliant working women, who had never asked for charitable assistance, and who were making their way."[57]

The oratory of these and other radicalized young women garment workers of the self-described "1909 vintage" thus revealed a political engagement and self-invention that predated the Triangle fire itself. In fact, they historicized the Triangle Company's ruthless practices when they invoked the 1909–1910 Shirtwaist Strike. The so-called Uprising of the 20,000 was initiated at the Triangle Shirtwaist Company and grew to a five-month resistance that led to benefits for workers, many of them male. Triangle was among the companies that remained obdurate, and workers did not win union recognition there.

Novels on the strike, most male-authored, such as James Oppenheim's *The Nine-Tenths* (1911) or Arthur Bullard's *Comrade Yetta* (1913), were written from the perspective of the woman-martyring fire. As such, these books either rearranged or conflated the two events so that the so-called modern shop was a site of protest and conflagration alike. Recognizing the superannuation of this sweated site, male novelists rewrote the old turn tenement novel and assumed that women workers had the right to strike. Still, while they point to the oppressions of the "speeder," or quick worker, in the vest and coat factories of the Lower East Side, they have little to say about the longevity of the women's political action. Another fictionalized account of the uprising, Theresa Serber Malkiel's *Diary of a Shirtwaist Striker*, originally published in the *Call* the year after that seminal event (1911), proclaimed a triumphant spirit. Malkiel, a former garment worker herself, upheld the view of the Shirtwaist Strike as "the first real girls' strike" and attempted to reclaim the narrative from the many male commentators who had questioned whether women could sustain a labor initiative of that magnitude. Her sweatshop is as much a site of political apprenticeship as of unfit conditions. Deliberately avoiding a Jewish heroine in the name of cross-ethnic female solidarity, she moves her protagonist Mary from tepid sweatshop talk of fiancés and clothes to awe of real-life activist Clara Lemlich's union oratory. Mary's transit is through countless picket lines, brawls with the police, and a workhouse stint, all standard in Shirtwaist Strike novels by both male and female authors. But when Mary converts her paternalistic fiancé, an artisan distrustful of Jews and Italians, Malkiel makes her point. In so doing she also memorializes women's struggles at Triangle two years before.

But despite the Shirtwaist Strike and the Triangle disaster, as the ILGWU made advances for its male members, officials espoused protecting women rather than granting them parity. The resistant consciousness of early-twentieth-century women sweatshop workers continues to be the subject of much debate.[58] They may well have resented the Pittsburgh Survey's pejorative view of them as inefficient ethnic females, just as their predecessors suffered from the Triangle era's emphasis on a masculine discourse in which skill and advancement were the province of men.

With the arrival of the superficially prosperous, anti-"Red" 1920s, billed as the era of the "tired radical," the sweatshop narrative would both recede and take new forms. Up-from-the-ghetto memoirs and fiction were heralded by Zoe Beckley's significantly titled novel *A Chance to Live* (1918), in which the heroine chooses careerism over organizing clothing workers. Ushering in a postwar cadre of literature on breadwinning women's individuality, such tales would offer alternative arguments for ethnic women garment workers' entry into modern life. A new set of social surveys on Old World conditions in the New would review earlier assumptions about men's and women's industrial efficiency in a post-sweatshop era. And Yiddish theater's swan song to the landsmen-toilers and the sweatshop of yore would mark the New Deal decade's scrutiny of the Depression-era workscape.

WOMANHOOD, MODERN OR SWEATED: ASSIMILATORS AND DEVIANTS IN THE 1920S

By the early 1920s, the split between social work and social science widened. A new field, particularly as practiced under the aegis of the University of Chicago graduate division of sociology, the Chicago School, complicated the Pittsburgh Survey's perceptions of Darwinian ethnic-industrial neighborhoods in the shadow of the mills or the yards. The venues now became "a mosaic of social worlds," to quote Louis Wirth, one of the Chicago School's prime movers.[59] Redirecting rather than shedding the Progressives' emphasis on the necessity of acculturation, the sociological researchers Robert E. Park, Florian Znaniecki, Ernest Burgess, and W. I. Thomas did not dismiss as atavistic or inefficient the work and life habits of marginalized groups. Rather they were fascinated by the relationships between such groups and those habits. It was imperative, they argued, to do extensive field research on the links between individuals and the "group mind"—the way the individual's conception of himself is formed by community and migration.

These men tried for more detachment than their Progressive predecessors had brought to critiques of the provincialism of ghetto groups. They sought to understand the divided loyalties of the acculturated who live in two worlds and feel marginal in both. Like the Pittsburgh social engineers, they avoided discussion of class conflict, but they did recognize a clash in values between the dominant American culture and those of marginalized groups, including ethnic ones. Such an approach figured in the Old World to New studies of the Polish peasant, the Russian Jew, the Italian paisan, and the Jewish ghetto dweller—all populations inured to the sweatshop.[60] (The phrase "Polish sweatshop girl," furthermore, was often interchangeable with "Jewish immigrant seamstress.")[61] In such studies, the process whereby groups moved first in an "accommodation" stage was central to the breakdown of ethnic insularity. Having gained greater access to civic, cultural, and economic life, they then advanced to integration into the larger society.[62]

Even as members of these groups transplanted to America became "modern," gaps in this process tended to be studied in terms of the social and psychological dislocation, ethnic and otherwise, that emerged from other members' sense of marginalization. But in the search for resistance to mainstream modernity, Chicago authors found that sweatshop injustice was sociologically less compelling than the city venues in which marginalized ethnic behavior could be observed: barrooms, cheap hotels, amusement parks, and gang-ruled neighborhood streets. Thus, rather than examine the sites in terms of oppressive labor relations, these researchers shifted their focus from economic struggle to what Park called the "laboratory" city's behavior out of the mainstream. Deviant modernity, about which much was written, could ironically either be the result of psychic confusion about New World values or the dangerous loss of identity consequent on moving into the mass culture and the impersonality of city life.[63] In studying those who overturned the dominant moral order, Park was particularly, but not exclusively, interested in hobos, gangs, wayward women, prisoners, dance-hall women, prostitutes—all from working-class backgrounds. Park also addressed the unorthodox conduct of the American-born bourgeoise who sought luxuries and sensual experiences that her daytime husband could not provide. Hidden from scrutiny was the sweatshop, although it nominally belonged to antisocial institutions.

In his analysis of Chicago's various Jewish work groups in *The Ghetto* (1927), Louis Wirth revisited this fading cultural site. A German Jew, Wirth had a particular interest in the problems of minorities. He was aristocratically perplexed by the often unruly and sectarian behavior of the East European Jewish working class. He skirted the Chicago School's description of Jewish racial-ethnic atavism as indigenous to the slum by envisioning the outmodedness of the ghetto itself. When he narrowed his focus to concentrate on Chicago's poorer Russian Jews, he simply listed the 1880s sweatshop as one of a number of early trades—among them peddling and shopkeeping—plied by these East European immigrants. Thus, Wirth touristically included the surviving sweatshops with tenements, missions, and street markets as quaint neighborhood sights soon to disappear entirely.[64]

Others studying Italians in Chicago used a similar set of descriptors. Largely unconcerned with the Progressive dictum that sweated garment shops were out of step with history, the 1920s observers trivialized the difficult experience in the name of local color. In the "sociology noir" of the Chicago underworld, Wirth's precept that "the clustering of Jews in a particular space made them what they were" was extended by his Chicago colleagues to unskilled factory women and servant girls gone wayward.[65] In W. Isaac Thomas's *The Unadjusted Girl* (1923), one extensive case history concerns Esther, a Jewish prison inmate who was an industrious worker at low-level women's jobs but was unable to "adjust to American customs" and was constantly picked up for soliciting and petty theft.[66] Despite the association of such resistance to mainstream values with the lower-class factory women engaged in drab and joyless sewing jobs, Park, Thomas, and other Chicago School researchers, in their sociological life histories of "maladjusted" women, did not think of the sweatshop as a launching pad. The very term "sweated labor" was passé, to be replaced by "deviants" who peopled women's prisons and reform houses and looked only to theft, the use of drugs and alcohol, and commercialized prostitution. Using the new lexicon of mental and physical instability, Thomas and Park saw exploited toilers as prey to economic determinism yet consumed with the desire to meet their needs and wishes.

In their very passing over of the sweatshop because it embodied neither deviant nor liberating modernism, the Park-Thomas group missed
the feminine frustration generated by dead-end work. Interestingly, their
studies of low-wage male occupations, including seasonal day labor, examine the men's wanderlust and lack of tolerance for routine. In the classic study *Hobos and Homelessness* (1927), Nels Anderson pointed out that
the derelict, though contemptuous of organized society, was still productive. These men worked more often than not for their keep, and did
much of the marginal field work that more settled men would not. In
contrast to such mitigations of the male social deviant, the dissatisfied
woman worker was worth scrutiny only when she found a safety valve—
or a dangerous existence—in the sex trade.

More popular writing directed at mass-culture audiences did reinvoke
the sweatshop motif to address women's thwarted self-development. One
such form was the women's assimilation memoir, as generated by Rose
Cohen, Elizabeth Hasanovitz, Bella Cohen Spewack, and Anzia Yezierska, its major practitioner.[67] Sometimes labeled the "historian of Hester
Street" because of her eyewitness ethnography, Yezierska was most often
identified as the "sweatshop Cinderella."[68] To supply the oral testimony
that Chicago-style sociologists left unreported, she rebutted the case
study approach on which Park, Burgess, Thomas, and Dewey (Park had
studied with Dewey at Chicago) prided themselves.[69]

Anzia Yezierska's stories create an alternative documentary in this regard. She provides clues to what the Park group left unreported. She incorporates into tales with titles like "Hunger," "Wings," and *Salome of the
Tenements* her heroines' dislike of the "old witch" owner, as they spend all
day sewing "dead" buttons onto clothing.[70] Not only does she indicate
the old-time shop's gender division—women "finishing" clothes by
hand, men running up garments at machines—but for the "objectivity"
of the Chicago School she substitutes scathing analysis. Garment work
joins an array of "women's" occupations. Her immigrant everywomen
work in paper-box factories (*Bread Givers*) and as janitors ("Hunger,"
1920), laundresses ("Soap and Water," 1920), and household help, both
paid and unpaid ("Wings" and "The Lost 'Beautifulness,'" both 1920).[71]
She exposes them to bad rooms, nasty landlords, grasping employers,
tyrannical rabbinical fathers, manipulative, self-subordinating mothers,
and snobbish philanthropists and bureaucrats.

But it is the sweatshop that animates her greatest indignation, or rather her own arduous climb out of it. In one of her most famous stories, "Hunger," she is the subject of her own work biography. As, still a green-horn, she walks the "Hands Wanted" New York City streets, Shenah Pessah pits her "vigorous, young hands—made strong through toil" (41) against the "whirr of machine—flying belt—clicking clatter of whirring wheels" (42) encountered in the shop. Progressive rules bear no weight: the lunch break is taken atop (illegally placed) bundles of cloth, on window sills; there is no overtime pay; and the word "union" is not thought of.

But Shenah's solidarity is with her ambitions alone. The theme is familiar enough: Shenah feels at first inadequate, then competent, later disgusted at the meager pay and work-floor gossip about hairstyles and husbands. She speeds up the pace of immigrant assimilation even as she sews. When, near story's end, Shenah speaks passionately about her longing to fashion a successful American self, her dungeon shop becomes an operatic stage. Addressing the reader without need of a Chicago School intermediary, she recounts how anger at her lowly job produces only strength to triumph over the shop.

In "Soap and Water," Yezierska's alter-ego heroine, her English now fluent and her upward climb more certain, is nearer her goal but still far from it. She is a night school émigré berated by a Columbia woman dean for perspiring after a sweated shop day. In a narrative revenge, she berates the dean years later, using much the same resentful language as she used with her former sweatshop bosses.

Eventually she educates herself up and out of Hester Street clothing shops to participate in "enlightened" studies of much the same people. Here, years after she graduates from college, her signature anger can finally take narrative revenge on those slumming. There is a fitting irony here, for the sweatshop Cinderella can redefine sweatshop exploitation as social survey. She recounts her negative experiences in assisting the Chicago School professor John Dewey in his research on Polish working-class Philadelphia. Dewey's 1919 study was undertaken in the same years as the classic Thomas-Znaniecki study, *The Polish Peasant in Europe and America* (1918–1920).[72] Her dislike of Dewey's survey and the urban sociology of which it was a part was so intense that it was still central fifteen years later in the 1930s retrospective roman à clef *All I Could Never Be* (1932). As she had done for decades, Yezierska added Dewey to the cast of Protestant, native-born, educated surveyors sent out from the university to settlement houses and poor communities.[73] Her outspoken protagonist alter ego angrily chides this man slumming for exotic ethnics rather than addressing the conditions that make the shops, but Yezierska herself implicitly extols the language of acculturation and assimilation in a complicated way. Many of her tales recount the protagonist's departure from sweatshop work. Her great subject, after all, is herself in all her "hoarse-throated orality."[74] In her emphasis on selective ascension, she does not spend much time arguing for the eradication of the shop. In all of her sweatshop writings, for instance, she never mentions the Triangle strike or the subsequent fire.

As one of the first U.S. labor writers to capture the urgency, agency, and post-sweatshop regrets of the immigrant ghetto, Yezierska also exposes some of the falsities of assimilation purveyed by mass-market explicators. Phrased another way, it was not so easy to live out the Chicago School theories. Pervasive in her writings is the dialectic between the remorse of success and hatred of the past. This conflict plays out in everything Yezierska wrote, and her solutions are deliberately artificial. That is, she knew that the sweatshop was the rock on which her literary reputation was built, yet her popularity was also based on her fantasy plots in which Old World passion melts (or fails to melt) WASP ice. The ghetto Cinderella story was such a popular prism through which the sweatshop girl was seen that Yezierska wrote book after book, went to Hollywood, and eventually lived on Fifth Avenue with a maid as she told and retold it.

Bella Cohen Spewack, whose escape from obscurity lasted longer than Yezierska's, revisited her brief sweated experience in a similar way. Her unfinished 1923 memoir, *Streets,* looks satirically at the sweatshop pay divisions between male pants pressers and oppressed finishing girls.[75] Like Yezierska, Spewack subordinated her savaging of women's sweatshop sufferings to deploring the way young ethnic women too often accepted mainstream disdain of foreign-born seamstresses. In her memoir and swan song to her unhappy youth, she gives a bitter indictment of the real America. A few days' apprenticeship at the sewing table alerted her to the groping hands and economic meanness of the bosses. It is significant, however, that Spewack made a point of her limited experience of sweated labor. As a high school girl working for a few Sundays in a men's coat shop on the loft-top floor of her Lower East Side block, she escaped the degrading work and noxious odors of dirt and perspiration after each day. Her knowledge of the shop is thus mostly observation: an uncouth pants presser marries her mother, who does piecework at home before, during, and after marriage to this violent man. Aside from some chapters of *Streets,* she largely mutes the bitterness of the unfinished memoir, as if she knew that even had she completed the book, it could not compete with Yezierska's happy-ending message of assimilation for a post-sweatshop era.

Spewack told the alternative women's story that the culture would not publish, much less reward: no girl at her needle, however talented, could live a modern existence. For her, as for Yezierska, the remembered sweatshop existed only to brand the women who stayed there.[76] Not surprisingly, narratives of the male sweatshop experience would find far more receptive audiences.

Sweatshop Moses in the Promised Land: Manhood and Retrospection, 1918–1930

By the 1920s the male sweatshop sufferings of Morris Rosenfeld's frail East Side tailors, the "bearers of burdens," seemed more remote than ever.[77] Chicago ethnography had not chosen to acknowledge the persistence of sweated men's garment work. Neither had women memoirists, who instead cast tailors, pressers, and cutters as workers who were oppressive to women, whether small-time harassers or bosslike profiteers.

In remasculinizing the sweatshop, Jewish men of letters and their Yiddish theater interpreters provided an alternative to the views of both Robert Parks and Anzia Yezierska. While acknowledging the death of the shop, these writers resurrected the "inside" shop and repeopled it with skilled male tailors. They complicated the vanished site to make it a setting that could accommodate two periods: the Triangle/early ILGWU years and the onset of the Great Depression.

Sholem Asch, one of the foremost Yiddish authors of the time even in non-Jewish circles, devoted a lengthy novel to the superannuated sweatshop. Asch's novel *Uncle Moses* is concerned with the sweatshop culture of the landsmen, or Old World shtetl neighbors, and the patriarchal bosses who, having escaped from the shops themselves, return to impose their will on less fortunate landsmen. His novel mixes acute observation and melodrama to examine Lower East Side power relations among transplanted clothing workers.[78] As such, it played a vital role in reasserting Yiddish themes in prose and periodical literature. Serialized in Abraham Cahan's *Forward,* the chief Yiddish-language daily in the United States, in 1917, it was published in book form in Yiddish the next year. Its English translation appeared in the early 1920s. Capitalizing on the nostalgic power of the work, the actor-director-screenwriter Maurice Schwartz reinterpreted it for a late 1920s generation that included more affluent factory workers and their American-born children. Identified with the coming of age of the Yiddish theater in the 1920s and the Yiddish cinema in America in the early 1930s, Schwartz took the principal role in both the stage and movie productions. He adapted the Asch novel first for the Yiddish Art Theater in 1930 and then as a Yiddish sound film in 1931.[79] Even today, as a theatrical ethnography of displaced shtetl tailors on the Lower East Side, it stands up far better than Joan Micklin Silver's *Hester Street* (1975), based on Cahan's *Yekl,* or the 1979 Hollywood costume picture, *The Triangle Factory Fire Scandal.*

The enduring significance of each version of the story lies in the complex portrait of the passing of the old Jewish shops. Schwartz emphasized how the boss's cynical nostalgia defined this transitional phase for acculturating Jews who were initially unused to their American surrounding. The shops were staffed by overeducated immigrants forced by economic dependence to be deferential to uncultured types whose superior they would have been in the Old World. Asch observes that these men were "refined fathers of Kuzmin captive in this stifling shop enslaved to the needle."[80] When the narrative begins, they have not severed their ties to the shtetl or to their boss, Moses Melnick, who had arranged for them to be brought over to work in his shop. Initially it seems that this brotherhood of memory cuts across class lines: the owner is a living reminder of the Pale of settlement where they were all born.

Unlike the novel, the play and film versions "directly engaged the progressive currents of the day—political and aesthetic."[81] The stage set for the Yiddish Art Theater version, for instance, used the latest social realist artistic techniques to portray the prisonlike work space of Melnick's shop. The film built on the captivity theme by making explicit Moses's will to control all aspects of his employees' lives. To adjust to the 1920s labor reality of the strengthening ILGWU, Schwartz makes Moses's union-busting views more vocal. "Union people don't work in my shop," he asserts as he jocularly lays down the law to his beaten-down tailors. "Only townsmen."[82]

By retaining Asch's eponymous title in both the play and the film, Schwartz inscribes the novel's pity for Uncle Moses as a fading sweatshop Jew. Schwartz's play and film adaptations also background the "sweatshop plot" of the loft-size venue piled with clothing-laden tables for the landsmen cutters and operators. The real focus is the melodrama of a self-styled Moses doomed to wander a sweatshop wilderness. The core of the plot is the undoing of Moses Melnick. Anxious to lord it over his men, he loses credibility; foolishly in love with a young woman employee who detests him, he is doubly dethroned when she betrays him for a better man.

As one of the most enduring pieces of 1920s sweatshop Yiddishkeit, Uncle Moses reminded its East European shtetl audience that the passing of the shop was no simple thing. The site that enchained and the boss who trafficked in loyalty fell with the rise of the garment unions. At the same time, this tyrant had his own pathos. The legendary Schwartz inhabited the role on film, producing sympathy for Asch's grasping but paternalistically generous figure. In the final scenes, broken and Learlike (Schwartz had early on immortalized that Shakespearean role on the Yiddish stage), he haunts his former shop and reminisces with his onetime subjects.

With the coming of the 1920s, the old Jewish sweatshop boss was a Dickensian curiosity. Even the influential *Forward* editor Abraham Cahan had altered his signature sweatshop fables of ambitious bottom-rung tailors in favor of the factory-owning title character in his novel *David Levinsky*. This garment trades autocrat, far from chiding his workers for disloyalty, as Asch's Melnick does, disclaims any Old World co-religionist's identification with them. Rather, he boasts of draining them of strength as he climbs to the status of a manufacturer. Modernizing his workplace in the name of brisk efficiency, he also disdains the old role of paternalistically controlling relations with employees.

Cahan's heartless Levinsky is an updated version of the uncouth cockroach contractors of his own 1890s sweatshop fiction. Cahan thus illuminates Asch/Schwartz's difficulty in the post-sweatshop 1910s and 1920s with imbuing the anachronistic Moses Melnick with grandeur. There is no tragedy in the downfall of the landsman's quasi-religious shop culture as depicted by Asch and Schwartz, for Moses is simply not modern enough. Neither a proponent of Triangle-like state-of-the-art equipment nor a successful tyrant over unionism, Moses cannot keep up with American progress, unlike the self-styled lawgiver of Cahan's garment shop world. As the Great Depression approaches, Moses, like his sweated jobsite, is passé. Whatever sympathy this old-time boss generates, Moses and his ilk would soon be among the capitalistic villains of 1930s social protest art.

In the opening decades of the twentieth century, a succession of interpreters declared the death of the shop. The Pittsburgh Survey-era Progressives "proved" the sweatshop's obsolescence by representing the shop as a pretechnological throwback and its toilers as woefully out of step with American self-forging and optimism. With rare exceptions, Progressive-era reformers followed the late nineteenth century's nativist predecessors who blamed the poor for their sweated plight. Equally crucial was that the sweatshop served larger ideological purposes. Progressives impatient with the ethnic inability to climb out of the shop associated sweated labor with a lack of ambition. In this vision of the sweatshop, the will to succeed remained the alternative to succumbing to exploitation. In either case, the American Dream remained intact.

This willful forgetting of sweatshops helped characterize the fitfully affluent 1920s. By the era of the Chicago School's "maladjusted" working class, few in the social work establishment saw the enduring sweatshop as a rebuttal of American upward mobility rhetoric. One lonely holdout was the iconoclastic idealist Lewis Hine. Throughout the two and one-half decades preceding the rise of the Chicago School, he was the preeminent photo-historian of manual work. Ubiquitous, he photographed disoriented but hopeful Ellis Island immigrants; workers in substandard Buffalo, New York, canneries; those in similarly illegal Illinois and Delaware factories; and a thousand industrial communities from Massachusetts to the Southwest. He chronicled the prematurely aged breaker boys of the Pennsylvania coal mines, the stunted mill children of the textile South, the underaged boys and mature men debilitated alike by the Pittsburgh steel mills, and what he termed the "prevailing type of garment workroom," the American sweatshop.[83] Always careful to provide subtexts or descriptive labels, he widened his purview in thousands more photo-documents for the National Child Labor Committee, the

Pittsburgh Survey, and the *Survey* (later the *Survey Graphic*) magazine. It was thus no surprise that in his own lean years, the 1920s, he was still touring tenement house apartments of artificial flower makers, millinery workers, and other ethnic seamstresses.[84]

But these photographs rarely achieved the signature status of his Progressive-era work. In an antisweatshop essay for the *Child Labor Bulletin* in 1915, Hine had warned, "The home is for the family—Industry Keep Out."[85] But to many in the culture at large, his photo-stories on the impoverished single mothers unwillingly carrying on the sweatshop tradition seemed jeremiads rather than timely documents.[86]

By the late 1920s, to those who were not allied to the dominant society's professional (and usually Protestant) social reformers, the sweatshop discussion appeared at a vanishing point. Interested in deviance rather than labor oppressiveness, the Chicago School of sociology all but succeeded in erasing it from public discussion and reform campaigns alike. In a different kind of erasure, eyewitness narrators who had climbed up from the shop, like Yezierska and Spewack, cast contemptuous backward looks at it. Jewish male sentimentality revived the shop as a witness to fledgling Jewish garment trade unionism. Indeed, in revivifying Asch's tale of paternalistic boss and increasingly hostile workers, those like Maurice Schwartz transiently heralded the early needle-trades labor movement. Yet, by casting the boss as a semitragic figure, even the workers' limited labor activity was a reminder the bygone shop.

Just as the vision dimmed, Depression-era social realism, dedicated to honoring the worker, signaled both a return to and a reinvention of the sweatshop of memory. Nowhere was this more visible than in the artists' and photographers' sections of the Works Progress Administration (WPA). The next chapter examines how, from the New Deal years onward, sweatshop aesthetics arose to represent the "colorful" sweatshops of Wirth, the transplanted shtetl tailors of Asch/Schwartz, and the unhappy seamstresses of the Jewish woman author's Lower East Side. The heyday of the Congress of Industrial Organizations and the American Communist Party would also see the rise of a leftist sweatshop iconography and a lumpenproletariat.

With the sweatshop branded legally and morally unacceptable in the New Deal order, the 1930s era generated new representations. But to what extent did visual artists historicize it? Conversely, how did the anachronistic sweatshop acquire a very real 1930s face?

PART TWO

 Sweatshop Aesthetics

CHAPTER 4

Newsreel of Memory

THE WPA SWEATSHOP IN THE GREAT DEPRESSION

I paint my time using the people as evidence.
—Portraitist Alice Neel, quoted in "I Paint My Time
Using the People as Evidence,"
Chronicle of Higher Education (2000)

Late at night I came home completely exhausted. My
mother was still bent over her sewing machine. A
mountain of work lay around her, and she was on her
last piece. She was so weary she could hardly lift her
head. I looked at her, sat down next to her, and put my
arms around her. Tears filled my eyes.
—WPA muralist William Gropper, "Home Work,"
Freiheit (1948)

THE SWEATSHOP MEETS the New Deal in Ben Shahn's
epic mural in Roosevelt, New Jersey (1935–1936), commissioned for the
resettlement and renaming of the former Jersey Homesteads (figure 1).
The reinvented town was designed to provide jobs and sanctuary for displaced European garment workers during the Depression and to aid the
ethnic needle trades in New York City, where the labor market had been
devastated by the Depression. The Roosevelt mural exemplifies unionist
idealism in a kind of utopian re-visioning of present-day conditions. In
his portrayal of the end of sweatshops in times so troubled that these
places were again flourishing, Ben Shahn reaffirmed the New Deal's belief in an empowered and upwardly mobile proletariat freed, finally, from
history.

Shahn's understanding of the persistence of sweated labor into the
1930s appears in a coded way in the mural. Superficially he depicts in

roseate terms the plant and the cooperative farm where garment workers, through a marriage of ILGWU and government subsidies, would labor part time at each work site. Yet Shahn's artwork also suggests that those fleeing to America in the 1930s to escape the Nazis may have been the means of perpetuating the shop: the lofts and tenement apartments in the middle of his canvas are in American cities. Nor is the time in his mural only historical: the workers he portrays could well have staffed 1930s sweatshops. Although new colonies and government camps might have been a partial solution to poverty, the conditions that formed the shop preceded the 1930s and were common during that time.

Shahn and the WPA artists considered in this chapter were well aware that the needle trades still lagged behind basic industry. The limited victories of the post–Triangle fire era were forgotten when the protocols agreed on by unions and clothing manufacturers lost momentum in the 1920s; at the same time, schisms between Communists and Socialists threatened to tear apart powerful entities like the ILGWU. The unionist battle against the sweatshop was revivified in the early militance of the 1930s, when battles for collective bargaining and the minimum wage also intensified. Enduring benefits were gained for skilled male workers, and the indignities of being clocked for going to the bathroom or charged for renting one's machine were eliminated. But many of the clothing shops in large industrial cities remained, in the words of the son of a veteran, "ratty." Remarked one Italian woman veteran of the Progressive era shops still working in the 1930s: "It used to be twelve people crowded around a sewing table; now it's ten."[1]

The unions themselves often turned a blind eye to the clothing contractors whose shops employed their members but engaged in dubious labor policies. Publicly both David Dubinsky of the ILGWU and the head of the Amalgamated Clothing Workers, Sidney Hillman, welcomed the National Recovery Act of 1934 and its attacks on sweatshop and child labor.[2] Yet, especially before the rise of the Congress of Industrial Organizations (CIO), the "slashing of [NRA] code standards," observes one recent historian of the garment industry, "was the rule, not the exception."[3]

The charge of engaging in sweatshop practices had limited resonance, however, in a time of vast joblessness; people welcomed any kind of work. By the late 1930s, with the coming of job-creating agencies like the Works Progress Administration (which included the Federal Artists' Project [FAP]), and the rise of the CIO, whose focus was on autos, rubber, coal, and steel, Hillman and Dubinsky had become needle-trade allies. Whether in their speeches or in the recollections of their own rank and file, the sweated work of the decade's second half emerged as more than a renascent site or a disturbing throwback. The sweated workplace became part of a debate on how to help the nation as a whole find decent jobs.

Visual artists also placed the sweatshop in a much larger landscape, one fraught with symbolic meaning. A great many easel painters, illustrators, and muralists bypassed the subject in favor of hope-inspiring Americanist portraits and murals of forward-looking workers.[4] Yet some who sought an "art for the people" came from working-class backgrounds and had done shop and organizing work in the needle trades and elsewhere. For them, sweatshop subject matter had the pictorial potential to challenge the official optimism of Franklin Delano Roosevelt's artist-employing Works Progress (later Work Projects) Administration, created in the spring of 1935. In artistic circles, in fact, the WPA was synonymous with the Federal Artists' Project, "the most important patron of the visual arts in the United States during the Depression."[5] Particularly powerful were the large-scale installations of "public art" for venues as diverse as the Department of the Interior and the nation's post offices, commemorating everything from the building of Hoover Dam to the factory floor of Ford Motor Company.

The muralists who were producing paintings and frescoes for the Public Works of Art Project (PWAP, later subsumed under WPA) knew better than to depict the strikes, demonstrations, and breadlines—in short, the inequities of capitalism—that were widespread at the time.[6] But new visual possibilities were available to the artists who were working on sweatshop paintings. They could both employ this industrial throwback to mark the urgency of 1930s poverty and despair and critique the New Deal's funding for artists, to the extent that their sweatshop portraits were backward-looking.

Among the New York artists who surrealistically reminded viewers of the luckless Singer sewing machine operators or home pieceworkers whose pinched lives served as metaphors for the Depression's economic traumas were Ilya Bolotowsky, Philip Evergood, and Lew Davis.

Bolotowsky's retrospection about his motives might serve for them all: "They told us to paint urban scenes," he remarked matter-of-factly forty years later.[7] By then a celebrated Abstract Expressionist, he had exhibited easel paintings completed under the WPA in shows held by Art Front, a Communist Party artists' "union" which also published an eponymous journal. (His colleague Philip Evergood recalled being roughed up during a sit-in at the New York WPA headquarters.) Bolotowsky's 1934–1935 painting *Sweatshop* was described by an *Art Front* critic as a "very fine . . . Expressionist painting of needleworkers."[8] To modern re-visions there is much chaos but little of the shop. A portly, androgynous figure bends over a sewing table while other distorted background figures and a dressmaker's dummy compete for cubist space. The psychic dislocations of sweated work rather than the actual conditions of labor are well captured, but there is little in the pictorial rhetoric that is easily comprehensible. More accessible is Philip Evergood's *The Toiler* (1938). A skeletal mother sits in an emaciated daze at her sewing machine, oblivious to her spindly, ghostlike son sitting on the floor in front of her sewing table. A pile of unfinished garments dwarfs those finished, and human time is as suspended as maternal concern. Lew Davis's *Eight Figures* (1935) seats similarly anomic seamstresses, fixated on their machines, with a ghoulish fluorescent half-light obscuring or distorting their faces. Even in their rounded backs and tensed postures, they seem motionless, as if both bereft of sympathy and unable to accept it.

Despite their dual allegiance to the WPA and leftism, these and other artists were understandably more interested in experimentation with pictorial styles than in offering recognizable representations of the sweated workplace. Other quite different WPA artists, who worked with or knew of one another and were loosely called Social Realists, balanced documentary impulses with aesthetic ones. To assess how these painters defined sweatshop verisimilitude for the 1930s, we turn to four of the most representative, William Gropper (1897–1977), Moses Soyer (1900–1974), George Biddle (1885–1973), and Ben Shahn (1885–1973). Joining Gropper, who continued what had become an unpopular sweatshop tradition into the Cold War era, the worker-artist Eugene Salamin (1912–) provided a WPA coda to Depression-era visual narrative.

THE HUMPENPROLETARIAT:
WILLIAM GROPPER

No other WPA artist, indeed no other artist of the time, did more than William Gropper to insert the sweatshop into social realist iconography. If he is remembered now, it is for his monumental oil paintings of industrial heroism, such as the 1940–1941 frieze *Auto Industry*. This Detroit post office mural is a celebration of the CIO: machinists of various types engage in a kind of group labor dance, each manning his drill press or pulley with complete concentration and focused energy. They are union men all, looking toward the light of the factory ceiling. Illuminated by the vast industrial windows, many even wear white shirts (in a repudiation of the "blue-collar" stereotype) as they put their shoulders to the work of the nation. As a tribute to the collective bargaining shop of the then-powerful United Auto Workers (UAW), *Auto Industry* is unparalleled.

In artistic terms, the central figure in the frieze is a factory-floor athlete of great muscularity, reminiscent of discus throwers. A similarly athletic display characterizes the figures who are at one with their drill presses and work routines. Gropper was an art school veteran who had been taught by academically trained artists and later by the groundbreakers of the Ashcan School of urban painting, Robert Henri and George Bellows.[9] From them he learned to ground his portrait art in a tradition of working-class subjects. Furthermore, like his contemporaries Isabel Bishop, Reginald Marsh, and Kenneth Hayes Miller (the Fourteenth Street School), Gropper combined classical poses and fluid yet idealized motions to render the worker figures of his day.

Yet unlike the older Ashcan painters and Fourteenth Street artists, Gropper was an artist whose politics had always been rooted in his hardscrabble garment trades youth. "Work Like Hell and Be Happy," showing bent-over men and their machines, was the title of a 1922 early cartoon he drew for the *Liberator*.[10] By 1925 he was contributing to *Advance,* the publication of the Amalgamated Clothing Workers Union (ACWU). In the years that followed, as evidenced by his satiric pictures of rich men and politicians, he expanded his "red" graphic art. Gropper thought of himself, as did many Communist Party members, as a cultural worker, and by 1927 he was a delegate to a ten-year celebration of the Russian Revolution. Still desperately poor when hired in 1934 for the short-lived

Public Works of Art Project, he had little admiration for Franklin Delano Roosevelt and was no doubt aware of the strictures to produce pro–New Deal art.[11] Like other artists whose work contained controversial political images, he did not always turn in the prescribed work. One example, his satirical 1930s drawing, *Capitalism Tries to Smash the WPA,* aptly reveals his wry understanding of the opposition to government support for the arts.

His fellow WPA artist Louis Lozowick wrote in a posthumous homage that Gropper "inherited the legacy of the industrial sweatshop system."[12] Born in 1897 on the Lower East Side's Pitt Street, he was the son of Harry and Jenny Gropper, who met in garment district sweatshops and worked there for years. As the oldest of six, William early on became a breadwinner, working as a bushel boy in the kind of sordid loft factory so brilliantly captured by the sweatshop photojournalist Lewis Hine. Throughout his grammar school years he hauled bundles home for his mother, who did extra piecework at home.[13] "The sweatshop gave us our livelihood," he reminisced, with the House Un-American Activities Committee (HUAC) looming, in *Freiheit,* the Yiddish-language organ of the Communist Party, "but robbed us of our mother."[14]

Gropper was haunted all of his life by memories of his slaving mother.[15] *Seamstress* pictures her sewing near a dangerous scissors. Executed in 1938, the painting is the result of many studio sketches dating from the mid-1920s. It portrays her as she runs her machine and concentrates on hemming, her back to the viewer. She wears the flowing white shirt of the workers in the Detroit mural, but the inverted "V" shape made by the blouse seems to cut into her bent back. A pincerlike pair of sewing scissors rests near her left hand as she guides the machine needle over a garment so long it seems to extend from outside the room to the remnant-scattered floor. A parallel fold to the right of her work table demarcates her imprisoning sewing area. She retains her femininity—the outline of her face is pleasing and soft—but the darkness that seems to emanate from her black Singer sewing machine envelops the lower part of her face and renders her more a shadow of a pretty woman than a corporeal presence.

In a quite different painting executed the same year with the same title, another Gropper seamstress, a desexed being compared with his feminine mother, sews by hand, stooping over her work, while a tailor at a machine, his bent back turned to us, sits at the operator's table. Ironies abound here too: although her face is visible, this seamstress is so absorbed in and chained to her sewing that the viewer's eyes move quickly from her rough-hewn features to the worn hands that encircle the material.[16] A light fixture with three ominous bulbs seems aflame, and the threadbare tenements outside the grim shop are cell-like.

His cartoon art for the *New Masses* often featured figures such as beggars on crutches hawking their misery or defiant dishwashers, their hands submerged in filthy water. In Gropper's satirical drawings these figures bend from the waist slightly, all the while arguing their case with the world: the beggar of "Steady Employment" balances on his homemade crutches while yelling at offstage bystanders. The slavey in the restaurant kitchen, with piles of dishes on the counter on the right and his back turned to a massive chef-boss who is heedlessly lighting a cigarette, speaks his discontent to the drying dishes on his left.[17] While portraying the exploitative work culture, these early cartoons explore body language as a form of resistance in itself. Viewed against the signature humpbacked figures of Gropper's sweatshop portraiture, these straight-backed figures are rebels indeed.[18]

For those drawings and paintings, Gropper drew on a nineteenth-century European tradition of depicting working subjects as allegories of toil. Jean François Millet's 1858 charcoal *Women Carrying Faggots* is completely defined by the backbreaking work.[19] If Millet focused on the solitary peasant laboring as one attuned to rural time, Goya's celebrated 1820s painting *The Forge* would establish a nineteenth-century industrial pattern imitated in Georges Seurat's *Stonebreakers* (1884) and *Men Hammering Stakes, Lumberjacks* (1882–1883). These works play not on mythic images of Hephaestus or Hercules but on peasant bodies displaying brutish strength: the principal figures are faceless, their powerful backs turned toward the viewer, their personalities subsumed under the task.

In what the proletarian author Mike Gold in a similar context termed the "newsreel of memory," Gropper's image of the shop coalesced around the bent, usually male worker. So prominent was the humped tailor in his many works of sweatshop representation that it could be said that his iconography was a re-vision of Marx's oxenish lumpenproletariat. I term Gropper's needle-trades workforce the "humpenproletariat," a term that combines the slang meaning of "humping it" with images of man-beasts in the industrial posture endemic to the tailoring trades (figures 2 and 3).[20]

One recent historian of sweatshops has noted that the term "hunched over" is pejorative.[21] Gropper's tailors certainly seem to personify slavish obedience. So akin to scholars in their concentration, and wearing their humps like a proletarian badge, they often exhibit the agonized face or the dementia of the tormented. Their suffering is further described by their sewing environs: knives and scissors are placed ominously near. Thus, these industry-made hunchbacks are inhabitants in a Proletkult sweatshop, the Communist Party's term for art that would educate the working classes in left-wing ideology.

Gropper's longtime connection to the Party's Yiddish organ, the *Freiheit*, suggests that his humpenproletarians are carrying Jewish ethnic memory on their backs as well. Marc Chagall's symbolic World War I painting, *Remembrance,* established a precedent: a shtetl peddler carrying in a knapsack slung over his bent back a miniature of his village home.[22] Gropper's manipulation of sweatshop images to address the persecution of the Jews will be addressed later in this chapter. Suffice it to say that he invested the East European refugees and displaced persons of the early World War II American sweatshop with an understanding that their psychic disorganization now had an added cause.

Gropper was far more in tune with his skilled male tailor figures during his WPA work-relief period than with the heroic workers in the murals he produced in the late 1930s. Like fellow WPA political satirist Philip Evergood, he felt that artists were cultural workers subjected to mistreatment and sweatshop conditions of their own: WPA had quotas (one painting a month) and timekeepers, artists never learned where their work was going, and they endured humiliations attached to WPA certification.[23] To those on the left, like Gropper, the exploited cultural worker could look to the Artists' Union, not government largesse, for redress of grievances. Making the garment analogy explicit, one local of artists affiliated with the CIO even proposed that a union label be placed on every member's artwork.[24]

Thus, Gropper offered the powerless sweatshop in his easel paintings and drawings as a rebuttal to the New Deal's empowered WPA factory workers. Ironically, powerful as its protest was, his art bypassed another set of power relations: the sexual politics of sweatshop art.

FEMINIZING THE SHOP: MOSES SOYER

Gropper, unlike most WPA artists and their allies on the agitprop left, did depict women engaged in work, whether tailoring or laboring in the more common industrial sites of mill and factory. Yet with the exception of his fragile, saintly mother, the sweatshop women of his WPA period are bereft of femininity. Gropper's fellow WPA artist Lew Davis, who abhorred the mixed-sex workplace and admired mining-town manhood, portrays the sweated seamstress to deplore her. His eerie *Eight Figures* (1935) groups underclad, psychically remote women around a rectangular sewing table. A faceless boss figure spies on them, and seated among them is a freakish East European tailor, his head shrouded. Pall-bearers at a labor funeral, these male figures stifle any nascent female work culture. Sewing was considered a "woman's job" by the New Deal agencies of the 1930s, and even the three Fourteenth Street School artists bypassed the subject, as if reluctant to illustrate drudges at the needle. The breadwinning women of Bishop, Marsh, and Miller are either taking a break from the office or plying the sex trade with sailors on leave.

This absence of seamstresses who were both women and workers in their toilsome milieus would be unremarkable had there not been a tradition of such figures that was well known to WPA era artists. Not only did they carefully apply the lessons of Renaissance and Baroque masters to their portrayals of plebeian 1930s women but their art school educations had also exposed them to the lady of leisure whiling away the hours with needlework in classic paintings and the woman holding the distaff in genre paintings of cottage industry.[25] Even if they had not seen the sentimental Victorian illustrations of the "Song of the Shirt," they would surely have known of Degas's laundresses bending to their tasks (their faces "anonymous, shadowy profiles") or been familiar with the work of the American impressionist Mary Cassatt, whose young seamstresses sew by lamplight or kneel to pin their ladies' garments.[26]

Moses Soyer, born in Czarist Russia and, like Gropper, a student at the National Academy of Art and the Ferrer Club, was the rare colleague who integrated the proletarian seamstress into the WPA canon.[27] Also like Gropper, Soyer broke away from the academy and began to study the radical graphics of the time—in his case those of the *New Masses* antecedent, the *Liberator*. For many years he taught at the Socialist-leaning Art Students' League.

He proclaimed in the radical trade union magazine and fine arts journal *Art Front* in 1935 that artists should "not glorify Main Street" but rather commit themselves to "paint[ing] America . . . as it is—mean, dirty, avaricious."[28] Some of his canvases bore witness to the passive despair of the breadline and the unemployment office. Yet Soyer's favorable vision of a social realism that included sweated labor spaces was at odds with his own artistic production. His paintings of seamstresses reversed Gropper's nightmare of his mother at endless piecework. Instead, Soyer offered a womanhood rescued by the New Deal. Superficially at least, his paintings seem to be placid depictions of sewing at home. They borrow from European genre scenes "virtuous working women, quasi-religious icons of domesticity . . . spinning, knitting or sewing."[29]

They also derive from more sophisticated renderings of sewing women's inwardness, most notably Edouard Vuillard's intimate interiors of his mother's workshop—twenty years of her patterning, cutting, stitching, and finishing of corsets.[30] Edward Hopper Americanized the intimacy and isolation of Vuillard in his own seamstress by her window, as in the 1921 drawing *New York Interior*.[31] Soyer and Hopper register a long-standing shift in the perception of seamstresses home alone. No longer the endangered virgin dreaming of a savior, she is now a casually sexual figure. Observed in a moment of reverie, she has an intense concentration not accounted for by the tailor's art.

Soyer's is a less subversive working-class portraiture than Gropper's. He once observed of his subjects that they give "the impression that there [is] no central story in the painting, no central direction. Each girl [in the urban scene paintings] is a world unto herself."[32] For instance, the viewer's eye follows the concentration of *Girl at Sewing Machine* as she bends delicately over the machine (figure 4). The eye takes in her curly hair swept up into a chignon of sorts and travels to the right foreground to take in a red remnant of cloth denoting the home piecework that awaits her skill. Respect for a 1930s seamstress's seriousness of purpose and her inner world, however, is played off against the overtly erotic details of her clinging orange sweater, her delicate neck, and her rouged or flushed cheek. The viewer's impression is not far removed from the glimpse into lower-class sensuality provided by Degas's pastel shadings of the bodies of laundresses and women taking baths: both artists catch the lower-class woman, who is often linked to sensuality, in a private moment, as if in repose.[33] The fleshly attractiveness and innocent sensuality of these female figures belie the 1930s work theme, much less the theme of 1930s economic peril.

Although Soyer eliminated the distinction between home and work, his women are "safe." His updated *Madonna of the Shirt* (see chapter 2) thus feminizes sweatshop portraiture but in the process sacrifices sweatshop history: Soyer provides no marks of labor and exhaustion, nor does he give us the prettified sewing machine girl of popular sweatshop melodrama. His is neither a Proletkult nor an eroticized shop. Still, by its very visual clues and its stark, pared-down background, Soyer's WPA work conveys a working-class quality. In their protected solitude his women are saved the economic misery of the starving Victorian garret seamstress. In Soyer's reading of Depression-era piecework, women's separateness from widespread economic suffering is their salvation. It remained for other artists to integrate the newsreel of memory and the mixed-gender sweatshop into a mural art that was acceptable in New Deal terms.

THE PATRIOTIC SHOP: GEORGE BIDDLE AND BEN SHAHN

When the sweatshop entered the world of WPA mural art, it did so as an institution left behind in the Old World. It was apt that George Biddle was commissioned to convey this patriotic message, since America had been far more generous to his family than to those of the other artists discussed here. Biddle was the scion of a wealthy Philadelphia family who convinced his former Harvard classmate Franklin Delano Roosevelt to fund a federal arts program. Although he lacked the working-class credentials of his colleagues Gropper, Soyer, and Shahn, he shared their interest in the revolutionary realism of the Mexican radicals Diego Rivera and José Orozco.[34]

Biddle's difficulty in balancing the Mexicans' attention to an oppressed underclass with the upbeat nationalism of the Federal Artists' Project is evident in much of his 1930s art. His homage to the execution of Sacco and Vanzetti and his 1933 painting *Starvation* are essentially pre-New Deal creations. But his memorable 1936 lithograph *Death on the*

Plains is similarly confrontational. Though his good friend Franklin Roosevelt was then in his second term as president, the drawing makes no room for New Deal hopefulness.[35] A dead steer, one of its hind legs grotesquely flung up in the rigor of death, seems to fill an entire portion of a drought-parched field. Bleached bones from another animal, an earlier victim of the Dust Bowl, loom over the corpse and intensify the theme of decomposition. An earlier painting, in contrast, *Family Beach Pavilion* (1931), pays Grosz-like attention to a group of overfed people who look like prosperous refugees from a European country. One man's dandified beret and green shirt and socks trumpet "un-American," as does a heavyset blonde wearing a fur piece to the summertime seashore. These works all defied the populist imagery that Biddle himself had claimed was necessary, whether the subject matter was American farmers, expatriate pleasure seekers, or the garment trades sweatshop.

Only in his five-part mural *Society Freed through Justice* does he tell an American story, the immigrant's flight to America, from a New Deal perspective. In two of the panels, Biddle's "European" sweatshop is optimistically entitled "The Tenement and Sweatshop of Yesterday Can Be the Life Planned with Justice of Tomorrow."[36] Its longtime residence in the halls of the Justice Department is a curious example of how to defang revolutionary art while treating the downtrodden.

Sweatshop, finished around 1935 (figure 5), positions a pair of sweatshop group portraits of small East Europeans with rounded faces and slightly Slavic features next to one of a more varied ethnic assortment landed in an industrial America where railroads deliver them to their new destinations. In the two sewing scenes the figures are clustered, indeed huddled, over tables with machines and shroudlike cloths. Their pallor, zombielike concentration, and somewhat old-fashioned clothes, combined with the empty hanging suits and unclothed dressmaker's dummies in the backgrounds of the respective parts, mark this portion of the mural as a set piece. Frozen in undemocratic European time, these workers seem as lifeless as the garments they create.

Their emigrant faces are only slightly more animated once they and their relatives land in America (the right-hand side of the first panel). If anything, the New World is a landscape of thwarted or deadened action. One family is barefoot, apart from the crowd. The faces look without seeing, grieving both their Old and New World lot.

However bleak the mural looks to postindustrial viewers, Biddle provided acceptable history, for his sweatshop is cordoned off from an American landscape.[37] Defanging Gropper's sweatshop portraits, Biddle demonstrates that garment workers in flight will assimilate to the American way.

Ben Shahn's sweatshop responded to WPA patriotism in a more dejected version of melting-pot history. As described above, the 1930s saw the establishment of a colony in tiny Roosevelt, New Jersey, for Jewish immigrant garment workers fleeing Nazi persecution.[38] The nature of that assimilation was fleshed out in Shahn's *Roosevelt Mural*. The panels depict the history of the town, from the Eastern European origins of the toilers in New York City's graphically depicted garment workers' shops to the founding of the cooperative community (where Shahn himself lived). The historical chronology is not a strict one, as the mural moves in and out of the European past, a device whereby Shahn reminds those looking past the uplift and rhetoric that the shop is a recurring threat. On the other hand, Shahn's is a fable of hoped-for prosperity. His sweated workers join the march of labor to a new life and the professions. This is upward mobility of the sort that enabled Shahn himself, the son of wood carvers, to pursue an art education and make a living through Federal Artists' Project work.[39]

Complicating Biddle's scenario, Shahn adds to the narrative of uplift and redemption the twinned evils of Nazi oppression and urban immigrant sweated labor, which are conquered in New Jersey. Two of the panels, "Immigration and Sweatshops," a homage to the Triangle fire workers, and the middle one, "Sweatshops and Union Organizing," move from the old evil to the proposed new CIO changes. Shahn undercuts Biddle's march of progress in some subtle ways: his Triangle fire images, for instance, melt into those of Great Depression turbulence. But this fusion of past and present is soon reversed by the third panel, "Building a Cooperative Community and New Deal Planning," which provides the New Deal coda.[40] The sweatshop fades in importance as the viewer sees the mine union luminary and CIO founder John L. Lewis on an East Side soapbox, cobbling together an alliance between basic industry and the garment trades. The mural concludes with the fruits of the CIO: schools, construction sites, college classrooms, engineers' meeting rooms, cooperative stores, and a suburban housing development.

But that was not the end of the CIO story. The next year Shahn reaffirmed the obsolescence of the sweatshop in his general industrial mural for the Bronx Post Office, *Resources of America* (1938–1939). As in the Homesteads fresco, he pictorialized a swath of occupations. The stand-ins for the shop were the sharecroppers' field and the textile industry, both of which appear, partly shorn of their arduous connotations, early in the mural. The New Deal explication was similarly optimistic. Despite the weary faces of the African American field hand and the wan textile operatives, Shahn was really engaged in "pairing panels to show the people and processes involved in transforming raw materials into finished products."[41] True progress, however, could occur with American industrial might. The heavy industry of the mines is particularly dominant, with muscular drillers. The motif is further represented by a massive steelmill hand in goggles.

As this is a Rooseveltian monument to a back-to-work nation, Shahn takes care to elide men (though not women) and machines and to praise the energy rather than the alienation of worker. He even resolves some contradictory tendencies in 1930s art in key panels whose Tennessee Valley Authority backgrounds herald industrial futurism. In a final set of panels, which conjures up Walt Whitman teaching workers of the future, the repeated Homesteads theme is that workers will have education and advance also. Sweated labor has been transmuted from present nightmare to past memory.

For all their differences, both Shahn and Biddle made the sweatshop visible but invisible. It was the muralist Ernest Fiene who brought closure to the optimistic sweatshop of the WPA years by eliminating it entirely. Known in his time for the 1939 mural *Harmony and Achievement,* in which Franklin Delano Roosevelt figures prominently, he included sewing shops under that rubric in another ambitious project: his *History of the Needlecraft Industry* (1938–1940) includes a shop that combines the two visions and is in effect no sweatshop at all.[42] The operators, cutters, and pressers of Fiene's vision stand or sit erect. Blond, robust, and large-framed, they are for the most part divested of the immigrant identity. They work contentedly and determinedly, neither victims nor rebels, but key players in the needlecraft industry. Nor do they seem allied with union strivings: if they are members of ACW or the ILGWU, the viewer does not know it. The patriotic shop could go no further. In the coming decades, as the very subject itself became suspect, the sweatshop would disappear altogether from American art for decades to come.

AFTER WPA: THE SWEATSHOPS OF WILLIAM GROPPER AND EUGENE SALAMIN

With the end of New Deal patronage and the looming war in Europe, art that depicted sweatshops or many other prolabor subjects was literally junked: canvases were thrown away and even burned at the direction of the government.[43] The newsreel of memory was now unpatriotic. As the war in Europe began to involve Americans, WPA artists supported the war effort by suppressing their radical leanings.

When artists resurrected the proletarian, they did so in the belief of the time that the subject matter of have-nots—and even more the old ethnic sweatshop—was no longer relevant in an economically reinvigorated postwar society. There were, of course, the ripostes of the marginalized, whose artistic expression was rapidly gaining currency. It was abstract expressionism that addressed the countercultural, the oppositional, and the rebellious, whose alienation was depicted as emotional rather than economic.

With representational art and social realism both out of fashion, sweatshop art had to defend its own relevance as much as that of its subject. To do so, it addressed the exile and psychic dislocation wrought by wartime evils. Some artists, like Gropper, were already established and simply strengthening their reputations. Others, like the still-obscure worker-artist Eugene Salamin, were unknown by the art world. Why Gropper's sweatshop portraiture succeeded and Salamin's was neglected reveals a great deal about the working-class toiler that postwar Americans found aesthetically palatable.

As Gropper made a living from his commercial art and escaped much of the fury of the House Un-American Activities Committee in the early 1950s, he created a number of works that forged a link between his mother's sweatshop and the Holocaust experience. The subject of sweatshop exploitation was reinstated to fit the post-Auschwitz context, and the shop became in these works of the 1950s and 1960s a metaphor for concentration camp slavery. The shop became a relocation site for displaced persons. In contrast to the patriotism of Biddle's and Shahn's murals, Gropper's site is one of psychic disaster: his tailors are free from the camps but not from their horrifying memories.

Visitors to the U.S. Holocaust Museum in Washington, D.C., can see a display of sewing machines that were found in the Lodz concentration camp; photos of the coerced tailors in assembly-line rows accompany the display. Gropper's postwar subjects are similarly removed from the world to engage in the punishments of the Nazi shop. They dwell in time frozen by their historical tragedy. The history, however, is twofold: they toil in the same chaotic, pre–World War II ethnic space of Gropper's prewar work. But their faces are now demented. Whereas at the beginning of the war canvases focused on work in the midst of chaos, a decade later, as in the lithograph *Sweatshop* (c. 1950), there are shaved heads and regimented clothing—signatures of the anti-Semitic incarceration.

Consonant with this death row theme, the sewing machines look like spikes, eyes seem sunken and sightless, and the disconnection among workers is complete. Even a reprise of Gropper's 1938 painting of his seamstress mother renders her as a body in a chair, her white blouse the only humanizing touch. In this tailor's cell block, two faces that resemble each other look particularly grotesque. Further signifying the evil sweatshop, the very materials on which the inmates work are difficult to recognize as garments in the making. Unlike the men's and women's clothes produced by his prewar tailor's piecework, the sewing here exists in an absurdist universe. In place of contracted, if exploited, sewing work is the doomed production commandeered by the Nazi regime.

Gropper went on in "Piece Work": *Capriccios* (1952), named for Goya's antiwar series (figure 3), to blur the difference between Holocaust victims and postwar survivors.[44] His humpenproletarians exist out of time, in a kind of tailor's hell. With its ominous visual references to penned enclosures, to larger-than-life bobbins, to skeletal tailor's hands, this work marking Gropper's return to his WPA period substitutes the exploitation of the Jews for their extermination.

If Gropper's widening referentiality shaped the sweatshop as a concentration camp, Eugene Salamin's sweatshop art returned it to a Depression-era focus on workers. Salamin was both left-wing activist and worker-artist "in hiding" in the wake of the Taft-Hartley Act's exclusion of left-wingers from trade unions. His paintings visually narrate the sweatshop in exile in more ways than one, and his earliest finished work, a series of oil paintings executed in the 1950s, sanctifies difficult lives in a sewing-trades context.[45]

A Party activist during the Depression, Salamin literally sought refuge in the garment trades in the 1940s after his efforts during the Second World War to organize machinists in the Brooklyn Navy Yard.[46] Vocal about his support for the Communist Party, he also retained a lifetime connection to the garment industry. He was a member of the Amalgamated Clothing Workers of America (which published Gropper's drawings) and supported his family as a tailor while attempting to find a foothold as an artist. Born in 1912 in Galicia in southeastern Poland, he emigrated to New York City in 1929 and did manual work while seeking a center for politically active artists.[47] Though a talented draftsman, he had neither the academy training nor the professional connections to the era's left magazines that most WPA artists enjoyed, and he would study with the urban scene printmaker Philip Reisman until after the war.[48]

In the 1950s, Salamin worked at Ripley's, a small men's clothing shop where Jewish refugees, such as those in Gropper's postwar drawings, worked as well. Ripley's, a union shop controlled by the ACW, was a piece-rate shop that employed not only Jews but many refugees from Poland, as well as Italians, a few Jamaicans, and, later, Latinos and Greeks.[49] It expanded from a small Brooklyn site into a large industrial building on the Upper West Side, which, in Salamin's rendering, resembles a sweated site. In its lack of amenities, Ripley's was the kind of place where Salamin could study the very conditions that as a Communist he had hoped to change. But his art does not excoriate or idealize the shop so much as it observes those who carved out a worklife there. Like others in the clothing industry, Salamin worked on a piecework basis in the 1930s. "Sometimes when I had to wait for the work to come," he recalled, "I would take out my sketching pad and sketch the people at work. Also, I sketched people at lunchtime, eating, reading, or playing cards. I have made hundreds of sketches of clothing workers and also paintings in oil and watercolors by the dozen."[50]

In a series of remarkable paintings executed by this "underground artist" in the 1950s, Salamin's shops are dingy and cramped, with dirty window panes, poor lighting, and nowhere to sit or take a break other than the sewing tables themselves.[51] The equipment is equally shabby: the sewing machines could well date from Hine's era or perhaps were purchased second-hand. In some paintings, the bright colors of the men's shirts—some violet, others blue—transcend the harsh fluorescent light and the absence of natural daylight produced by the covered-up windows (an old sweatshop ploy). The seediness of the setting, furthermore, is in marked contrast to the workers' patient concentration and quiet camaraderie. In one of his strongest works, the self-portrait *Lining Baster* (1955), the New Deal's ode to muscular labor acquires a secular holiness: the shaven-headed figure seems both martyr and hero (figure 6).

Salamin refutes Gropper's dystopian sweatshop. His figures are not shriveled Holocaust Jews but dedicated dwellers in a multiethnic shop. He paints real people, not types, and these figures are dignified and self-contained. Even the dehumanized or safely sheltered seamstresses of WPA artists fade before his vision of female operators, often black and Hispanic women, who ply their trade with respect for both their male colleagues and their own work ethic.

In recent interviews, Salamin, who is ninety-one years old at this writing, remembered how dismayed he was at the lack of worker consciousness in the shops. The fact that his paintings are not political lessons in Communist solidarity, however, harks back to the WPA workshop. His figures are not taking down the shop; they are simply better than their surroundings. The result is a collective workspace and hope. People hunched over machines or pieces of cloth are bathed in a secular equivalent of holy light. Their light is suffused from a mystical light source such as is found in conventional paintings of the scholar saint Saint Jerome (such as the medieval Boucicault Master's *Saint Jerome in His Study*).[52] Transmuting the context from saintly to proletarian, religious to socialistic, Salamin provides a glow or aura for each worker to illuminate, so to speak, the act of toil.

The irony is that in the midst of the McCarthy years, American art, for a moment in the history of sweatshop depiction, reconciled proletarian aesthetics and politics.[53] The weak lighting that is as endemic to the shop as its streaked windows is no more powerful than what would emanate from the bulb affixed to an aged machine or from such opaqued windows. Yet unlike such dim artificial illumination, the light is a hopeful one, filled with rather than bereft of proletarian meaning.

Gropper recovered from his own exclusion in the McCarthy years, although he refused to cooperate with HUAC and did not exhibit in New York until 1961.[54] Even had he been oblivious to the irony of that phoenixlike Social Realist recovering from the McCarthy period to resurrect an important reputation, Salamin, unlike Gropper, never had the time or capital to devote to publicizing his sweatshop paintings. The continued neglect of his oeuvre, however, is in no small part attributable to his choice of subject, which no nostalgia for WPA has touched.

William Gropper was dubbed the "workingman's protector," but by the 1970s, as the sweatshop disappeared from his art, workers themselves had ceased to be heroic to him. No longer undervalued labor, as they had been during the years when unions were struggling for recognition, they had become, if anything, too powerful. His demonizing painting *Hardhats* (1970) depicts workers with horned Viking helmets and ball and chain massacring young women.[55] The Vietnam War polarized protesters and blue-collar "hawks," and the era of the heroic 1930s worker gave way to the era of his force and brutishness.

THE ARTISTS DISCUSSED in this chapter harnessed the iconic power of the turn-of-the-century shop so as to convey larger and more immediate anxieties about labor, war, and global evil. Their sweatshop images express the economic repression and anxiety of their own period rather than that of their parents and grandparents. These WPA artists did not remember the shop so much as they created it, from the considerable materials of the day: their status as committed professional artists; their "red" politics; and their tenure on government-supported art projects. Soon new generations would extend and challenge the art of worker-painters like Salamin, reach back to Lewis Hine, and help reinvigorate the debate on the American sweatshop in a supposedly classless society. In the next decades, Ralph Fasanella, Sue Coe, and others would sew together a working-class community and, in so doing, remake the old sweatshop.

CHAPTER 5

The Sweatshop Returns

POSTINDUSTRIAL ART

The nearly 2,000 sweatshops [that] operate openly in
New York City [often] employ illegal immigrants. . . .
Most are owned by immigrants, too, now primarily
from China and Korea, just as their predecessors came
from Italy and Eastern Europe. Some of these [new]
sweatshops are remarkably bright and spacious, with
fluorescent lighting [and] freshly painted walls. . . . But
there are still those that rival the most sordid garment
factories [of] 1890.

—Alan Finder, "Despite Tough Laws, Sweatshops
Flourish," *New York Times* (1995)

I did these drawings as I accompanied three
investigators for the New York State Department of
Labor Apparel Industry Task Force. . . . We visited six
sweatshops, all non-union. . . . The sweatshop has re-
emerged as a fact of life for thousands of workers.

—Sue Coe, on her "Sweatshop Series" (1994)

I never start with the premise that we know more than
they [the sweatshop workers] do. . . . My film is a
series of "photographs in which people can speak."

—Author's interview with David Riker (2000)

THE WPA IMAGES of Shahn, Soyer, and their group re-
flected the historical shop of Jews and Italians, ethnics allied with rank-
and-file power in the garment trades by the late 1940s. As early as 1937,
however, nonwhites had entered the shops and the needle-trades locals
that staffed them: local 22 in New York City was 10 percent black before
the Depression was over.[1] By the late 1940s, the large-scale immigration
of Puerto Ricans to New York City and new waves of Asian immigration

had supplied workers for the city's many smaller garment shops. There the boundary between union shop and sweatshop was often nonexistent. This new sweatshop seemed, in effect, to be hiding in plain sight: blacks and Puerto Ricans in New York City, whether ILGWU members or not, received only $1.50 an hour.[2] Representative struggles erupted in 1947 when black and Spanish-speaking workers who wanted to join the venerable Italian Dress and Waistmakers' Union Local 89 were refused admission.[3] Despite the breakthroughs of the black activist Maida Kemp, who climbed to the executive board of the ILG in the 1950s, the predominantly female membership was very underrepresented.[4] The 1958 strike by Puerto Rican women in Brooklyn loudly proclaimed the economic disparities of the wider garment trades membership. For people of color and some of the less successful Jews and Italians, a union shop could house a mini-sweatshop.[5] On the same site, a white working class occupied the highly skilled and better-paying jobs, while for black, Puerto Rican, and, between 1970 and 1980, Asian workers, union membership provided some with a living wage but barely supported it for others.[6]

In the postwar decades, there was much criticism of the ILG for not combating such two-tiered shops in New York and elsewhere. Civil rights advocate Herbert Hill accused the union of being a guardian of the sweatshop. The 1984 semidocumentary film *Nightsongs,* based on five years of undercover work in New York's Chinatown, made the charge pointedly: its sweatshop, run by a smooth-talking Jewish boss, doubles as a recruiting ground for union workers. The film argues persuasively that, at least for Asian and Hispanic employees, some without green cards, management and union are in cahoots.[7] The Chinese women there go to ILGWU English classes and mouth lessons on grievance procedures for collecting back pay. The closed shop has deteriorated to a place where bosses recruit workers by urging them to work faster and the union contribution is to provide English classes where Christmas carols are taught to Asian and Hispanic workers. Yet the boss acts like a corrupt shop steward: he waves away their pleas and shortchanges them consistently. One veteran comments laconically, "We don't get much union protection."

Among poorly paid apparel workers, this complaint was to surface repeatedly in the three decades from the 1950s through the 1980s. Their complaints both presaged and continued to define the post-industrial job era. Outside of the garment trades, the term "postindustrial," signifying the decline of the American manufacturing base, would not be a common one until the mid-1970s, although other historians locate the "making of North America's Rust Belt" as early as 1969.[8] The plant-closing recession of 1974–1975 and that of 1982–1983 saw millions of factory jobs lost, including those in the industrial Northeast.

In a curious historical twist, in the midst of such mass firings, the ILG and Amalgamated Clothing Workers (ACW) effectively defended the good quality of life supplied for all of its members. The very charge of "sweated labor" invoked rhetorically in the mid-1930s to usher in collective bargaining was used less and less by the big garment trades unions. There had been almost no garment union strike activity since the early days of the 1935 Wagner Act. When, in 1958, 105,000 unionists went on strike in New York City, their language was that of enforcing contracts, gaining adequate severance pay, and the like. Using the watchword of the postwar era, "industrial peace," that strike saw a return to the interethnic solidarity of the pre–World War II years. Economic disparities among the members notwithstanding, there was the illusion, if not the reality, of a needle-trades brand of American exceptionalism. One seasoned Jewish veteran of the shop made the distinction between the past and present: "I was a kid, a greenhorn [in the 1930s], and the work I could get was in the sweatshops. You know sweatshops? Now I'm a man with a job I'm good at." Was the ILG important to him? "You bet your ass."[9]

Even as postindustrial decline waited in the wings to affect the U.S. factory force and the ILG rank and file, rank-and-file fidelity to the union was slow to change. When in 1962 Judy Bond, a New York City manufacturer of women's blouses with outlets elsewhere, ominously shifted production to Alabama despite ILGWU campaigns, chief David Dubinsky predicted runaway and "offshore" shops by the mid-1960s and also accurately predicted that sweatshops would return to the city in the decades to come.[10] Nevertheless, by 1993 there were only 86,000 garment workers in New York City, compared to 350,000 in 1947.

Artistic response to the threat of the shop was slow to incorporate Dubinsky's prescient warnings. From the passage of the antilabor Taft-Hartley Bill in 1947 until the sweatshop's return in the Reagan years, its resurgence in the 1980s, and proliferation by the mid-1990s, visual narratives, from paintings to graphics to cinematic art, took the cultural cue. With the exception of films like *Nightsongs*, with its delicately depressed

Chinese-Vietnamese seamstress, the sweatshop received scant artistic attention. Throughout the Vietnam War era, avant-garde artistic rebellions against representational art as well as a lukewarm interest in working-class politics made the visual narrative of sweated labor tenuous.

When it did resurface, the postindustrial art of these men and women had no less potential for social protest than it did in the WPA era. The artists themselves, however, were by then no longer the children and grandchildren of the old Jewish sweatshop workers: the most "traditional" artist among them was Ralph Fasanella, an Italian American labor radical with a lifetime of organizing activity in the United Electrical Workers (EW). More typical were Sue Coe, a British-born, New York–based artist whose political outrage proliferated in surrealist imagery of global subjects, including American ones, and David Riker, a Belgian-born filmmaker with a lengthy vita in American public-access television.

As blacks, Asians, and Hispanics who had once worked alongside the oldtime sweated Jewish and Italian laborers now replaced them, these new visual narrators recorded the "return" of the sweatshop in highly personal ways. Their art also commented as much on the decline of union crusades against the sweatshop as on the reemergence of the shop itself. As social critics, they played on contradictions in the enduring argument between homegrown versus inherently "un-American" sweatshops. Carrying on the traditions of Moses Soyer, Ben Shahn, and other 1930s painters and illustrators, their work juxtaposed working-class light and sweatshop darkness.

THE SWEATSHOP BEAUTIFUL:
RALPH FASANELLA'S ART

Few carried on the socially conscious representational tradition of working-class art better than Ralph Fasanella (1914–1997), whose work includes some classic retrospective canvases on home and factory sewing in the years before the Great Depression. In his own time, Fasanella's subjects form a virtual litany of New York worker life and leisure from World War II through the 1970s. He was a true son of the Italian sewing trades experience: his mother, Ginevra, took him to her Lower Manhattan sewing shop, exposed him to her unionist philosophy, and recounted the drama of the Lawrence Textile Strike of 1912, in which an immigrant workforce, many of them young women, exhibited militant unionism.[11] Ginevra Fasanella's socialism and antifascism would have mirrored that of Italian syndicalists in the ACW, of which she was a vocal member, and of the ILG's two "Italian" locals, local 48 and Luigi Antonini's fiery sister local, 89.[12] Following his mother's lead, Fasanella himself made common cause in the 1940s with socialist needle-trades politicos in the American Labor Party and even ran for office.

A son of the Lower East Side, Fasanella was very familiar with the East Harlem (at the time the largest Italian American community in the nation) and East Bronx tenements and apartments in which so many Italian American seamstresses did their piecework, and he depicted these locales repeatedly. The Singer sewing machine in his painting *Family Supper* (1972) is a visual shorthand for many of these experiences. The art critic John Berger offers a telling description of the scene: "The family is Fasanella's. In the center is his mother. On the right wall is one of his own paintings of his father, the iceman, his head clamped in the ice-tongs with which he worked. On the back wall is a second painting, this time of his mother with his sister and himself standing on chairs in front of another wooden cross, against a brick wall between window frames. Every person and object in this kitchen is a memorial to what happened within his family. . . . But the way it is painted makes everything in it continuous . . . with the exterior walls and [the city] that surrounds it."[13] This observant summation nevertheless overlooks a prominent piece of Fasanella—and Italian American—family history. Fasanella's reference to ill-paid piecework is clear enough: the canvas contains a sewing machine in the crowded living room/kitchen. More disturbing is a center background image of the crucifixion of his iceman father. When *Family Supper* was installed in the Ellis Island museum in the early 1990s, its depictions of both maternal and paternal labor were oratorically sanitized as it was feted for its vibrant recreation of immigrant work and family life.[14]

But like the officially upbeat art of the patriotic WPA sweatshops of George Biddle and Ben Shahn, this kind of public acceptance was a response to the perceived nostalgia of Fasanella's presentation of Italian American blue-collar struggles. Even the presence of the ILG chief David Dubinsky at the installation ceremony indicated the union position that the piecework sewing betokened by the Singer in the painting had been superseded by a strong needle-trades rank and file. As both a benevolent re-vision of the crowded tenement apartments of Riis and Hine and a quasi-documentary chronicle of the white, New York ethnic past, Fasanella's art was taken up by the ILG, among other labor organizations. To this day, postcards and posters with images like *Family Supper* from Fasanella's work raise money for the Union of Needletrades, Industrial and Textile Employees (UNITE), the new amalgamation of the ILG and service workers' unions.

Yet, like *Family Supper,* the painting *Dress Shop,* an exploration of sweatshops completed the same year, reveals the contradictions between a superficial reading of Fasanella as an "America the Beautiful" "melting pot" artist and his tumultuous political history that included disillusionment with "bread-and-butter unionism" and a highly critical attitude toward the ILG. As a former labor organizer (for the United Electrical Workers in the 1940s) and a HUAC victim from the 1940s onward, Fasanella formed his attitudes in his late 1930s Workers' Alliance days and through his allegiances to causes such as the Spanish Civil War. (He served in the Lincoln Brigade, also known as the "red" brigade.) As a member of EW, he had left the CIO, his umbrella organization, by 1940, after its implementation of an increasingly conservative, anti-Communist policy. The Fasanella of the early 1970s was still in many ways the same unrepentant leftist who, though he had briefly made common cause with the socialist needle-trades politicos of the American Labor Party, had steadfastly supported the pro-Communist congressman Vito Marcantonio.[15]

Fasanella's friend and biographer, Paul D'Ambrosio, has argued that *Dress Shop* builds on his radicalism as well as his identification with working people. The painting is neither agitprop nor politically neutral, but rather a work that raises the working-class's awareness of its own history.[16] Like his other labor paintings, it is a kind of homage, an act of faith, and a tribute to worker solidarity. Although Fasanella borrows iconography from his own religious background and uses it to describe the secular history of laboring people, his American clothing trades shop—where, in Fasanella's words, everyone is "sweating away"— nonetheless emerges as a quasi utopia where labor is energetic, vivid, and communal.

In tune with the advances in labor organizing in New York City's burgeoning union years, the 1940s through the 1960s, Fasanella's sweatshop is more apparitional than real. The clear reference to Triangle definitely invokes past abuses, but his vivid colorism and humanized, rather beaten-down space make his shop a worker hub. This urban American primitive's colorist landscape is no simple one but a terrain of contrasts. This is not the WPA shop of Gropper-like enslavement or Shahn's transit upward. In *Dress Shop*, to borrow a phrase from Alfred Kazin, "past and present become each other's faces."[17] The clothing factory Fasanella imagined is thus a place of paradox: past injuries seem indistinguishable from present gains, and harsh memories intersect with the visual beauty of the painted sweatshop.

One way in which Fasanella gives this paradox visual form is by suspending ordinary spatial and temporal rules. He pays his homage instead at a proletarian crossroads. He invokes four time periods, the most recent being 1968–1972, the years during which he worked on and finally completed the painting. Hence the allusions to the assassinations of JFK and Martin Luther King and the reelection of Richard Nixon and, consonant with immigrant garment trades history in New York, the fact that many of the workers pictured are Latino.

Yet, in a reference to Fasanella's own family past, these new arrivals sit side by side with the Italian seamstresses, who would have shared the space in the 1920s and 1930s with East Europeans. This retrospection is a tribute to Ginevra Fasanella's difficult work life as a seamstress living in the East Bronx and supporting six children in the 1920s and 1930s. Though Mrs. Fasanella made buttonholes in a New York City coat factory affiliated with the ACW, which represented the men's clothing field, it might well have been the Italian women's cloakmakers' local 48 of the ILG that provided her or her dressmaking neighbors with the union work it supplied to virtually all of New York City's Jewish and Italian garment workers. As a child living in the East Bronx, Ralph visited his mother's job site (Chatham Square and Bowery), during a time when Italian seamstresses worked either at home or, as widows or otherwise the sole support of their families, in clothing factories. In *Dress Shop,* women operators, who made up three-quarters of the workforce in the trades, were given lower-tier, lower-paid work, as witnessed by the assembly lines of the Fasanella picture.

A third temporal reference is to the legacy of martyred women. Note the banner in the painting's lower left: "In memory of the Triangle Shirt Workers." This post-1911 tribute resonates with the ethnic women at sewing machines seated in windows surrounding the logo and underneath the dress factory. Such symbolic placement of the seamstresses provides a colorful and dynamic folk art tribute, a quiltlike depiction of women at work. At the same time, however, Fasanella's placement of these workers in a crowded old tenement reminds labor audiences of the horrendous sweatshop conditions that led to the historic factory fire and the death of 146 workers.

The chronology is made even more complicated in that Fasanella contextualizes the Triangle years and Ginevra Fasanella's work years in the narrative of his own early work history: Fasanella and his sister both worked in clothing factories in the mid-1930s. The fourth and final time/place frame is Fasanella's stint as a presser in the mid-1930s, witnessed by a steam presser in the painting's lower right. His fellow garment workers sit in a loft space that might have been his old East Bronx shop or any of the "new" sweatshops bypassed by progress.

Geographically as well as temporally, this is indeed a "complex dialogue between past and present." By the 1970s, Fasanella's dress shop could just as well have been in the garment district, on the Lower East Side, in East Harlem, or in his own neighborhood. Always in search of local venues for his art, Fasanella visited dress shops in his East Bronx neighborhood during those years.[18] (As late as 1960, even Hollywood acknowledged this figure in *The Young Savages*, in which Shelley Winters plays a single mother struggling to bring up her "juvenile delinquent" son on the proceeds of her East Harlem home sewing.)[19]

In Fasanella's dress shop, as with many of his works, "dimensional limitations fall away."[20] His painting both invokes the sweatshop and celebrates the needle trades' past as if it has never passed away. This frozenness in time, in turn, belies the sweatshop as a site of industrial malaise. He denies the "death" of the working class and, with it, trade unionism. Historically, even as *Dress Shop* was completed, ILG organizing drives were muted in the 1970s and 1980s in the Midwest and on both coasts.[21] The labor movement, despite negotiating cost-of-living raises, was weaker than it had been in decades. Although Fasanella made iconoclastic statements about unions selling out, *Dress Shop* itself lies in a time warp where desolate suburbs and industrial ruins are irrelevant. Fasanella does not do "industrial decline" art, because his is a blue-collar city. However cheerful or solidarity-driven, that city remains a worker enclave.

The problem is that, as sweatshop iconography, Fasanella's work site is quite clearly the Sweatshop Beautiful. Fasanella's own sister complained that Fasanella did not do justice to the gloom and oppression of her dress-factory experience in the late 1940s, a time when garment unions were supposedly renewing their strength.[22] Having opened up the *Dress Shop* like a dollhouse to reveal the interior, Fasanella obviously rejects the darkened, hidden interiors of Jacob Riis and Lewis Hine. The painting thus chooses not to look at poor people's imprisonment and in fact is in a tradition of labor art that dignifies the worker, whatever the job. Fasanella's city has a human scale, and he continued to depict it as such even as it lost its industrial base. Linked to the American regional tradition of folk art, *Dress Shop* is a sweatshop painting with an American grain.

Fasanella also beautifies other troubling labor subjects, from his difficult tenement home to the 1917 Lawrence, Massachusetts, mill strike. But *Dress Shop* is important because it not only deals with his family's labor history but also questions just how substantially modern workers' lives differ from the hardscrabble life of Ginevra Fasanella. Fasanella's sweating workers, he often opined, can make good money. But they remain working people shut out from the embourgeoisement of the white-collar stratum that benefited Fasanella himself, and these contradictions are visible in *Dress Shop*. In an interview granted the year he finished the painting, he laid the blame at the union door: "These women, lots of women, Italian women, Puerto Rican women, black women, Jewish women, sweating away [in *Dress Shop*]. . . . I'm . . . mixing periods of time here. [But now in the 1970s] they're not galvanized into political action, because the unions have not made the people politically conscious. I think they lull them with economics—a lot of other things."[23]

Dress Shop was finished in 1972, the year Fasanella actually began to make a living from his art. Thereafter he had a successful and fairly lucrative career that lasted until his death in 1997. Yet in his lifetime artistic identification with workers, Fasanella rejected as unworthy that "narrow hunger for goods" in which "you . . . lose your class position."[24] One wonders to what extent his own "god that failed" informed his frequently voiced criticism of the labor movement for letting working people down in its preoccupation with power.[25] Fasanella knew well that the early ILG and ACW espoused a semi-socialist vision, and some of the icons of that vision appear in his canvases of the late 1940s and 1950s. *May Day* (1947), for instance, sports a bust of Karl Marx along with union mottoes and locales.

In *Dress Shop*, however, praise for organized labor is obviously absent. With its ambiguous historical time and depiction of working-class shop conditions, *Dress Shop* suggests Fasanella's suspicious ambivalence toward garment unionism. His paintings are firmly rooted in a working-class New York that Joshua Freeman, the historian of the metropolitan working class, argues persuasively was cemented by the proliferation of unions. Fasanella's sweatshop representation is tied to the very gains of working-class Italians as they carved a niche in the ILG and elsewhere.

Fasanella's task in unifying his painting, whether he was conscious of it or not, was to integrate the old Triangle era with the new era of the unionized sweatshop. His reconciliation of the good life with the ugly shop provided a new aesthetic of sweatshop representation. Opportunity exists in his paintings alongside the reminders of how close garment workers remain to their constricted labor past. By the time he painted *Dress Shop* he was weary of ILG's official truths and skeptical of even its closed-shop goals. Yet to the extent that Fasanella, who as late as the 1970s dreamed of returning to the trade union movement, portrays advances in workers' standards of living, his sewing machine operators remain in an ILG world.

GOING GLOBAL: SUE COE'S SWEATOPOLIS

With his depictions of clothing factories in historically working-class New York City, Ralph Fasanella kept his work worlds localized. *Dress Shop* conflates uptown and downtown sewing shops to reflect his own life spent entirely along the subway routes from the Bronx to downtown Manhattan. Lawrence, Massachusetts, was far away, and Indiana was completely alien terrain. By contrast, it is globally exploited labor that preoccupies the political satirist and artist-journalist Sue Coe, whose critique of the impact on people of the "economic crime of capitalism" is more severe than that of the older artist Fasanella.[26] Born near working-class Birmingham, England, in 1951, she relocated to New York City in 1972, the year Fasanella completed *Dress Shop*.[27] Her lithographic portfolio for the *New Yorker* magazine, "Sweatshop Series" (1994), like the more famous drawings of her "Porkopolis Series" (done in New York

in the 1970s and issued in book form as *Dead Meat*, 1993), returns to the
mutilating landscape of Upton Sinclair's meatpacking exposé *The Jungle*
(1904).[28] Porkopolis is a worker universe of terrified animals on a con-
veyor belt where workers on the sped-up disassembly line risk their own
lives as well.[29] Animals and workers exchange and share identities. As in
the Sinclair text, the lives of Coe's workers are eaten up by industrial exploitation, and their bodies ground up by the workplace accidents that
are all too routine in the factory megalith. The factory floor is no less
lethal than the sweatshop.

If Fasanella is a latter-day artist of the industrial "folk," Coe is
modernity itself. She deconstructs both proletarian solidarity and the individualism of the American Dream. Savagely anti-authoritarian, she is
ready to hijack from artistic tradition anything that can turn the business
mythologies of the day on their heads. Coe's ravaged postindustrial landscapes call into question American claims of stepped-up productivity and
the soundness of its manufacturing base. To her, industrial efficiency,
U. S.-style, changes so-called efficient factories into charnel houses.

Coe finds the jungle all over the world's industrial landscape, including the shadow cast by the factory across the sweatshop. She well knows
that the old Progressive distinction between factory and sweatshop is futile, whether applied to Armour Meat or the Triangle Shirtwaist factory.
She thus satirizes the term "light manufacturing" in her demonstration
of the assembly-line peonage that turns the sewing machine operator
into just another factory operative: haggard faces inhabit butcher and
needle-trades sketches alike. Workers in pork production exchange char-
acteristics with needle workers, and vice versa: each set of factory hands
faces the monotony of the assembly line and is anesthetized into rote activity, just like animals led to slaughter.

It is true that the "Porkopolis Series" includes far more horrendous
imagery, to wit, a tour of a hog's brief life from birth to market, highlighting the slaughtering process. What is noticeable, however, is that
only in a satire on the Fruit of the Loom textile company does the
worker meet the fate of pigs in Porkopolis.

Two themes converge in Coe's 1994 drawing *Garment Workers Exploited by Fruit of the Loom* (figure 7): corporate greed and the devouring
of workers. In the foreground, a monstrous figure eats up a woman
clothing worker, a clear reference to Saturn devouring his children lest

they challenge his authority, and a play on Goya's famous 1820 drawing on that subject. The textile giant's rubric and the factory in the background draw on another graphic tradition, that of the WPA illustrator so well known to readers of the *New Masses* and other left periodicals.

By placing *Garment Workers* in the context of the "Sweatshop Series," Coe reveals her worker-devouring sweatshop to be an American export as well. Fruit of the Loom resembles other giant textile companies that UNITE tried with little success to organize in the mid-1990s. In this, her art responds to the fact that "sweatshops in the U.S. are part of a complex global system of manufacturing and retailing." More and more textile production occurred abroad in the decade prior to her sweatshop drawings, manufacturers farmed out the sewing, and "the bulk of the actual production [was done by] an army of contractors in the United States and overseas."[30]

By using New York City as a key site, Coe emphasizes that the intercontinental sweatshop is certainly no worse than what she has witnessed. For the "Sweatshop Series," Coe toured six sites along with state Labor Department investigators. She accompanied Andy Chan, Magali Ramos, and Ellen Davidow to six sweatshops, all non-union, sketching the shops and investigators in a *New Yorker* magazine series in an issue on fashion. For years afterwards Coe repudiated the *New Yorker's* treatment of her piece: "[The *New Yorker* editor] Tina Brown had a huge party for all the fashion designers/models [featured in the issue]. There were tons of champagne, as was her way [then] . . . and they had a huge screen for Art Spiegelman's cover, then showed the entire contents of the issue, with the exception of my work. The labor that creates fashion was conveniently missing from this soiree."[31]

Although Coe's comment is directed to the staff rather than the *New Yorker's* treatment of her sketches, she is reflecting a grievance of another kind. For in the issue itself she is not listed prominently in the table of contents, as if her work is an afterthought.

What makes Coe's sweatshop art so arresting is that her "Sweatshop Series" applies her signature Porkopolis metaphor to the sewing and clothing trades. Rather than shrinking, her sweatshop proliferates in size and meaning in this vision. Notably, Coe's sewing-floor workers are not emaciated. Their bodies are plumped for capitalist slaughter even as their faces are expressionless, wary, frightened. They sew under morgue

lighting, and the only life in their surroundings emanates from the col-
ored cloth and threads. Yet, like Chicago's cattle and pigs, they are valuable food for the corporate maw even when they are dead-alive. Coe's
sweatopolis, in which workers may be spiritually dying, depicts economic slavery as the commodified body.

In its association with the killing floor of the slaughterhouse, Coe's
shop is no longer on a human scale. Her art in effect unifies First and
Third World sweatshops. Indeed, Coe's is an eternal shop, limited in nei
ther time nor space, a hellish complement to her many other nightmare
landscapes of fumes, gases, ghostly presences, and stockyard carcasses.

Witness her key series drawings *Chinese Floor Workers: Age 72 and
Still Working in a Sweat Shop[at][$]4.25 an Hour* and *Machine Workers from
El Salvador: They Wear Bandanas to Prevent the Inhalation of Dust* (1994)
(figures 8 and 9). Coe has ironically referred to herself as a gutter journalist, but the mesh here of picture and title invokes the best of Jacob
Riis and Lewis Hine. While the subtitles clarify that these are emigrants,
Coe plays as well on the fact that El Salvador and China were notorious
throughout the early 1990s as apparel industry "slavetraders"—the characterization of American labor councils of their use of cheap labor.[32]
Coe's sweatshop art dehumanizes while compelling the viewer to see the
seamstress and presser as oppressed people. And the locus is global: these
workers could be anywhere from New York's Chinatown to Indonesia.
In Coe's art, the Third World replicates not the old ascension myths but
the oppressions of the New World. The "Sweatshop Series" shows that
the shop, if anything, has come full circle: begun in America, disseminated abroad, it has now been resurrected on U.S. soil.

The mid and late 1990s revealed that Coe's truth was indeed no
stranger than reality. Her drawings appeared in magazines and galleries
prior to the scandal of the El Monte, California, sweatshop raid in 1995
(to be discussed in chapter 6). In a multiagency raid, federal investigators
discovered sixty-seven Thai women and five Thai men imprisoned in an
apartment complex. "Under the constant surveillance of armed guards
and confined behind a ring of razor wire, they had been held for several
years and forced to work . . . up to eighteen hours per day for far less than
the minimum wage." Coe could have written the stage directions:
beaten, threatened, incarcerated, these sweatshop workers were truly the

captives of the kind of clothing manufacturers she had already envisioned in her nightmare art.[33]

Viewed in the context of the "Sweatshop Series," Fasanella's message that the moral ugliness of the sweatshop was tempered by the beauty of the working-class spirit risks seeming sentimental. Another artist, however, working in the film medium, has succeeded in balancing the imperatives of idealism and realism.

DAVID RIKER'S *LA CIUDAD:* BRINGING IT ALL BACK HOME

> Inside the sweatshop the heat is suffocating, and the stale air hangs heavily in the room. Sitting in rows hunched over sewing machines, two dozen Latin American workers, mostly young women, feed the hungry machines an endless supply of cloth.
>
> —David Riker's stage directions, shooting script,
> *La Ciudad* (1998)

The movie camera exposes the ills of contemporary life in much the same way as the painter and the photographer do, and by the 1990s the filmmaker David Riker had gone through a personal and artistic odyssey that echoed Fasanella's and Coe's work. He too tries to convey, in his brilliant 1998 film *La Ciudad,* how the worker understands the experience of the shop. In his exploration of the contradictions between the beautiful sweatshop and the ugly one, Riker's humanism fills the space in a way reminiscent of Lewis Hine. The apparel shops and factories Hine photographed existed in a time when the few unions trying to reach the workers there were largely excluded. Hine's method of allowing the subject's self-expression made his photographs poignant reminders of how solitary was the suffering of workers, no matter how crowded into coal pits or closetlike tenements.

Whereas Hine's subjects were often the industrial fodder on which "free" immigration during the century's early decades was based, Riker's concern is the story of the undocumented workers who now take many of the dirty, ill-paid jobs performed by the workers of Hine's generation. *La Ciudad*'s characters work for pickup-truck hiring bosses who bid them down on street corners and cover the windows of their factories.

Because the workers in this film were given a total of only twenty-five minutes of break time each day and worked six days a week, Riker was often frustrated in his attempts to speak with them when they were not working. These differences aside, providing close-ups of worker faces is hardly distinctive to these two artists, but Riker's treatment strongly suggests the Hine influence. Like the Progressive-era photojournalist, Riker as a filmmaker concentrates on long-held shots of the faces of laborers and shoots footage using actual workers who volunteered to act in his film in ways that would mirror their actual work. Again like Hine, Riker aims his camera in a way that locates them in the workplace and pauses to take in their expressions, their sorrows.

Riker contextualizes the sweatshop in the world of the desperate and newly arrived day worker with a family to support. The film's first three vignettes concern street-corner construction workers vying, many unsuccessfully, for $5-an-hour jobs and the unemployed campesino recently arrived and bewildered by the web of regulations for work, school, and apartments. Riker's gritty shots show us a depressed Spanish-speaking neighborhood, viewed from both the street and the endless el trains that transport the workers to anonymous building sites and vast industrial parks in Queens. Riker's mise-en-scène of liquor stores, lottery ticket booths, bodegas, and sidewalk debris is reminiscent of the wartorn vistas of Rossellini's *Open City* and Fellini's *La Strada*.

Born in 1963 in Belgium, Riker came to New York City in the early 1990s and spent five years gaining the trust of the Spanish-speaking workers who would play the ensemble cast of his film. He had learned his art by photographing the construction sites where he worked over the years and later by filming documentary footage of both marine and paper workers' strikes. A stint in public-access television widened his understanding of the need for a timely American reportage that would also reinvigorate an American film art of conscience. He filled in his training by studying the social documentaries of Barbara Koppel, such as *Harlan County*, and engaging undocumented workers as collaborators in his film project. Riker added further authenticity in the sweatshop segment by "borrowing" a space (reminiscent of Hine's ruses for gaining entry to textile mills in the South) and converting an actual shop into a set. Setting up steam presses, moving machines around, even using seamstresses who had worked in (and not been paid by) other sweatshops, Riker in effect created his own shop on the site of an actual shop.[34]

Aware of the industrial decline that had left Hispanic immigrants doing piecework at home and in Brownsville, Sunset Park, and Long Island City lofts, Riker saw another kind of Latino sweatshop story. To continue the Fasanella saga of a draining apparel industry in which workers retain an innate dignity, Riker repositioned the shop at these new sites and repeopled Fasanella's ethnic working-class enclaves, updating the demographics of *Dress Shop*. Unlike Camilo Jose Vergara, the photographer of ruined American inner cities whose study of the *New American Ghetto* (1995) appeared while Riker was scouting locations and interviewing sweatshop workers, Riker took exterior shots of sweatshop factories that did not foreground the decayed neighborhoods of the new immigrant ghettos.[35]

Unlike Fasanella, Riker does not have a working-class background. To ensure the kind of authenticity that photographers from Lewis Hine to Sebastiao Salgado in his already-classic *Workers: An Archaeology of the Industrial Age* (1995) have created in their still photography, Riker knows that he must earn the trust of his subjects.[36] In a recent letter to the author, he described how rapidly his film became an unusually collaborative effort: "I wrote the screenplay in English, with little emphasis on the final dialogues. This screenplay serves as the basis for the improvisational work we do in the dramatic workshops—it gives us the structure, the characters, and a sense of the tone. Working with the non-actors—in this case with the garment workers—I begin to write out dialogues in Spanish based directly on the workshops. Slowly, the dialogues are worked out scene by scene."[37]

In the "Seamstress" episode (figure 10), the protagonist is Ana, who supports a mother and a sickly daughter in her home country and is owed back pay, as are her coworkers, by a type-A Korean couple who lease a loft in some Manhattan or outer-borough factory district. Exterior shots locate a silent industrial park whose façades are anonymous and identical. When the camera enters Ana's own shop, we get an impression of a Sweatshop City the size of the huge housing developments Ana sees from her elevated train on the commute home to her denser, more human-scale New York barrio.

The most prominent image of the "Seamstress" episode is of Dominican and Ecuadoran women laboring over machines. Bells ring to mark the day's beginning, the lunch hour, and the day's end. During the lengthy day, these women work quickly, as do the male pressers who line the walls of the massive, high-ceilinged factory room. A patrolling subcontractor behaves, as directed by Riker, much like a guard harassing convict labor, yelling, "Work!" and pushing a worker as he does so. He continues roving the floor, shouting over the industrial din: "Fastah, fastah!"; "What is this?"; "Make it straight, okay?"; and "Avanca!" Himself goaded by a British-accented contractor who rejects many of the finished garments, he spies one girl, picks up a dress from her finished work basket, and summarily commands, "Get out." Only occasionally does he commend a woman with "This is good—okay."

Ana's woes outside of her shop work organize much of the episode. Like so many of the working poor in the quartet of *Ciudad* vignettes, she cannot find emergency money to send home, even though she is steadily employed. Her unyielding bosses haven't paid their workers in four weeks, possibly because they themselves are waiting for money, although they are svelte and well-dressed and seem driven to accumulate rather than share the profits. "No money this week," they inform Ana and her coworkers. A collection at the shop yields a pittance for Ana, as does beseeching her cousin, a presser in the shop who drinks away his own sadness.

Ana's futile search soon extends to the owner of a dress shop who refuses the handmade garments of Consuelo, a friend of Ana's who would lend her money if she herself could find commissions. "We don't buy dresses from people in the street," he tells the two seamstresses, suggesting that large manufacturers control not only their subcontractors but a wide network of small store owners and vendors. In a scene at what looks like a union hall or workers' defense league venue but is left ambiguous—in keeping with the film's hard-headed understanding of union separation from such workers—Ana asks laid-off workers from other sweatshops how to collect her money. The grim news is that when "we . . . arrive . . . the factory will be closed." Returning to her job, she grieves at her machine. The subcontractor sees her idle and, as he has done so many times before with other workers, tells her to "get out." In a powerful segment, Ana clutches her machine as if it were her dying child, and the faces of nearby workers are tearful.

Fellow workers stop their machines and cease ironing in sympathy, and the shop falls silent. As the camera lingers on each worker, even including the for-once-silenced subcontractor as if he too is caught in the market economy that dictates he fire less productive workers, there is the sense of a quiet, transient mutiny. But it is the silence of despair, not of a concerted job action. The scene ends with shots of bosses, workers, and Ana herself silent and hurt: no redress, no salvation. In this not fully mobilized sweatshop, there is no victory: a woman who has to pay her daughter's medical expenses loses her factory sewing job and no union benefits accrue. This is not an overthrow of servitude: no organizer enters this frozen shop, nor is there a bid for control over the workplace.

It is a remarkable scene nonetheless, simply because the workers are so moved by the plight of Ana yet the traditions of organized labor that would express their solidarity are completely absent. It is difficult to know what their faces reveal: sorrow, resignation, dawning resolve. Yet Riker has indelibly revealed the face of the modern shop.[38]

In recent interviews, Riker described his sweatshop scenarios in *La Ciudad* as allegories of victory as well as defeat. An implicit criticism of ILGWU's betrayal and abandonment, he pointed out, is built into the film narrative. What he learned from his five years of research prior to making the film was that UNITE was not serving the least skilled workers well but rather making deals with contractors: "UNITE organizers undermine workers' democratic processes, doing deals and negotiating behind their backs. . . . You are paid if you are loyal to the union [rather than] developing an activist shop. . . . Unions don't organize workers. Workers organize unions. . . . [That is why] the Garment Workers' Solidarity Center [a still-struggling New York City organization for undocumented garment workers] broke from UNITE."[39]

Although there are only hints in "Seamstress" of the coming of the Solidarity Center—to this day an organization repudiated by UNITE—Riker's sweatshop is graced by the beauty of the workers' faces and spirits. This is not the dystopia of Coe: the large corporation is not even a shadowy presence, and indeed the viewer is struck by the light-filled space of the garment factory. In those interviews, Riker often remarked that he wanted to learn who the workers were. Compared to Coe, he emphasizes his respect for his subjects rather than their permanent status as injured creatures. His sweatshop inevitably partakes of that insight.

If one views the work of the 1930s sweatshop artists from the perspective of the trio discussed here, these WPA forebears, themselves influenced by sweatshop representation from Lowell onward, embraced a fairly unitary idea of the shop. They all perpetuated a dingy late-Victorian stereotype of sweatshop workers that has been well described by Alfred Kazin, the brilliantly successful son of a Jewish dressmaker mother and a tailor father: his own relatives, he said, were "bent and cadaverous and pale [in their] garment lofts on Seventh Avenue."[40]

Neither Kazin nor the WPA school leavened their imaginings of the misery of the old Jewish shop, however, with the dead-endedness of the wider Latino and Asian sewing trades of, for instance, 1930s Los Angeles. The California women of color toiling and striking with the help of the ILG maverick Rose Pesotta received little cultural attention in the New Deal era and for many decades afterward. For generations of postsweatshop artists, the question instead was how and even whether to continue the protest mode. As the *New York Times* critic Charles Hagen commented in 1995—after the publication of Coe's drawings and before the release of Riker's film—on a Museum of the City of New York photo exhibit pairing the photos of Jacob Riis with contemporary photographs of the poor, modern artists "are wary of taking on the role of social crusader."[41] Some artists made sporadic references to Chicano sweatshops in the era of the United Farm Workers, and the Asian presence in the sweatshop was honored in the "people's art" murals of the Los Angeles and New York City Chinatowns, including those of the Lower East Side muralist Martin Wong (*Henry Chong Laundry*, 1994).[42]

Mention should also be made of *Hidden Labor: Uncovering L.A.'s Garment Industry*, an unusual 1998 exhibit funded by a partnership of humanities councils, philanthropies, and redevelopment agencies.[43] A multimedia women's project of the Common Threads Artist Group, it was mounted in a local storefront space. Through photographs, a mural, shop objects, and texts in Spanish and English, it ambitiously surveyed the entire social history of the Los Angeles sweatshop. Subsections like "To the Land of Sunshine and Sweatshops" and "They Took Our Jobs and Sent Them Overseas" counterposed garment workers' union history with the actual material culture of the sweatshop, such as dressmakers' dummies plastered with signs contrasting business profits and labor's meager share. As a counternarrative to the careful avoidance of blame characterizing the then-current Smithsonian Exhibition's show in Washington, D.C., on the history of sweatshops, the subject of chapter 6, it was a satiric reproof that could have used greater exposure.[44]

At the end of the twentieth century, then, it was largely through the work of Fasanella, Coe, and Riker that a wider ethnic vision of the American sweatshop and its art came into its own. All of these artists were working, as Sue Coe remarked, in a time when labor art was unpopular, but each nevertheless saw the sweatshop as a labor site reflecting its time. The loft spaces depicted in the works of these three artists suggest different degrees of disillusionment with the unionist claims to workplace democracy of the late twentieth century. In each artist's ethnic story, the sweatshop proves the need for working-class consciousness. Though casting a cold eye on the materialism endemic to the post-HUAC American Dream, Fasanella's shop is a kind of haven, incorporating a labor past and a once-vibrant working-class culture. Yet his workers, even those of color, are caught in a postwar time warp. Coe, on the other hand, is very much of the moment. She trumpets the urgency and immediacy of growing exploitation. Riker's sweatshop, neither melting pot nor slaughterhouse, depicts a new working poor who find no comfort in Fasanella's union-generated boons but who also avoid the dehumanization of Coe's corporate-induced sufferings.

However unpopular their subject, these artists have demonstrated that the "new" sweatshop could come into its own artistically. All three, often relegated to marginality, have carved a new sweatshop aesthetics. Their work incorporates and re-visions the dialectic between humanized and grotesque space at the heart of the classic American shop. These artists have continued the transmutation of the sweatshop context already under way in the 1930s. Employing personal iconographies for the resurgent sweatshop, their representations also address both the role and the invisibility of the Asian and Latino worker.

Like so many imaginers and observers of the sweatshop before them, they bring to that work site their own labor vision. Although they disagree on the (limited) opportunity the sweated site provides, both Fasanella and Riker create an art of social idealism. They challenge the notion of the ugly shop in which workers' concern for one another is submerged in a debasingly competitive ethic. The older man invokes a somewhat romanticized proletarian past while the younger reiterates the dignity of labor. Coe's denunciations of business leave little room for either sentiment. In her social-surrealistic revision, the sweatshop remains as American and ugly as ever, the hub of a devilish local and global network.

Their interpretations mirror more, however, than personal preoccupations. All three deplore the treatment of labor in a country so mythically devoted to the abolition of class division. To some extent in Fasanella and more dramatically in Riker and Coe, the American union is all but invisible. And the art that challenges, repositions geopolitically as well. Whether the workforce is global or local, unionized or green card-less, the postindustrial sweatshop is, most definitely, made in the U.S.A.

PART THREE

Spinning the Shop

CHAPTER 6

Spinning the New Shop

El Monte and the Smithsonian Furor

Sweatshops are not a suitable subject for the Smithsonian.
>—Tracy Mullin, president of the National Retail
>Federation, quoted in George White,
>"Sweatshop Exhibit Rends Garment Industry,"
>*Los Angeles Times* (1997)

The use of sweatshops is not a . . . footnote in American history.
>—California Congressman George Miller, defending
>the Smithsonian Institution in a Pacifica Radio debate
>with an American Apparel Manufacturing Association
>spokesman (1997)

I felt like I was really living in hell.
>—Freed El Monte worker, quoted in Michael Krikorian,
>"Two Brothers Sentenced to Six Years in Thai
>Slavery Case," *Los Angeles Times* (1996)

WHILE IN THE MID and late 1990s socially conscious artists Sue Coe and David Riker waged their solitary battles in New York to reawaken awareness of the sweatshop, a 1995 Immigration and Naturalization Service (INS) raid on an illegal shop in suburban El Monte, near Los Angeles, so ignited popular sentiment that by the end of the decade it had found a prominent place in the history of sweated labor as presented in a national museum exhibition.

With its flood of immigrant labor, southern California had been home to much sweatshop activity since the 1960s. The El Monte shop, flagrantly illegal and even known to authorities, had been in existence since 1988 and was run by a villainous family of Thai contractors who held their illegal immigrant workers in a barbed-wire barracks complex and worked them twelve to eighteen hours daily. The sentences in the court cases that followed were "among the largest . . . ever agreed to in a modern slavery case."[1]

The El Monte story as told in the press was rightly one of coercion, chicanery, and immense profit. Yet because the El Monte saga contained a spiraling scandal that eventually involved brand-name manufacturers as well known as Guess, it may have been the story that the photographer and critic Alan Sekula was thinking of when he wrote, "Mass media portray a wholly spectacular political realm."[2] So notorious did El Monte become that the plot of an episode of *Law and Order,* one of the highest-rated television shows, drew on its raid-indictment-vindication story. It was almost as if Sue Coe's vision met David Riker's in a cop show version of the "classic sweatshop." Using New York City's antiquated tenements in its early scenes, the show focused on the peonage of Latina dress shop workers and only alluded to Thai workers in the scenes where the NYPD found evidence that workers had been tortured and murdered for trying to escape their sweatshop confinement.[3]

In the exhibit "Between a Rock and a Hard Place: A History of Sweatshops, 1820 to the Present," which ran from April 22 to October 30, 1998, the Smithsonian Institution's National Museum of American History, in its dedication to the public interest and the re-creation of the American past, was obviously dedicated to a more sober and reflective approach. The El Monte scandal inspired the museum's staff in a way that was not singular so much as timely.[4] Nevertheless, the scandal came to be identified as the exhibit's controversial centerpiece by the media, by the garment industry, and by the lively public debate months before the show opened.

The exhibit aroused nearly universal criticism: unions found it too sanitized, and management disliked the recital of a long string of sweatshop tragedies, from Triangle to El Monte.[5] Arousing liberals' criticism, the Smithsonian Institution displayed in its halls carefully phrased self-advertisements for name-recognition clothing manufacturers who claimed they followed a "workplace code of conduct" that obviated union or government inspection. Although it was encouraging the public to learn about a negative aspect of our national heritage, the National

Museum took care to preface the show with a disclaimer: the Smithsonian had no desire to be "unpatriotic," "cause pain," or "embarrass," but it did feel "a responsibility to convey a fuller, more inclusive history."[6] With El Monte as its token sweatshop, the museum discovered that this noble set of goals was impossible to achieve, given the charged nature of the very phrase "American sweatshop."

Exploring the reasons why the El Monte scandal attracted widespread media coverage and a few years later became the centerpiece of an exhibit at the National Museum of American History uncovers much about the nature of recent American responses to sweatshops, the power of apparel makers to revise sweatshop history, and the politics of exhibits designed to create a reasoned dialogue on sweated labor in the United States. This chapter analyzes the battle over how to tell the story and how to honor the shop. Such an analysis must begin with a brief summary of the spin that various parties put on the exhibit and the large-circulation daily press coverage of both the sweatshop and the museum exhibit. How much did the show adopt the familiar dialectic between the sweatshop as a rite of ethnic urban passage and as a continuing shame? Did the media and the museum "spin" the shop as a permanent or transitory site in the American experience and obscure the shop itself, as has so often happened in the history of the sweatshop idea?

TELLING EL MONTE: LOS ANGELES GOTHIC

El Monte was front-page news during the first week of August 1995. While in nearby Los Angeles the August 2 INS raid did not receive anything like the coverage of the O. J. Simpson trial, even as late as August 15, 1995, a *Los Angeles Times* editorial roundup had three pieces on the raid to one on the police villain of the Simpson trial, Officer Mark Fuhrman, and his preferential use of the "n-word." As journals throughout the nation carried the hard-news story, and editorials deplored it, newspaper readers had an opportunity to see the "real" sweatshop unmasked in 1995.

In early August, authorities raided the shop, liberating a workforce of mostly women and a few men. Some had been there six years, wearing drab yellow uniforms and sewing designer labels on high-end, mass-produced clothing. They had been under guard around the clock, made as little as $0.60 an hour and at most $2.00 (curiously, accounts differed greatly), and were threatened with death if they tried to escape. In literary terms, this story might have issued from the "wrongs of the shopgirls" plot of antebellum Gothic novelists like George Lippard. But in reality it was a troubling story of forced labor in the contemporary United States.

At its core was a matriarchal family of "sweaters." Suni Manasurangkun was a sixty-five-year-old woman whose outsize greed contrasted with her appearance as a fairly benevolent shop forelady. With her five sons, two daughters-in-law, and two guards, she had institutionalized sweatshop slavery. By 1988, the operation ran at various locations in downtown Los Angeles. "Together [they] constituted one business operation sharing common ownership, control, coordination and assets [joined by] other unregistered production sites."[7] Under the family aegis, sewing, ironing, finishing, checking, and packaging operations were efficiency itself.

A story of this kind could not help being sensational, for it contained enough melodrama for a nineteenth-century dime novel. Adding to the drama was the nontraditional site of this American sweatshop—southern California, not New York or Chicago. El Monte is a working-class suburban community with a largely multicultural Hispanic and Asian population. The raided apartment complex was hiding several anomalies under this mantle of upward-mobility respectability: the building had been converted into a prisonlike garment factory rather than a loft or an industrial park; subcontractors were atypically wealthy rather than subsisting from week to week; it was Thais, not other ethnics, who were running this business in the United States; the compensation system was based on slavery rather than piecework; and more than seventy people worked at the site, rather than the usual twenty or thirty. Not featured in most coverage, perhaps because it was less dramatic, was the fact that twenty-two Latina workers were there voluntarily, and both Thais and Latinos worked in a "front" shop in downtown Los Angeles that was open to inspection. The real operations were elsewhere in the area.[8]

Numbers told a story: owners who were worth $750,000 in cash and jewels forced workers to make department store garments for an average of eighty-four hours a week. With actual—and poetic—justice, all of the workers joined in a lawsuit for back pay. Some years later, in a final deviation from Triangle victimization, they won millions.[9] The out-of-court settlement with the clothing manufacturers included, however, a provision absolving them of any legal liability.[10]

The media collaborated in telling the El Monte story, for with only some exceptions, they emphasized the same talking points: the entry into the United States of indentured workers, mostly country girls tricked by Bangkok recruiters, with false passports paid for at exorbitant rates to the El Monte operators; their imprisonment, both monetary and psychic, which included garnishing their wages to repay their "debt" to the owners for smuggling them in with false passports; and the company store in the El Monte compound that, like mining companies of old, inflated prices for food and other necessities. El Monte was, in fact, a company town of sorts. Much was made of the crowded rooms in which workers slept on mats stuffed with fabric, the denial of medical treatment, and the chain-link fence in the evil compound. The media especially emphasized the fact that these women toiled making designer-label clothes for prestigious manufacturers.[11] Although the press consensus was that "the scene should never be repeated in the United States (or anywhere else for that matter),"[12] reporters covering the story were slow to reveal these manufacturers' names and those of the retail chains that sold clothes produced at El Monte.[13] On the eve of the Smithsonian show, the roster of firms actively fighting sweatshops was not much longer than it had been before El Monte.[14]

El Monte was more than a sweatshop; it was a prison. Court papers alleged that immigrant workers were subject to "false imprisonment in a system of peonage and involuntary servitude." Included in the suit were those manufacturers "who contracted with 'operators' to produce garments at prices too low to permit payment of minimum wages and overtime."[15] The owners were also charged with harboring illegal aliens and conspiracy. The cases all cited a brutal conspiracy, and seven Thai nationals eventually pled guilty to "federal slavery charges stemming from a sweatshop in El Monte where about six dozen fellow immigrants were forced to manufacture garments."[16] Most of the conspirators named in the suit, which was settled within a year, received stiff fines—eventually totaling millions of dollars—and some were also sentenced to years in federal prison.[17]

But El Monte's story is far more stark and complicated than the story told by the newspapers' raid-liberation-justice tale. Alan Sekula remarks of American tabloid-style reportage: "The importance of the framing discourse is masked, context is hidden."[18] Only a few media observers charged that various agencies, including the INS, had known for years about the place.[19] Far more common were the less liberal interpretations that El Monte was an illegal immigration issue and that the immigrant operators named in the suits should serve longer prison terms.[20] Few besides the *New York Times* saw the features of a bigger picture: the widening circle of legal liabilities; the problems endemic to the apparel industry; and the shame of retail outlets stocking sweatshop goods.[21]

Briefly incorporating the El Monte events and fallout, the Smithsonian show had its own story to tell.

THE BUILD-UP

For eight months prior to the exhibit, the Smithsonian consistently listed its subtitle as "A Dialogue." Yet that aim became increasingly ephemeral, and just before the opening it was changed to "A History." The reasons were by then clear to the battling adversaries. The apparel industry during those months had mounted a campaign to block, then to censor, then to cancel the touring show. Anti-sweatshop groups made common cause with the Smithsonian senior staff. Although the curators took care to consult industry representatives as they prepared the show and "tried to design the exhibit in a way that would head off controversy," the very topic seemed to guarantee a hostile business response.[22]

The intense media scrutiny began long before the mid-April 1998 opening. The National Museum had been defending itself in the press for months.[23] There were also press releases and, more than a year after the Smithsonian exhibit, a catalog keyed to a Los Angeles Museum of Tolerance version of it.

Had one looked only at early lists of financial supporters, the Smithsonian's cast of contributors would have seemed to cut a wide swath. K-mart CEO Floyd Miller provided a statement in the "Dialogue" section, and there was support from retailers like Calvin Klein and Levi Strauss.[24] Labor sponsors included the National Labor Committee and the powerful Union of Needletrades, Industrial and Textile Employees (UNITE). Bipartisan politics played out behind the scenes: both Democrats and Republicans were all too aware that taxpayers were funding the museum's show, that sweatshops were an ongoing problem, and that

1. Ben Shahn, Detail, center section, *Jersey Homesteads Mural*, 1935–1936, Special Collections and University Archives, Rutgers University, New Brunswick, N.J.

2. William Gropper, *Tailor*, c. 1940, Hirshhorn Museum and Sculpture Garden, Smithsonian Institution, Gift of Josephine H. Hirshhorn, 1966. Photo by Lee Stalsworth.

3. William Gropper, "Piece Work," from *Capriccios*, 1952. Los Angeles County Museum of Art, Gift of William Gropper. Photo © 2000 Museum Associates, LACMA.

4. Moses Soyer, *Girl at Sewing Machine,* c. 1939. Metropolitan Museum of Art.

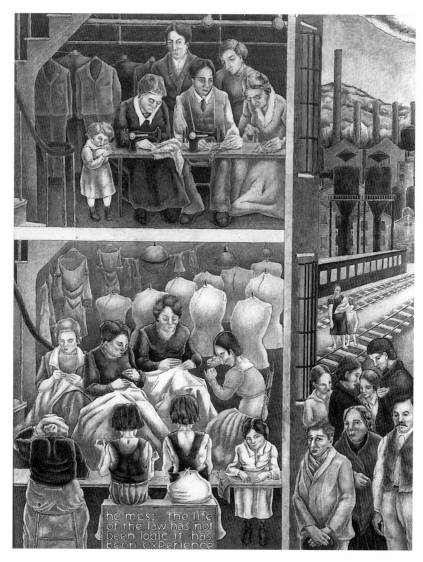

5. George Biddle, Study for *Sweatshop*, c. 1935, Smithsonian American Art Museum, transfer from the General Services Administration, on loan to the University of Maryland.

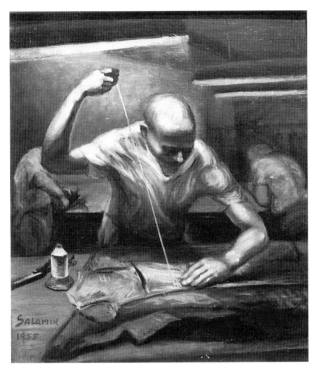

6. Eugene Salamin, *Lining Baster,* 1955. Author's collection.

7. Sue Coe, *Garment Workers Exploited by Fruit of the Loom,* 1994. Galerie St. Etienne.

8. Sue Coe, *Chinese Floor Workers*, 1994. Galerie St. Etienne.

9. Sue Coe, *Machine Workers from El Salvador.* 1994. Galerie St. Etienne.

10. Still from the "Seamstress" episode, *The City/La Ciudad,* 1999. Photo by Victor Sira. Released by Zeitgeist Films.

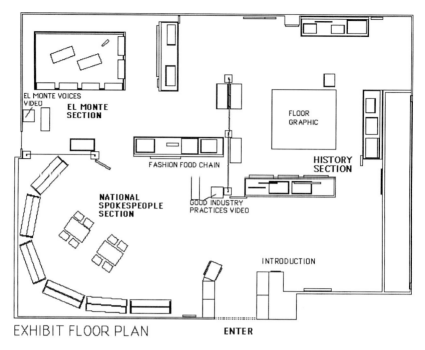

EXHIBIT FLOOR PLAN   ENTER

11. Floorplan of the exhibit. Smithsonian Institution, National Museum of American History.

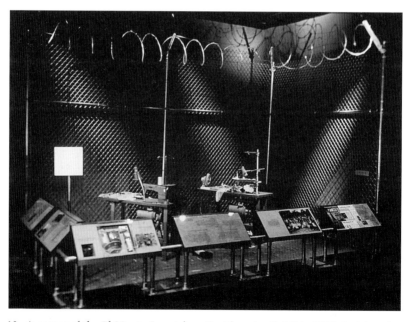

12. A corner of the El Monte Sweatshop, Smithsonian Exhibit, 1998. Smithsonian Institution, National Museum of American History.

there were real gaps in enforcement of sweatshop as well as immigration law. And both sides well knew the power of the manufacturing lobby to curtail a national museum's efforts to probe an unattractive aspect of American business history.

The apparel industry objected to business being linked with sweated labor, saying that the exhibit promoted guilt by association, ignored the 800,000 people in the apparel industry, and "let down" the American public.[25] The industry lobbied Republicans in the House, since Congress provided almost three-quarters of the Smithsonian's funding. These accusations of the exhibit's negativity toward the apparel industry were echoed by key Washington Republicans, including Sam Johnson, appointed by House Speaker Newt Gingrich to the Smithsonian Board of Regents to represent managerial views and those of many of his fellow Republicans as well. Johnson promptly charged the Smithsonian with "historical revisionism," turning left-wing rhetoric back against those presumed leftists. Democratic Congressman George Miller, who had chaired hearings on sweatshops like El Monte, was one of forty-six Democratic lawmakers (admittedly a House minority) to sign a petition presented to the government to support government funding for the exhibit.[26]

Throughout these pre-exhibit debates, the El Monte segment generated more press coverage than all of the other parts of the exhibit put together. "This isn't about history at all. . . . It's about contemporary policy," Jack Morgan complained publicly. Its "focus is so much on labor and the image of El Monte" that it "tars us with same brush as El Monte."[27] But if it was obvious to all concerned that the sweatshop present was the real issue in the debate over the National Museum exhibit, the museum's handling of the sweatshop past proved problematic as well.

FACTS AND ARTIFACTS:
WHAT THE EXHIBIT WAS AND WAS NOT

It was not only their pro- or antilabor views that prevented reviewers from being able to agree on which controversy the exhibit was generating: the perceived slur on the apparel industry, the supposed politicization of the show in its inclusion of El Monte, or the very nature of sweatshop history itself.

The content of the Smithsonian show itself was problematic to almost everyone. Following signs, visitors entered the National Museum to find an introductory section that explained the historical framework of dividing the show into three subgroups, "1820–1880: The Seamstress," "1880–1940: Tenement Sweatshops," and "1940–Present: The Resurgence of Sweatshops" (figure 11).

This three-pronged historical section preceded "El Monte," "Good Industry Practices," "The Fashion Food Chain," and a section labeled (but not acting as) "Dialogue," which was no doubt meant to establish the longevity and continuity of the shop in American life. It featured graphics and documents on the rise of ready-to-wear clothing and the proliferation of underpaid tailors and seamstresses, many of them solo operators. Posters and banners supplemented this section as well as the second one, which highlighted the immigrant repopulating of sewing shops; the classic sweatshop and its industrial toll; and the New Deal's legislative cleanup efforts, which ushered in an era of union benefits.

The much-disputed modern-sweatshop section took the story from the quiescent (and underground) post–World War II shops to the hidden, shameful ones like El Monte. The physical plant was depicted with nothing more than barbed wire and two lone sewing machines, a conflation of one corner of the notorious site and the outer limits of the grounds. Foregrounded instead was the material culture of El Monte—workers' quarters, company-store purchases, letters home. Most important were the few post–El Monte video interviews with workers, whose voices, through these interviews with Smithsonian researchers, were finally heard. (These taped comments would later be excised from the Web site versions.) Since the Thai men and women who granted these interviews were the only expert witnesses offered by the show, the museum might have taken more care to privilege them in the exhibit. Ex-sweatshop workers, many still without green cards, would admittedly be reluctant to come forward; nevertheless, the museum seemed to make no attempt to expand the El Monte testimony with that of others who had endured and fled similar situations.

A transitional section located between "El Monte" and "The Fashion Food Chain" on the advantages and disadvantages of domestic and off-shore production did include a 1997 *Doonesbury* cartoon by Garry Trudeau that lampooned Nike, a *Bobbin* (the industry magazine) advertisement soliciting offshore clients, and lists of the pitiful wages paid by countries outside the United States. Yet it gave more exhibit floor space to industry representatives and their statements opposing sweatshops.

This was a highly pictorial rather than a scholarly show. Yet if their aim had been to help visitors envision the literal and spiritual darkness of the El Monte world, the curators could well have consulted a Sue Coe or a David Riker, whose imaginative underworlds brilliantly convey contrasting but somehow complementary versions of the El Monte deprivations. If, on the other hand, their intent was to give the exhibit a factual rather than an artistic spin, they could have taken excerpts from court records, social welfare case studies, Ellis Island immigrant letters home, accounts of a history of sweatshop raids, or the writings of industrial physicians; no such documents, however, were used. Rare literary excerpts provided some dramatic texture, such as a truncated passage from Abraham Cahan's "A Sweatshop Romance" (1898), but no curator thought to tap the wealth of Yankee seamstress, Jewish sweatshop, and Triangle fire fiction, which might have made the National Museum's display of oft-seen Riis photos and UNITE pamphlets come alive.

More important, the Smithsonian curators made no real attempt to rethink the American sweatshop by examining cultural prejudices about it, chronicling the museum's own difficulties by mounting a sweatshop tribute, or employing the authority of the museum experience in experimental ways. (One reporter semi-seriously suggested that the show "could have included a few visualizing exercises" explaining the lure of the El Monte shop to a fourteen-year-old girl living in the Thai countryside and facing the choices of servitude, prostitution, or "work in an American sweatshop to pay back your travel expenses.")[28] Instead, the exhibit prefaced sections and subsections with brief, fact-filled descriptions to provide historical and narrative continuity. There were necessarily many gaps in sewing-trades time—between, for instance, the antebellum 1850s and the ethnic 1880s, between the Triangle era of 1910 and the New Deal. In tune with trade union history, the post–World War II period of sweatshop quiescence was given short shrift, and any criticism of the ILGWU and ACW (UNITE was listed at the end of the exhibit for providing "advice and assistance") for their inequitable membership policies during those decades was omitted in the name of prudence.

As a simplifying exhibition, the show's emphasis on material culture worked to a degree. The artifacts ranged chronologically from a tailor's shears from 1820 to a long-knife cutter of the late nineteenth century, to a badge worn at the Triangle fire mourners' parade, to a phony time card (undated) used to deceive government inspectors, to a 1970s UNITE poster and a photo of a 1997 Queens knitwear sweatshop. One problem even here, however, was that the presentation of these artifacts made no distinction between a history of the sewing trades and a history of the sweatshop. The excerpts from period documents to some extent helped to clarify the shop experience: Horace Greeley sympathizing with the genteel poverty of pre–Civil War seamstresses; a Civil War–era ad for cheap clothing; a *Harper's Bazaar* poem from 1870 on women's continued suffering in the trades; a brief statement from Rose Schneiderman on the Triangle fire victims; a strike broadside in Spanish and English from the 1930s; a 1938 *Life* magazine blurb extolling the collective bargaining gains of garment workers; an INS badge; a 1980s pamphlet from Haiti luring U.S. apparel manufacturers to set up factories in that country at a time when Americans made $26.00 a day to Haitian workers' $2.60.

One problem with the National Museum's presentation of facts and artifacts alike was that there seemed, as one museum critic phrased it in a related context, no "interplay of insights" among the photos, the imagery, and the textual sections.[29] Perhaps one reason was the virtual absence of any thematic and cross-media unity that might have been generated by workers' observations. Worker activities outside the work site, therefore, are relegated to a few "official" union dates: the 1909 "Uprising of the 20,000" (meriting half a sentence), the 1915 Chicago ACW strike parade (one sentence), and a vague reference to strikers "from 1900 into 1930," as if strike activity ended there. No dates or venues at all were attached to many exhibit ephemera, nor was any scholarly attempt made to estimate decades or sites. "The Rise of the Needle Trade Union" section was particularly weak. Carefully removing the radical taint, this part of the exhibit made no linkage between the Jewish labor movement and the formation of the Socialist and Communist garment trades. As if to head off industry ire, inflammatory words like "socialism" and "communism" were excised from sweatshop history at the National Museum. The Triangle fire, a tragedy that generated worker testimonials, speeches, novels, and poems, received similarly tepid treatment.

Despite available interviews, even those excerpted from Andrew Ross's *No Sweat* and its spiritual forebear, Stein's *Out of the Sweatshop*, the National Museum seemed to have made no real attempt to turn the spotlight from the material culture of the sweatshop, as produced by the owners themselves in the plethora of tools, locales, ephemera, and advertisements for workers or goods. Similarly, the reformers' broadsides and pamphlets displayed were the product of middle-class reformers, with only a few Rose Schneidermans, herself a veteran organizer, speaking for the silent rank and file.

The effect of all this was to give the impression of the shop as a series of disconnected historical events rather than a continuous underclass labor history. Absent was the flavor of felt experience. The announced goal of the curators was to "expand the number of voices, or points of view, heard or seen by the viewer."[30] But it was the curatorial voice that controlled the show, with assists from other highly educated, articulate commentators who had never been sweated workers. The only words of workers themselves were five quotations from letters home written by El Monte workers in 1992 and 1993. Their attempts to define their own experience, presented through curators' chosen excerpts rather than entire letters, came late in the National Museum's history of the sweatshop. Like the carefully choreographed one-day visit of a few former workers to the exhibit when it opened at the Los Angeles Museum of Tolerance in 1999, the inclusion of these workers' words seemed more ceremonial than real. Omitted as well—in pursuit of or as a sop to the manufacturers' approval—were the names of the manufacturers that had traditionally or recently been the worst offenders. (The catalog, published in 1999 as part of the Los Angeles museum's reprise of the Smithsonian show, did not equivocate so much on casting blame, but it veered between anti-sweatshop advocacy and calculated neutrality.)

In fact, the desire to placate the apparel industry watered down a sweatshop history that, despite the gaps and omissions, had the beginnings of a radical critique. The Smithsonian curators chose instead to handle the nearly impossible task of making a balanced presentation of the sweatshop as "a logistical problem" rather than an opportunity to create "an affective drama."[31] They felt obligated to convey information so as to include the manufacturing voice by allowing the industry to speak entirely for itself. Initially, the curators had tried to exert some control over the self-aggrandizing content of an industry video that featured modern textile factories and denied U.S. linkage to sweatshops; ultimately the video was included verbatim.

In the "Good Industry Practices" section, the curators tried to appease controversy. Wrote Mary Alexander, one critic doubtful of this motive, "The theme of this section seems to be that contemporary management and government officials abhor sweatshops and are vigilant in refusing goods produced by laborers in such conditions." "Kathie Lee Gifford's inclusion," Alexander continued, "leaves one musing over her recent public exposure as an exploiter of workers. Does this mark her rehabilitation?"[32] Assuming, apparently, that any muckraking story is incomplete without sanitizing rebuttals from the targeted industry, the curators, in the final section, "The Fashion Food Chain," privileged six "professional" voices—representatives of business, labor, and government, community activists, and celebrity endorsers—at greater length than they gave to the El Monte five. Giving up the attempt to engage manufacturers in a conversation with anti-sweatshop groups, the show ended with none of the "dialogue" originally envisioned. Wal-Mart, Kathie Lee, and Levi Strauss provided disclaimers for an apparel industry that otherwise had refused to speak at all.

The Smithsonian's El Monte section was placed, chronologically, near the end of the show (figure 12). Six dresslike racks provided a chorus of management, labor, and government perspectives. The actual sweatshop, however, represented by the two sewing machines placed within the infamous barbed wire of the compound, was ghostly at best. To the pair of work stations and barbed wire were added bundles of seized clothing. There were no models of people at work in this shop, no miniatures of the onetime workplace. If the key to understanding sweatshop toil is witnessing the laboring body at work, this was in every way an ethereal shop. Within that disembodied context was a selection of "El Monte Voices." In the background the voices of freed workers and law enforcement officials described the conditions uncovered by the August 2 raid three years before. A tapestry of witnesses offered powerful recollections of peonage.

In their placement of El Monte just before the "Dialogue" section, as the finale to the historical survey of sweatshops, and opposite a set of voices for change (excluding activist ones, however), the curators no doubt intended to suggest continuity while highlighting reform. The result was emblematic, however, of the entire exhibit: the reform was muted at best and the continuity forgotten.

Thus, the exhibition's search for compromise rather than dialectic or capitalist critique informed this block quotation regarding El Monte's significance: "The El Monte sweatshop, like the Triangle disaster, has become a powerful symbol in American history. Although many sweatshops have been raided in recent years, El Monte has been used as a media event by U.S. Secretary of Labor Robert Reich; Victoria L. Bradshaw, State Labor Commissioner, California Department of Industrial Relations; and others to galvanize the American public into action. Some industry representatives suggested the situation has been blown out of proportion. Others wondered [if] it was just the tip of the iceberg." The cursory quality of the El Monte section, however, was most attributable to the museum's decision not to visualize too much of the shop. Of the wealth of material culture extracted from El Monte, little was shown. Toilet articles bought at high commissary prices gave no sense of "the crowded, noisy, smelly conditions."[33] Nor did the curators make any effort to dramatize the overheated work and living quarters and the nearly absolute control of the patrolling guards. Only a lone, stained cup, indicating that workers drank large amounts of tea to stay awake for marathon days and nights, symbolized a set of conditions that the exhibit chose not to make graphic.

Although they recognized that the exhibit would not be able to mount a "dialogue" between labor and business on the sweatshop, the Smithsonian curators did try to incorporate controversy into the exhibit in a number of ways. Their afterword to the exhibit stated that the subject had proved more complex than they originally thought. The final section also cited ways in which viewers could make comments or read articles about the furor the exhibit was generating. In the name of a dialogue with the sweatshop, the California Fashion Association (CFA) and others concluded the El Monte section. (It should be noted that fifteen manufacturers, the bulwark of the CFA, controlled four-fifths of the contractor base in southern California.)[34] Fact sheets and videos reminded visitors of the economy-sustaining importance of sales volumes, worker employment, and salaries allegedly well above minimum wage. Also celebrated was "the can-do competitiveness of the American apparel industry boasting about the trained workforce, excellent technology, and ability to quickly respond to . . . the fast changing fashion industry."[35] Another reviewer commented, "Because so much spin had preceded the April 1998 opening, reviews seemed anticlimactic. Commentators found the show tame or controversial, bowing to pro-labor or pro-business ideology depending largely on the periodicals they were writing for and their own viewpoints one way or the other."[36]

AFTERMATH: THE MUSEUM OF TOLERANCE AND THE KATHIE LEE FACTOR

In July 1998, with three months of the show still to run, the curators announced that the exhibit would not be touring the country. The months of industry lobbying and threats to withhold funds from future exhibits had paid off. "I feel vindicated that someone heard us," Ilse Melchek, executive director of the California Fashion Association, which had boycotted the show, commented disingenuously.[37] The liberal-minded *San Francisco Chronicle* explained: "The Smithsonian couldn't scrape together the $100,000 or so needed to put the two truckloads of historic artifacts on the road. . . . Manufacturers [in addition] had already denounced the show as a taxpayer-funded smear of the U.S. apparel industry. Those protests, in turn, had museums in both San Francisco and Los Angeles reluctant to carry the exhibit because they feared that corporate donors would pull the plug on future shows."[38]

This preemption by a coalition of three hundred garment manufacturers that could not forestall the Washington show accelerated from the day it opened until mid-July, when the touring exhibit was derailed.[39] Wrote one satiric *Los Angeles Weekly* reporter, "If you missed the Smithsonian Sweatshop Exhibit or don't remember hearing about it, you're not alone."[40]

Cyberspace also felt the curtailment. Although a virtual version of the exhibit continued to be available with textual overviews and photographs of documents, exhibit spaces, and artifacts, the voices of El Monte were silenced. There was apparently no funding available to retain the taped interviews with those who had once been trapped in the facility.

Although the show was dead, the ghosts of El Monte continued to haunt it. The scandal was brought up reproachfully by the press during the year after the show closed.[41] "Sweatshops Continue but Nobody Is to

Blame" ran one satirical headline satirizing manufacturers' arguments.[42] Anti-sweatshop groups, with new allies, were busy trying to revive the Smithsonian show and finally publish a book catalog to memorialize and distill the exhibition. Because the Smithsonian would provide no funds for a reprise of "Between a Rock and a Hard Place," these groups found a new sponsor, the Simon Wiesenthal Center and Museum of Tolerance in Los Angeles. The reprised exhibit added sponsors such as the University of California at Los Angeles Asian American Studies Center and gave more credit than the original to the Asian Pacific Law Center, which had represented the El Monte workers in 1995.[43]

As revealed by the catalog that appeared during the Los Angeles version of the exhibit, the process of remounting the show was not without hitches. The selection of catalog essays by historians and labor voices revived the question of what was a balanced narrative—not to mention museum exhibit—of the sweatshop's troubled history. An essay early in the book by the co-curators was more detailed and forceful than any in the original show, although it still halted short of calling manufacturers and retailers to account.[44] Essays by various other hands quoted from the exhibit and even sometimes expanded on historical background. Although some of the comments about corporate responsibility were more pointed, the old equivocation remained: "The importance of El Monte and the prevalence of sweatshops is hotly contested," more than one author asserted.[45]

Industry spokespeople like Kathie Lee Gifford also received gentle treatment. Gifford had helped sponsor the original show in return for a spot denouncing sweatshops and disclaiming any of the involvement in them that her clothing line had once been accused of. In the original show Gifford (or her expensive publicist) had described herself as a "consummate woman of the 90s." In the catalog the prose was more sedate: she was now an "entertainer and businesswoman."[46] Building on their court settlement of no liability, management voices reminded readers that only contractors, not manufacturers or retailers, were responsible for the modern sweatshop (although retailers were not above pointing blame at manufacturers).[47]

The show at Los Angeles's Museum of Tolerance ran from November 15, 1999, to March 31, 2000. The Washington exhibit had been dismantled for more than a year, and to recapture public attention after such a hiatus, the curators had a kind of "El Monte reunion." There was little media coverage, however, when former workers visited the recreated compound, and virtually no comment from the clothing industry community. The *Los Angeles Times* conclusion to its coverage was succinct and upbeat: "Since their ordeal in El Monte, the Thai workers have moved on."[48]

FINAL THOUGHTS ON THE SMITHSONIAN SPIN

Even the Smithsonian imprimatur as a cultural archive could not overcome the perennial unpopularity of characterizing the United States as a site of exploitation rather than liberation. As students of the politics of museum exhibits have pointed out, no matter how a museum exhibit dealing with race, class, ethnicity, or gender is organized and mounted, it will be disputed.[49] It was disingenuous of the clothing industry, however, to charge that the Smithsonian, a museum dedicated to telling an "objective" history of and for the American people, was guilty of partisanship. These business interests correctly understood that throughout American industrial history the sweatshop has been cultural shorthand for the inequities of capitalism.

A 1995 Smithsonian exhibit on Hiroshima, "The Last Act: The Atomic Bomb and the End of World War II," was first softened and then canceled entirely. It had been judged unpatriotic for being too sympathetic to Japanese suffering and not sensitive enough to the suffering of the American military, especially POWs. The resistance to the sweatshop show was not as emotionally charged, but there was some justice in comparing the negative responses to each of these events, as many articles prior to the latter show did.

In a 1988 conference at the National Museum of American History entitled "Poetics and Politics of Representation," Ivan Karp, in his paper "Culture and Representation," presciently detailed the problems that would weigh down "Between a Rock and a Hard Place": "All exhibitions are inevitably organized on the basis of assumptions about the intentions of the objects' producers, the cultural skills and qualifications of the audience, the claims to authoritativeness made by the exhibition, and judgments of the aesthetic merit or authenticity of the objects or settings exhibited."[50]

The "intentions of the objects' producers" may well stand for the clothing manufacturers' stance of denial of culpability or complicity. When the concessions made by the curators caused the National Retail Federation to reverse its position, the museum had compromised for viewers and sweatshop workers alike those necessary "claims to authoritativeness." The show's selected facts and artifacts may have provided an air of "authenticity," but such deal-making further clouded the museum's mission and guiding principles.

The exhibit did accommodate alternative perspectives that challenged the official one of the inevitable abolition of sweatshops in a democratic and pluralistic society that welcomes all immigrants. By reincarnating El Monte, "Between a Rock and a Hard Place" entered the larger debate about the role of people's history in accounts of American laboring life. But it was the controversy about the flaws in the exhibition, ironically, that provided evidence of the continued historical refusal to acknowledge that "sweatshops, like the one in El Monte, are a home-grown problem with peculiarly American roots."[51]

As we have seen, the sweatshop has stood for and generated many cultural anxieties over a century and a half of public discourse about it. The Smithsonian exhibit revealed yet another dimension: the sweatshop symbolizes American history itself. For reasons of self-interest, and with help from Republican lawmakers, retailers and manufacturers spearheaded the assault on the exhibit's presentation of sweatshop history. But the passions generated by the exhibit signified more than just a positive or negative view of the role of the apparel industry.

The many difficulties in maintaining objectivity about the subject of the sweatshop have been traced throughout this study. While it lasted, the Smithsonian exhibit added a new chapter to the quest for an accurate history of sweatshops. The problems it faced remind us of the larger difficulty of presenting a balanced narrative of the sweatshop. In the end, the National Museum itself exhibited the familiar dialectic between historicization of the shop in the name of American exceptionalism and acknowledgment of its continued existence in the name of American class struggle.

Looking at both the press coverage of El Monte and its Smithsonian commemoration as a cultural phenomenon, we see a concerted media effort to uphold the American Dream. The "undoing" of El Monte was accomplished by the media coverage—particularly in Los Angeles papers, which had covered the August 1995 raid extensively—of former workers' subsequent success. The escapees who were spotlighted did achieve a measure of affluence, as in this representative headline: "From Virtual Slavery to Being Boss: Couple Once Indentured in a Garment Sweatshop Now Run Their Own Successful Restaurant." In many other pieces of this nature, El Monte became a familiar launching pad for reasserting the American Dream.

Despite the litigation following the raid of El Monte and subsequent legislation, in the end no one authenticated it as a shop. The exhibit, its supporters, critics, and many visitors instead joined the long history of knowledge production about this contested American site. To the prolabor forces, it was important to look beyond the press releases and Web sites of Nike, Reebok, and Guess. In their responses over the next few years, these organizations would develop a managerial narrative of the sweatshop that not only completely changed the terms of the debate but also launched preemptive strikes on future antisweatshop campaigns.

CHAPTER 7

Nike's Sweatshop Quandary
and the Industrial Sublime

The Nike cachet has been clouded by a new image of
Asian workers in hot, noisy factories, stitching
together shoes for as little as 80 cents a day.

—William McCall, "Nike Battles Backlash from
Overseas Sweatshops," *Marketing News* (1998)

A POWERFUL COALITION of apparel industries engi-
neered a halt to the 1998 sweatshop retrospective exhibition at the Smithsonian, arguing that it defamed a self-regulating industry, but they took a
different tack with the Clinton White House's Apparel Industry Partnership. This task force, which targeted enforcement in major garment center companies and notified manufacturers of violations, had emerged
from a 1995 "Trendsetter List" that praised "good guy" retailers and
manufacturers. By 1996 and 1997 it was pinning "Garment Enforcement
Reports" on those contractors and firms that were out of compliance in
the previous two or three years.[1]

Because it provided a fairly easy way to look like "good guys," the
report soon gained the assent of key factories and suppliers in the apparel
and footwear trades. Chief among them were Nike and Gap, which
signed on to a "No Sweat" agreement in which retailers that subcon-
tracted work to foreign factories had to post a "Code of Conduct" in the
language of the host country.

This widely publicized measure made for good press, but its voluntary nature did little to appease the antisweatshop activists and trade
unionists who were dissatisfied with the Clinton administration's re-
quests for accountability. The television personality Kathie Lee Gifford
hired publicists to distance her from Global, the subcontractor she

worked with in the mid-1990s to produce her clothing line in Honduran sweatshops.[2] In the late 1990s, firms like Donna Karan tried to disavow their own contractors but took swipes at unions as well, pointing out that corrupt contractors employed union shops.[3] And though Guess was roundly denounced on the basis of the frequent raids on its contractors' illegal piecework shops in Los Angeles, the company continued to argue that its self-policing was largely effective.[4]

Of the many large firms engaging in plausible deniability, including Gap, Guess, and Ralph Lauren, Nike emerged as a leading symbol of this brand of garment industry hypocrisy—limned most scathingly in 1997 by the veteran New York Times labor reporter Bob Herbert: "Because the company is so high-profile, so successful, so admired and envied, it has become, like the swoosh, a symbol. It's the ugly multinational, buying and selling people almost at will. . . . Nike . . . epitomizes the triumph of monetary values over all others, and the corresponding devaluation of . . . values we once thought of as human."[5] Garry Trudeau, whose Doonesbury cartoon on sweatshops was included in the 1998 Smithsonian show, produced another one in which Nike was a "guest villain."[6] Garment industry representatives were quick to launch a countercampaign for the public's hearts and minds in which they deplored the "scapegoating" of firms like Nike and Reebok.[7]

Stung by the criticism, Nike gradually began a defensive compliance with antisweatshop enforcement in its home and global factories.[8] Read one Business Week headline playing on the company's oft-used advertising slogan, "Nike finally does it."[9] But Nike didn't stop there. Unlike Lauren, Gap, and others, whose Web sites read like order forms, the shoe company quickly constructed an informational Web site, complete with frequently asked questions, statements of purpose, and a virtual tour of a Nike plant. Nike CEO Phil Knight appeared frequently at stockholders' meetings and elsewhere to rebut accusations and condemn watchdog groups for denying a role to companies such as his own in the creation of protocols. He has remained highly critical of antisweatshop groups.[10] By the end of the White House Apparel Industry Partnership initiative in 1997, Nike had released a statistic-laden report claiming that workers at its Vietnamese and Indonesian plants were paid and treated well.[11]

It remains to be seen whether corporate America has fully enforced the many provisions of the initiative that emanated from the Clinton administration Department of Labor. Phillips–Van Heusen, for instance, on March 8, 1999, signed an Apparel Industry Partnership "preliminary agreement" promising to recognize employees' right to collective bargaining in Guatemalan *maquiladoras*, or low-wage manufacturing plants, and then reneged.[12] The much-touted Code of Conduct was indeed placed in worldwide clothing factories, but few unions were permitted on the premises, and company unions were not likely to register complaints with management.

It was during the years of the Clinton White House task force on the apparel industry that Nike became concerned with "changing its image."[13] The shoe company and its corporate colleagues continued to argue that their workers cooperated with bosses loyally, and even smoothly, in workplace productivity. Yet somewhat inconsistently they now acknowledged a public responsibility to address what in business language was variously termed "the sweatshop quandary" or "sustainable development." The question had now become: How were they to protect corporate property rights, gain a competitive advantage, and still ensure workers their most basic rights?[14] Such a question generated others about how to spin the shop. For if offshore and scattered national subpar shops were somehow necessary for industry growth and corporate profitability, how could such shops be publicly explained? In other words, how would businesses define the problem rather than let their enemies do so?

The early chapters of this study have chronicled the early decades of the sewing trades, when there was no name yet for the sweatshop. By the 1920s a combination of Progressive and management forces had persuaded the popular mind that sweatshops, a transitional development of the ethnic turn of the century, had come and gone in this country.

Yet these old-style factories have much in common with those at home and abroad today. This chapter looks at the dominant arguments and rhetorical strategies perfected by one of the premier garment manufacturers reliant on Third World factories. Moreover, as detailed in chapter 6, immigration, legal and otherwise, has been reinvigorating sweatshops in the United States ever since the 1960s. How have the garment industry corporations dependent on these sites continued to work to erase the term for them? The Nike Web site will help answer such questions. As a form of literature, it exemplifies the most sophisticated corporate spin, a narrated history, complete with virtual factory tour, that skillfully rebuts current accusations from critics. Let us first contextualize that narrative within the larger rhetoric of today's corporate apparel community.

BUSINESS RHETORICS AND
MANAGERIAL NARRATIVES

There is little doubt that the language of manufacturers, most of which rely on outsourced production in discount-labor regions, has changed. In assessing the range of profactory and proefficiency literature of the 1920s, when scientific management came to the Ford Motor Factory in the form of Taylorism (engineered assembly lines), the cultural historian Martha Banta has coined the term "managerial narrative." That discourse approvingly allied speedups with firm workplace control. Remarks Banta, "Even when they state their intention to speak on behalf of [assemblyline workers], they report from *on high*" (author's italics).[15]

To its critics, Ford's "human engineering," with the aim of turning workers into mechanical entities who were continually in motion, came to define management control of the effect of technological production on the factory worker. To defenders, a higher wage packet and a better standard of living for Ford workers were rightly dependent on a fully automated workplace in which workers respected all management decisions and "unions [were] kept away at all costs."[16]

Economists who defend the practices of discount-labor regions from southern California to Indonesia, Taiwan, and South Korea often refuse to employ sweatshop or antisweatshop rhetoric at all. They contend that the morality of the sweatshop should be debated only by international rights organizations and consumer protest groups. Their belief is that human rights–related concerns have no place in the trade context and that corporate officials need not accept any social responsibility.[17] To those who deplore the low wages and poor conditions, speedups, and old, unsafe equipment, they argue that, however weak the local norms, "imposition of labor standard[s] . . . would render these third world factories non-competitive" and business would leave, as a 1998 study by the nonpartisan Investor Responsibility Research Center, which conducts research on controversial aspects of corporate policy, *The Sweatshop Quandary,* has noted.[18] In any event, the argument continues, these are the best available jobs in the countries involved and will enable production workers to climb up the economic ladder eventually. Thus, this argument concludes, garment factory globalization successfully exports American values.

Although an implied opportunity ethic is embodied in the raised living standard brought to these countries, those making this argument from conservative economic and management quarters are still reluctant to use the term "sweatshop" and prefer phrases like "this kind of employment" and "good news for the world's poor." They protest the term "sweatshop" to describe the "legitimate" employment fostered by "global capitalism and free trade" by calling it "vague and pejorative."[19]

One such conservative voice in the garment industry is *Bobbin* magazine, which describes itself as "the business and technology authority for the sewn products industry." Its mission statement continues: "With an emphasis on innovative management and production strategies . . . our goal is to serve as a forum for insightful exchange among sewn products executives."[20] In its issue published immediately after the World Trade Organization meeting in Seattle in late 1999, a feature essay makes no mention of the protesters who had decried the free trade practices put in place in the wake of the GATT agreement. Rather, the writer focuses on how globalization will "make it in the brave new millennium."[21] Another article praises *maquiladoras*. Titled "Mexican Firms Concentrate on Capital Investment," it informs readers that Mexico is a "hotbed of activity for the sewn products industry." The reasons are diverse: the installation of a great deal of new equipment, for instance, has recently boosted "production capacity," enabling Mexican manufacturers to "compete on a global scale."[22] Much is made of the innovations of the Mexican apparel industry to remain competitive, meet customer needs, and reduce production times.

Of particular interest to the writer—who is the associate editor of *La Bobina,* the Spanish-language version of *Bobbin*—are Mexico's Industrias Argaman plants, where pants, shirts, and jackets (often embroidered) are produced. The company is proud of its "two fully automatic and four semiautomatic machines." Although the cutting is done with sixteen manual cutters, two new automatic ones herald a more automated future.[23]

The article exudes an entrepreneur's optimism and enthusiasm. The United States, an export hub for Argaman Industries, receiving one-third of its goods, is the lodestar of its enterprise, and the Mexican factories are presented as eager to compete with Costa Rica and Colombia—two other countries, incidentally, that are notorious for sweated labor.

Interestingly, phrases like "diversity of styles" (24) adorn the article with a vestige of the language of inclusiveness that has become so much a cliché of the new millennium. These are not references to a multiethnic workforce, however, but to the variety of fabrics from which buyers may choose.

Absent from the piece is any acknowledgment that factories are staffed with human workers. By using the passive voice in the phrase "cutting is done with 16 manual machines" (21), the author avoids stating who performs this skilled work. The factories seem fully automated, as if robotics have come of age. The author makes no allusions to laborers, sewers, or operators, not even in reference to the labor-intensive "raw materials warehouse" (21).

In this futuristic brave new managed world, the union presence has been extinguished along with the working-class staff. Such is also the case in a "Q&A" later in the issue on equipping a Latin American plant. The discussion apparently bundles the cost of employing people into "capital investments" and "investment in machinery and technology" (42). Here at least workers are recognized, if only as an expense, for the apparel executive interviewed, Luis Sagastume, regional director of operations for Kurt Salmon Associates, assures readers that the new machines will result in "labor savings and quality control" (42).

Bobbin provides many other "tips for excellence" to retailers, manufacturers, and contractors (60). In contrast, the dark side of managing the factory is rhetorically erased. Omitting references to labor obviates the need to take note of the sweatshop at all. In these pages, labor is an abstraction, reduced to a series of costs.

The industry magazine even routinely dispenses with a standard business term like "labor capacity" in favor of "firm profitability."[24] This realpolitik of survivalism in the apparel industry is marked as well by a concern about "sourcing options": "offshore" (11) versus "rural-non-union, landed import, New York metropolitan areas" (15). The technical language of trade does pause to include people rather than strategies or geography in an allusion to "bottom line benefits through better customer service" (11), but nowhere are workers mentioned.[25]

In other industry sources, insider language can be more forthcoming about the problems of the textile industry. A piece in *Chain Store Executive*'s May 2002 issue complains that not following fair business practices could "get [you] caught in the crosshairs of labor-rights activists." "It does not take long," the author confides to his specialized readership, "for locating activists and rights campaigners to get out the story about a police crackdown on labor organizers or a child found working in a dress factory."[26]

In the spirit of not giving the enemy any ammunition, the *Chain Store Executive* article lists a number of methods "to address this new challenge." Rather than be caught "using factories where abusive workplace conditions could potentially put [a company's] reputation and brand at risk," the company should resort to one of many certification organizations that can give it the validation it needs. These are voluntary actions that can enhance a company's image and ensure its compliance with workplace codes of conduct. A broad range of names are provided, including the business-allied Fair Labor Standards Association and the student-activist Worker Rights Consortium, as well as Web sites and some statistics on the degree of company change customarily required by each certification. Although this piece reflects an awareness of "making it right"—it even mentions "workers" from time to time—the rationale for such ethical behavior is not to improve the lives of the company workforce. Rather, the author argues, avoiding the scandal-seeking antisweatshop activists makes good monetary sense as a strategy "for risk prevention and brand protection in the global economy" (195).

NIKE AND THE "INDUSTRIAL SUBLIME"

Another aspect of the discussion of the garment trades' public image is the rhetoric aimed at retail customers. This language also dwells on the necessary excellence of physical plants and management techniques. Yet, instead of using the insider's vernacular of *Bobbin* and *Chain Store Executive,* these user-friendly public relations campaigns focus on presenting pride in business as "accolades and graphic representations of the industrial sublime." The images are still of "property rather than persons, progress rather than social problems, managerial rather than working-class perspectives."[27] But with an eye to the visitor—whether to store, Web site, or even, on a conducted tour, an offshore plant—the company offers itself as a beautifully and humanely run community of shared interests. In this vision, worker, buyer, and manager join in applauding the recognition earned by name brands such as Nike, Gap, and Ralph Lauren.

Even as late as the El Monte raids in 1995, garment trade corporations disclaimed responsibility for the sweatshop conditions of their subcontractors at home and offshore. But when these firms began to understand in the late 1990s that this had become an era for serviceable corporate strategies to rationalize the rapid turnover in production, the downsizing of the U.S. workforce, and the farming out to discount-labor regions or to southern California, they revised their self-portrayals. Nike's promotional material, for instance, now invokes amity to describe its Vietnam subcontractor plants as "giant sewing factories" in which everyone from labor to upper management works as a team.[28]

Nike is well aware that where it remains vulnerable is in protecting its "good name."[29] This enhanced image of respect for more than profit margins is neither new nor confined to the apparel industry. From automotive Ford to tobacco giant Philip Morris to Dow Chemical, the large corporation dedicated to social service and public-spiritedness is a familiar presence. Few museum openings for the middlebrow audience or athletic events for poor children lack a corporate sponsor, among whom is often Nike itself. But in its efforts to protect its reputation, Nike not only joined other multinationals to defend the corporate entity but virtually revoked 170 years of sweatshop discourse.

Nike's image crafters realized from El Monte onward that choosing the right language was a crucial strategy in deflecting criticism. When superstar Michael Jordan was criticized as indifferent to the labor violations of the company for which he was a spokesman, he was widely quoted as saying he always counted on Nike to do the right thing—and left it at that. In turn, Nike quickly created a press release photo with the basketball legend posing with some recipients of its philanthropic largesse—in this case, educational grants. In a neat piece of circular reasoning, the subheading read, "Nike Re-Affirms Its Relationship with Michael Jordan."[30]

This reciprocity of salesmanship between sponsor and spokesman is one of the many ways in which Nike contains the "bad shop" through the language of the good one. The dominant trope, however, is not the shop at all but rather the family of man. This linguistic strategy presents

Nike as concerned with the betterment of all underprivileged people and provides the frame for telling what it terms on its Web site www.nikebiz.com—dispensing with capitalization to seem more user-friendly—"the inside story." A bevy of linguistic devices appear in the large Web site section "Manufacturing Practices." Noteworthy is the mission statement that appears up front: "To lead in corporate citizenship through proactive programs that reflect caring for the world family of Nike, our teammates, our consumers, and those who provide services to Nike." Notably absent is the iconography of sweated laborers hunched over machines or tables in overcrowded space. Instead, Nike shows us photos of workers chatting happily at a lunch table with stylish wooden benches and a flowering plant; one of them waves gaily to the photographer. (Wire mesh gates are partly visible in the bleak background.) Other photos feature smiling girls on their way to work, mugging for the camera, and workers lunching at McDonald's. Lists of statistics about the superior wages offered by American firms in foreign countries are also prominently displayed. We see only one lone photo of two women actually working: intent on their jobs, they are posed in a well-lit loft space; the stamping or sewing machines on which they work are not pictured, leaving it to the viewer to imagine the state of the machinery itself.

Other "Manufacturing Practices" subsections are more mindful of the critics: among the many mission statements and histories of Nike— "to provide workers making our products with the best workplaces possible"—is an annotated bibliography of reviews and case studies of third-party examiners, among them the prestigious Dartmouth Amos Tuck School and the industrially savvy *Sport Marketing Quarterly*. Nike cleverly bundles those highly critical of Nike's practices with Verite Evaluators' "Remediation Plan" of recommended improvements.

Nike excerpts nothing from the extensive "recommendations and findings" of the plan conducted by Verite, independent auditors hired by the company, and with good reason. Those who take the time to read the text of the plan itself, published in March 2001 (available on Nike's Web site and in hard copy), see a litany of abuses at one of the flagship Nike factories, in Kukdong International in Mexico. Among the findings were that armed guards patrol the gates; other security guards patrol and have the power to dismiss workers on assembly lines; workers younger than sixteen and as young as thirteen are employed at the factory; workers reported unfair or severe disciplinary actions; workers engaged in a work stoppage were summarily dismissed with no chance of being rehired; and workers reported no overtime pay for extra work.[31]

Rather than address these problems in its "Frequently Asked Questions" section, Nike's Web site directs the visitor to an online factory tour during which Nike rehearses many of the arguments about its contribution to employment abroad by paying the prevailing wage of a given country. In responding to the question of why Nike contract factories do not pay a "living wage," the fact sheets carefully reply that Nike pays a "fair wage." Whether one reads this Web document approvingly or critically, it is clear that Nike is paying scrupulous attention to the rhetoric of its self-presentation.

The online tour is of particular interest for its dramatization of the worker-friendly philosophy outlined in the other promotional materials. Chosen from among Nike's 750 contract factories employing 500,000 workers, the one we visit on the tour is in Vietnam, the site of more than a dozen Nike factories that account for 6 percent of Vietnam's total exports since 1995. We are told that Nike workers can make more than a teacher or any other worker in the country.

Another focus of the video is Nike's extreme concern for worker safety. While the word "sweatshop" is never mentioned, this carefully monitored work space is a riposte to critics of Nike's unsafe practices in the early 1990s. The film makes much of its water- rather than oil-based sneaker sole adhesives, the clean air in the factory, and the clinic on site to handle the rare untoward accident.

Like the photos described earlier, the shots of workers at work are very quick, and machines are viewed momentarily, as are sewing rooms. The tour spells out what is implied in those earlier photos, that Nike chooses to operate the "factory . . . as a community" and freely offers its workers a clinic, free meals, dorms, after-hours schools, even aid to the surrounding community by helping to build schools and hospitals and funding a grant program to serve "economically disadvantaged students."

This is an excellent industrial video, beautifully produced, with upbeat background music and careful attention to the subject of safety, the Nike Code of Conduct for labor standards, and the factory as a series of "places where Nike corporate responsibility comes together." As in many of the other sections of the Web site, the online tour gives only cursory

attention to worker responses to the labor situation and grievance procedures. An opening remark suggests that the on-site union offices will be
visited in the course of the tour; they never are. It is likewise misleading
that the Vietnamese "union" referred to is in fact a government-run entity that was never voted in by workers or empowered for collective
bargaining.[32] Most likely it is a company union such as that criticized
everywhere from a report on Nike factories in Mexico to the *New York
Times* ("Mexico's May Day March Shows Worker Anger at Official
Unions" read a May 1996 headline).[33] Nike also prudently omitted facts
such as that in the *maquiladoras* of Guatemala, another host country in
which many of its factories are located, most plants have no unionized
workforce or contractual provisions of any kind for workers. Such truths
would be difficult to glean from the Nike video claims.

AN INTERESTING CODA: Nike's clever self-representation might be punc-
tured by the Supreme Court's June 26, 2003, announcement that it will
not rule on the *Nike v. Kasky* case at this point, but remand the case to a
lower court.[34] A consumer activist, Marc Kasky, had brought suit against
the sneaker giant in 1998, arguing that the company misled the public by
denying that its shoes were made under sweatshop conditions at factories
in China, Vietnam, and Indonesia.[35] The suit further contended that the
public relations efforts were commercial speech and thus not entitled to
First Amendment protections. In response, Nike took its customary spin
one step further. Its statements on and off the Web that there were no
sweatshops concerned labor practices, not products, and should be protected political speech.[36] As such, the company's attorneys contended—
unsuccessfully thus far—that commercial speech applies only to paid
advertisement or product warranty.

    Although Nike hoped that the U.S. Supreme Court would rule in its
favor, that false statements in news releases are "political" and enjoy First
Amendment protections, this doubtful argument has of this writing not
been upheld by the California Supreme Court.[37] The linguistic circle
drawn by Nike's managerial narrative to enclose a sympathetic sweatshop
has, for the moment, been broken. But the Supreme Court has also said
that, in dismissing the case, it is simply not ruling on its merits at this
time. In judicial time, as on the Web, consumers may expect a new series
of twists and turns.

LABOR CHIC

Companies outside the clothing trades orbit also use language to preempt or cover over criticism, one aspect of the industrial sublime perfected by Nike, but the garment industry sweatshop initiatives are part of a particular kind of self-congratulation on its treatment of workers. Nike's logo, for instance, provides instant consumer recognition: its "swoosh," a red demi-sickle symbol, adorns the company headquarters and the products themselves, not to mention the manifold electronic and nonvirtual billboards worldwide.

But the use of a company symbol is only one part of what the French sociologist Guy Debord has called the "society of the spectacle."[38] Applied to corporations, this is a staging of a company's business practices in venues from cyberspace to print media. We have observed how the happy, chatty workers on the Nike Web site embody a rhetoric of benevolence. Nike's interest in worker imagery outside of the factory tour is often secondary, however, to promotional press conferences in which it affirms its financial support for emerging sports stars. To find other corporate co-optings of worker imagery, we can turn to clothing ads by other garment industry companies in which worker imagery is used in ways startlingly reminiscent of WPA art to sell the newest fashions.

In these advertisements, the pop-culturization of working-class life acquires a cultural value among bourgeois buyers. One student of the process has written, "The very sites—labor, uniform clothing, forced (im)mobility that traditionally represent class [exploitation] to working-class subjects are being recast as sites of freedom from oppression . . . [from] being middle-class."[39] Thus, blue-collar-inspired designer clothes are on sale at the store Working Class in New York City's Soho, where many items are sold with the fashion imprimatur of Workers for Freedom. In labels like Amsterdam Laundry and Laundry Industry, the sweatshop has become a logo.

White aspirations to wear blue-collar designer clothing are equally played upon in a full-page color advertisement in a 1999 issue of the *New York Times Magazine* in which a onetime proletarian apparently remains proud of his origins.[40] This ad for Slates shirts and sweaters, "available at better stores," has it both ways, praising the American Dream process by which a son and grandson of blue-collar Italian labor makes it out of the worker class while presenting what are clearly upper-class subjects in a lower-class milieu. The ad features a welder-designer, Frank Carfaro. The handsome, sports-club athletically trim Carfaro smiles while poised perilously with a blowtorch, goggles up, atop an aluminum frame for a black-leather-covered bed. Departing entirely from an iron worker's stance, he has his legs crossed and sports a black lounge lizard shirt and shoes. This supposed "third generation welder, first generation designer" with his white capped teeth is the poster boy for a paradoxically new iconography of labor: the worker in touch with his roots and completely separated from them. Oblivious to the fact that his clothes may have been products of blue-collar labor exploitation, Carfaro becomes a part of a promotional system that converts everything it handles into fashion.[41]

The immensely popular Tommy Hilfiger "hip hop" line of fashion clothes incorporates a stylishly oversized pair of pantaloons, hooded sweatshirt, and gargantuan leather jacket. By using rap musicians or look-alike models to advertise this line, Hilfiger links the "hood" origins of the style with immense commercial success. It is no wonder that ghetto youths are among the most avid buyers. Sean Jean sells his allegedly ghetto radicalism in his clothing collection, Revolution, as a kind of revolt against white plutocrats. Ironically, this style, rooted in black inner-city life, is legitimized for working-class youth only when worn by celebrity bodies. Yet Jean's handlers, like Hilfiger's designers, have so contrived it that this expensive clothing seems like a bearer of black identity rather than the result of a slick business agreement between music stars and fashion design.[42]

Outside the clothing industry, Phillips Petroleum, accused of employing immigrants in sweated oil fields, aired an op-ed page ad in the 2001 *New York Times* as Nike and other companies were reshaping their own images.[43] The slogan at the top of the ad is "Sweat on our Brow . . ." and on the next line, "Oil on Our Gloves." Beneath the working man who is the titular subject of the ad, the phrase is completed: ". . . And Geological Imaging on our Computers."

Pictured in this quarter-page ad on the last page of the first section of the daily *Times* is a worker figure costumed in a hard hat and blue-collar dress, stalwart and brawny, who has taken off his protective goggles, his most fashionable attire, to wipe his forehead as he looks presumably with confidence into the middle distance. Instead of the union badge or red button, this figure, drawn in the lithographic style of Louis Lozowick or Philip Reisman, wears on his left-hand pocket—over his heart—a "Phillips 66" badge. Below the badge the reference to computer imaging hooks this worker not only to brawn but to the brain power needed to run Phillips Petroleum. The "our" of the "sweat on our brow" and the "oil on our gloves" is vague: Does "our" refer to the partnership between worker and company? Or is the company speaking of the worker as one of its possessions, like its state-of-the-art computers?

The range of reference to blue-collardom expands further in the very small print following the imaging phrase. "Everyone has been sweating higher energy costs," it reads. It advertises virtual-reality software to suggest that geoscientists are searching for oil in the most sophisticated new ways. Such a method earns Phillips, it is claimed, the logo of the "performance company."

On the Phillips Web site, identified in small print at the bottom of this ad, this seeming paradox is extended. On the one hand, it is clearly the worker portrait that fuels this ad, just as worker sweat makes the industry run. But since the ad runs on a newspaper page read predominantly by middle-class stockholders and others with money to invest in the petroleum industry, another inference is more likely.

What Phillips has done here—and what many other firms do today—is to use the old revolutionary images of the heroic worker and discard their incendiary significance. The worker stands for energy, performance, sweat. Because he is so loyal to the company, he poses no threat of a strike. In fact, it may be that he is not a worker at all, but a field engineer who is out to survey and who spends his valuable geoscientific time at a nearby computer station. Is this a sweatshop image at the core? Or a complete obliteration of sweatshops as well as of any possible collective bargaining agreements to escape them? Whatever the answer, this is a cynical use of worker images in an age when factory pay has lagged behind inflation and worker termination rates are increasing.[44]

IMAGE IS ALL

The right to organize U.S. workers under the National Labor Relations Act of 1935 is not a reality to the many manufacturers and clothing firms that make their own public relations use of labor imagery in which there is no labor movement, only workers as service providers. In 2000, and not for the first time, the University of Chicago hosted a two-day, for-profit seminar to teach corporations the legal maneuvers they need to stay union-free.[45] Many such seminars have followed.

Overseas, in 2002, Nike, fearful of Indonesia's union movement, shut factories and cut back production with a plan to move on to underdeveloped sites in China and Vietnam where worker rights are not so hotly contested.[46] At the same time, Nike continues to lead the way in using an "image world" to make apparently factual statements about the real world.[47] Again using equivocal speech, Nike joins Reebok and Adidas in pointing out that thousands of factories "have [been] brought up to levels we are comfortable with."[48] Years before the sweatshop debates heated up, Albert Z. Carr argued in the *Harvard Business Review* that a corporation's ethical standards should not solely be based on the productivity argument. Yet his argument that companies might find a way to increase cost-effectiveness was at odds with the announced "focus on right behavior rather than avoiding wrongdoing."[49] We have seen briefly how a chorus of industry voices has answered Carr by disseminating a counterideology of upward mobility, efficiency, and the industrial sublime. A fitting coda to this one is an examination of how Sweatshop Watch, the Campaign for Labor Rights, and Students against Sweatshops reverse the industrial sublime to fashion counternarratives of their own.

CHAPTER 8

Watching Out for the Shop

To some, the Nike swoosh is now as scary as the
hammer and sickle.
—Thomas L. Friedman, "Foreign Affairs:
The New Human Rights," *New York Times* (1999)

NIKE'S PUBLIC RELATIONS campaign from the late 1990s
onward to deny the existence of sweatshops among its contractors was
answered in kind by opponents like the National Labor Committee,
Sweatshop Watch, the Center for Economic and Social Rights, the National Mobilization Against Sweatshops, and United Students Against
Sweatshops. These were but some of the dominant groups that had
joined a widespread sweatshop-watching effort that included labor, civil
rights, immigrant rights, women's, religious, and student organizations.
Another representative alliance of antisweatshop activists, the Global
Sweatshop Coalition, found that Nike had simply created "a world view
in which sweatshops are ok."[1] To counter the cyber-spin of Nike, the
group established a Boycott Nike Web site.[2] The site was one of many
anchoring a movement that, in fighting the global garment site, transformed the sweatshop itself into a world-class issue and saw Nike as "a
case study in international strategies for organizing." Nike's own insistence on "a code of conduct" for its plants was overturned, at least
rhetorically, by plans to enlist universities to agree, through the Worker
Rights Consortium (WRC), not to buy Nike products and to "enforce
university licensing codes of conduct."[3]

Americans are no strangers to industrial protest actions. They spearheaded campaigns against white slavery and child prostitution in the
Progressive era and led widespread consumer boycotts of clothing made
by child labor in the 1920s. In the name of defeating the "military-

industrial complex," the student-fueled anti–Vietnam War protests during the American 1960s acquired a worldwide dimension. But until the late 1990s, the U.S. sweatshop had not been the target of any such rallying cry. The goals of the sweatshop-watching movement are arguably even more ambitious than earlier efforts: to transform the wage relationship between Third World and oppressed U.S. garment workers and their employers, and to uphold the dignity of all exploited workers, both at home and abroad. Thomas L. Friedman wrote with customary eloquence in his *New York Times* op-ed column: "The only answer is for activists to learn how to use globalization to their advantage—to super-empower themselves—so there can be global governance, even without global government. They have to learn how to compel companies to behave better by mobilizing consumers and the Internet. I'm talking about a network solution for human rights, and it's the future of social advocacy. Precisely such a solution is now being tested with the apparel industry."[4] Friedman's comments bring up questions for another book-length inquiry. To what extent is this an American story and to what extent one of global capitalist restructuring? And how can students harness their own power as concerned citizen-consumers to form international networks against corporate global villages?

Many organizations with student constituencies are indeed currently watching the shop, from the Campaign for Labor Rights to Sweatshop Warriors, a group of immigrant women workers in Asian shops organized by worker-activist Miriam Ching Yoon Louie.[5] This chapter, however, concerns how American students or those studying in the United States are using the campus as an activist venue. The focus is on the anti-sweatshop movement of young collegians, most of whom neither have ties to the labor movement nor are workers themselves. Students Against Sweatshops and similar organizations not only turn corporate rhetoric on its head. As with other campaigns, they boycott sweated products, picket stores that sell them, and call on the authorities to cut ties with Nike and other garment manufacturers. But a new form of course credit, dubbed "service learning" or "community outreach," supplements these activities. In their challenge to the Nike version of the factory, collegians' interview-visits to sweatshops and research reports on college ties to dubious garment firms superficially recall the activist marches and demonstrations of the 1960s. This chapter briefly examines whether this affluent, pragmatic new generation's awareness of the Nike "spin" is a true counternarrative or an extracurricular lesson in the novelty of the shop itself.

Students Against Sweatshops:
Reigniting Activism

As late as the mid-1990s, there was no significant student involvement in antisweatshop activities. By 2000, however, university grounds had become the site of anticorporate chants, sit-ins, e-mailings by activists, and a push on administrators to join the Worker Rights Consortium, a sister organization of the United Students Against Sweatshops. The WRC's adoption at Purdue University in Indiana was the result of a successful twelve-day hunger strike. With fewer dramatics, colleges as far-flung as the University of California at Berkeley, the University of Iowa, and the University of North Carolina at Chapel Hill have been prodded to join the WRC.[6]

Among the best-publicized recent international academic conferences was that held by the New York University American Studies Program on April 7–8, 2000, ambitiously titled "Labor's Next Century: New Alliances, Sweatshops, and the Global South." The program described the event as "an international conference on the future of post-Seattle alliances, international organizing and the struggle for human rights."

The conferees, many of them NYU students, reaffirmed the WRC goal through workshops on barring sweated items from college bookstores, but sweatshops were not the only target. Speakers also advocated for the rights of underpaid, non-union clerical staff, graduate students, and adjunct teachers at NYU and other colleges and universities. More important was the emphasis on what the conference program termed in its plenary a "red/green alliance"—that is, an amalgamation of the New(est) Left with Green Party adherents dedicated to a nonpolluting environment. With the message that opposition to sweatshops freely crosses class lines, this widened antisweatshop mandate seemed remote from the old labor base of the radical Jewish and Italian 1920s. Trade unions were not a dominant presence at the conference, although the United Steelworkers of America (USW), trying in the postindustrial era to attract new constituencies to its locals, sent an eloquent organizer, Tim Waters. A graduate students' local recently installed at NYU, local 3882 of the American Federation of Teachers, was in attendance, as was a speaker from the powerful municipal union, District Council 37 of the Association of Federal, State, City, and Municipal Employees. Apparent too was a stock-in-trade activity of traditional labor rallies—fervent speakers generating energy for mass protests. Academic activists and their traditions were more dominant, however—for instance, there was a teach-in on sweatshops, a common event at the conference in 2000. The message that the sweatshop issue crosses class (and vocational) lines was carried not by workers themselves so much as by a revived 1960s college counterculture. Conferees narrated the new antisweatshop movement by recalling recent occupations of the president's office, a boycott, and other teach-ins.

Overlaying this reminder of militance in the antiwar era (though Vietnam was only briefly mentioned) was the conference's awareness of its historical roots. It was held largely, and symbolically, in the sanctuary of the Judson Memorial Church, a longtime liberal venue. It was no accident either that the conference was within walking distance of the garment trades' Lower East Side and the Cooper Union hall where girlish firebrands listened to Clara Lemlich call (in Yiddish and English) for the 1910 "Uprising of the 20,000."

Two radical traditions intersected at this assembly to consider "Labor's Next Century": the tradition of the pre-Communist Left and that of the New Left of the 1960s. Tim Waters, the USW speaker, invoked them both, if obliquely. Referring to clerical workers on strike for better pay at an Ivy League college, he opened with: "Have you heard about the struggles at Yale?" Likening the injustices of three decades past with those of pre–Cold War antiracial, antiworker feeling, he then invoked the framing of young black men in 1920s Scottsboro and the late 1920s execution of the Italian anarchists Nicolo Sacco and Bartolomeo Vanzetti. To much applause, he reminded his youthful audience that, in the tradition of such predecessors, they were the conscience of the new labor movement in the "fight for fairness in the global economy."[7]

The meeting itself had other historical precedents, though most of them were the inspiration of middle-class reformers. Florence Kelley, a Hull House intimate and for many years president of the Consumers' League, had at the twentieth century's turn and afterward rallied consumers of conscience to shun clothes made by overtime workers in cities like New York and

Chicago, especially women and children. In the 1910s, the Women's Trade Union League had made common cause with the socialist journal the *New York Call*, union pamphlets, and city, state, and federal inquiries into the "sweatshop evil" in ways that prefigured the United Students Against Sweatshops, a group that today can send "thousands of letters to a [criticized] factory" and whose student volunteers join "university officials, brand executives, and officials from a consortium of colleges . . . to visit with union and factory managers in countries like the Dominican Republic."[8]

This welter of activity prompted one *Business Week* column to ask: "Who Says Student Protests Don't Matter?"[9] Their impact is felt not least in their ability, on Web sites as in rallies and at conferences, to point out that the sweatshop stands for a host of injustices. On the Sweatshop Watch site, the sweatshop becomes cyber-shorthand for all wrongs against labor.[10] After summarizing its goals and ethical grounding in antisweatshop activity, the site lists abusers by brand name and highlights a wealth of resources, from newsletters to videos, from bibliographies to information on the much-opposed North American Free Trade Agreement.

The voice of this site is one of quiet righteousness—in deliberate contrast perhaps to Nike's communal and philanthropic rhetoric. Sweatshop Watch distinctly avoids hyperbole, and its aim is to strike a reasonable rather than zealous tone. One or two satiric cartoons contain the only inflammatory rhetoric. For instance, a graphic features "Evil Strauss & Co."—a version of the trademark label that Levi Strauss uses for its clothing lines.

Sweatshop Watch also provides a link to an organization it sponsors, the Garment Worker Center in Los Angeles. Established in 2001 by a coalition of immigrant rights groups, the center's aim is to help garment workers organize around the issues unique to their workplace. Its introductory statement gives these workers an eloquently simple voice: "We are the Garment Worker Center in Los Angeles. We are women and men. We are immigrants from Mexico, China, El Salvador, Guatemala, and Honduras. We are workers."[11]

OFF THE PAGE: THE QUIET VOICE

At the headquarters of UNITE in New York City, another organization, the Garment Workers' Justice Center, occupied a floor with a Martin Luther King poster, an old blackboard and classroom chairs, some En-

glish tutors, and organizers like Mayra Mendoza.[12] She had no college
degree when I interviewed her a few years back, but she possessed a deep
understanding of the Latina/Asian sweatshops of Guatemala and Brooklyn's Sunset Park, Honduras and Queens's Long Island City. "If you come
to the U.S., you have to work in a factory," she said in that interview. "To
have something better for yourself, for your family." Describing a job she
held early on at a clothing factory that produced labels for Donna Karan,
she said that management "played mind games" to persuade workers that
the quality of their work was not good. Moreover, there were "huge rats"
in the building, thanks to "paid-off inspectors," and no emergency exits.
Mendoza became angry about the conditions in the factory and "tried
to motivate others to clean the place." But because she was indebted to
her cousin, who got her the job in 1991, she restricted her campaign at
first to issues of cleanliness—such as the lack of a lunchroom and the dis-
gusting bathrooms.

Mendoza eventually became an investigator in the kind of Sunset
Park factory she had once deplored. It was undercover work: she pre-
tended to look for a job while observing the union-busting owner. By
1996, when she helped call a strike, he had called Immigration and Naturalization Service, which deported the organizers in the shop. Illegally,
he did not tell them they had a right to be notified of an impending raid
three days in advance. Reflecting on her onetime undercover life, Mendoza quietly characterized the garment bosses she had met and worked
for in one word: "greed."

Quite another voice emerges from *Sweatshops in Chicago*, a year 2000
report of a cross-religious-ethnic association, the Sweatshop Working
Group of Chicago.[13] This pamphlet demonstrates a continuity of rhetoric
and approach dating back to the Pittsburgh Survey days. Surveyors gave
worker-participants a page of questions, using the language of the poli-
cymaker. The third question, for instance, is: "Are there problematic work
conditions that are not violations of law or regulations?" As with the
Pittsburgh Survey, the Chicago report has no single author but speaks in
the voice of the reformer as it tabulates such things as the percentage of
respondents experiencing sweatshop labor violations, sweatshop employment by age, terms of employment, ethnicity rates, and so on.

The report does, however, include worker "voices" from interviews
with union members, those who had contacted the Department of

Labor with complaints, and those surveyed in their Chicago neighborhoods. Even allowing for interviewees' diffidence or self-censorship, the excerpts from these conversations seem bland, and the long tradition of regularizing workers' diction, whether in their native English or translated from another language, prevailed in this commission of inquiry, as it has in so many others before and since. Indeed, those questioned may well have wished to speak as fluently a "standard" language as possible. The interviews focused on working conditions, violations of law, and people's responses. But given that the subject was often sexual harassment or the terrible workplace accidents that resulted from a lack of protective clothing or training, the interviewees, donning the educated voice, gave their remarks a certain blandness of expression:

> It gets really bad. Sometimes the workers complain about the conditions to the boss and sometimes he'll do something about it, or sometimes he says he will and he'll never do anything about it. (34)

> I was working at the factory. I was given five minutes for bathroom break. I spoke up about how that was not reasonable. When I returned to work, I was fired. (34)

> It is nothing special. It is ok. (38)

Certainly one can understand that these are somewhat stilted translations in the case of the first two speakers, who are Spanish, and the third, who is Chinese. Also the carefulness with which workers replied to their interlocutors is not surprising. Yet in the twelve pages of excerpted comments from over fifty food processing, factory, and restaurant workers, the people interviewed do not seem differentiated from one another, nor do they emerge as people with lives and concerns outside of the workplace. As in the Pittsburgh Survey, to a great extent the reported conversations are not the workers' language and thus not their story.

SWEATSHOP SEMESTER

Of late, in return for college credit, some organizations like the Labor Resource Center at Queens College are offering a union semester—often a summer internship—in which students work on boycotts of sweated products or help garment industry workers organize their own union local. Labor organizations such as the AFL-CIO are cosponsors, and the students are urged to use Web sites like those of the Industrial and Labor Relations (ILR) School at Cornell University, the LaborNet compendium of sweatshop links, and the University of California's Berkeley Institute of Industrial Relations, which also offer Internet research guides to labor-oriented research organizations.[14]

In this "explosion of union-friendly websites," to quote the August 14, 2000, LaborNet Web site, the Triangle Web site is particularly useful supplementary reading for summer garment trade interns.[15] It contains student projects, related Web sites, photos, illustrations of the story of the fire, and ways to send user-friendly messages to a friend or to contact the ILR Webmaster.[16]

These programs provide a balanced combination of participation in the field and essential readings on the sweatshop and its history. Fact-gathering visits to a sweatshop, as defined through the eyes of idealistic college students "looking for something to support," is an initial hands-on lesson in labor organizing.[17] Titled "Union Summer," it is sponsored by the AFL-CIO. For a weekly stipend (incidentally, more than the exploited workers themselves earn), students in the past have helped organize strawberry pickers and hotel and newspaper workers. But they have not termed these work sites "sweatshops," nor has the parent union; sweatshops still retain a garment-district association. In 2000, for instance, students picketed Just Cynthia, a garment-center dressmaker, and several others to ensure that clothes were not made by sweated labor. They even forged an agreement with Just Cynthia to that effect.[18]

Realistically, links between student protest against and academic study of sweated labor, both nationally and in the global village, will be difficult to forge. The field is carefully moving toward oral history initiatives, both in and out of cyberspace, and pursuing initiatives like the development of learning resources on the Internet and courses for working people to learn asynchronously after or before the job.[19]

These are but some of the new educational ways to complete one's education through civic engagement. Yet, absent on-site conversations with laborers, reports and Web sites do not provide students with a sense of either the work done or the workers who engage in it. In 1998 there was a showing at the Museum of the City of New York of David Riker's *La Ciudad*, which had a cast of Latino workers, among them sweated laborers, but only a few members of the cast came to the showing. Those who did apologized for the scant number: their co-workers, they explained, were on the job.

Life-learning programs on the sweatshop are inevitably tied to earning college credit or a résumé line or two. One example is the Texas-based Center for Inter-American Policy Research. It is affiliated with the Lozano Long Institute of Latin American Studies at the University of Texas and the Equal Justice Center of Austin and its counterpart in Mississippi, both legal groups that defend the working poor and other coalitions of labor, religion, and civil rights. Students who apply do research on the treatment of workers in the poultry industry. The aim is to close the gap between academic research and advocacy. Student research associates spend summers doing study projects that result in co-authored reports that are used to assist in policymaking.[20]

The value of this summer labor research is undeniable, and students obviously develop research and writing skills that will last them a lifetime. Some doubtless decide on advocacy or organizing careers as a result of the experience. But from the inception of the call for student involvement, the rhetoric of the enterprise has been one that transforms the filth and dangers of the poultry industry into a kind of reading material. As in the AFL Union Semester, students seem to be warned by the tone of the project description to keep a distance from the objects of investigation. Without denying the value of the college sweatshop experience, it must also be said that the sweatshop has become a college text—providing opportunity for students to advance in their own careers. A heated exchange on the Listserv H-labor a few years ago sounded a note of caution for all sweatshop semesters: Labor historians predicted a time not far off when students would "hang out with the unemployed while doing clandestine . . . ethnography."[21]

There is a danger to presenting United Students Against Sweatshops (USAS) too monolithically. Some chapters are developing true ties to local labor movements and to working-class struggles in their areas. Students at Yale University, New York University, and elsewhere have been quite effective in supporting the campus strikes of clerical workers. This is not just slumming, but a forging of a cadre of dedicated social justice organizers among students.

Still, other students impressed by USAS merely seek to round out their undergraduate education by researching the other half. One example is the recent "up from sweatshop" film *Real Women Have Curves*.[22]

This film narrative provides an ironic context for the recent student involvement in antisweatshop work. Like many children of immigrant parents, Ana wants to leave the sweatshop behind. Ordered by her mother,
Carmen, to help with the family wage, she does so for a time, only to
defy her mother, who works alongside her in the Los Angeles sweatshop.
In the end, Ana takes her chance to go to Columbia University on a
scholarship, but before she does, the exasperated young Latina declares of
the dead-end sewing work that her mother and sister have been trapped
in for years, "This is a sweatshop! Can't you see that?" The film does
complicate the exploitation plot in that Ana's sister is a contractor to
clothing firms and the boss of the shop, but Ana's comment remains accurate. These women have little power over their own lives, and the
sewing shop venue—where they make evening and college prom gowns
for rich (white) women—is the proof.

In the context of the new student movements, Ana's transit to New
York City, another sweatshop city, at film's end, acquires an ironic dimension. College members of Students Against Sweatshops, unaware of
barrio Cinderellas, have been given opportunities to observe, learn from,
and write academic papers on the sweated workplace. Ana, overturning
this "life learning" story, observes the world outside the shop with as
much interest as those student investigators of the other half. It is true
that the movie gives her a wealthy college boyfriend who has little understanding of her life. But it is almost certain that she will never en-
lighten him. As a student against sweatshops, her crusade is to move
upward on her own.

THE LESSONS OF TRIANGLE

The International Ladies' Garment Workers Union's celebration of the
seventy-fifth anniversary of the Triangle shirt factory fire was, once again,
more than a respectful nod to the past: "The 75th anniversary of the fire for
the past two decades has been an occasion for the ILG, now UNITE, to
commemorate the past and link it to the underground economy of the
present. UNITE sponsors a wreath laying at the Triangle Site, the former
Asch, now the Brown Building, and New York University property." Tying
the long-ago tragedy deliberately to present conditions, one flier inviting
the public in 1995 to attend stated: "Unbridled competition on a global
scale has led to the rebirth of apparel sweatshops in the United States . . .
[which] unfairly compete with legitimate employers [and] undermine

wages and working conditions. Join us for a discussion by union and government leaders on how to protect the rights of workers."[23]

In the new age of alliances of labor and academics, events like the recent New York City Rally for Global Fairness have been held near the Triangle fire site and cosponsored by UNITE on the eighty-third anniversary of the fire in 2003. Such staged links to current events are deliberate. A flier circulated before the event said that the "modern" American sweatshop, ironically, is the result of twentieth-century improvements in technological change that have been in no way paralleled by improvements in conditions for workers.

Certainly a machine-age modernity with little provision for worker safety only made the Triangle shirtwaist factory more dangerous. The most notorious sweatshop of the American immigrant years, it was neither sunk in a tenement basement nor housed in a diminutive apartment. Rather, it was on a high floor of the Asch, a loft building next to a New York University Law School edifice. Period coverage after the fire named it a "hell-hole" and a "fire trap."[24] As is now well known, its employees were harassed and underpaid, its exit doors were locked, and the physical plant was a tinderbox of flammable liquids and materials waiting for an accident. Some eight decades after it went up in flames on March 25, 1911, New York University did not choose to provide a commemorative plaque; it was as if exerting the noblesse oblige of permitting the two tributes was enough disturbance of the expensive academic peace encoded in its army of buildings circling Washington Square Park. At any given time, furthermore, this urban university is itself embroiled in disputes with the unions. For instance, in July 2000, the United Brotherhood of Carpenters protested the hiring by New York University's chosen building contractor, Forkosh Construction, of non-union labor paid substandard wages. Soon, too, a Forkosh worker died, owing to poor safety standards. It was a Triangle fire in miniature.[25]

To honor the victims of Triangle, the university permitted others to provide two memorial plaques, one from the ILGWU and the other from the U.S. Park Service. In these two fairly small plaques—public representations of sweatshop labor installed on the southwest corner of the Brown building—the language used to narrate the event continues to suggest the contradictions between a passing and a consistent evil. The ILGWU plaque is understated. The second plaque, put in place more recently by the Park Service, is shinier, with enlarged upper-case letters telling the story in a way that seems to cancel out the tragedy itself.

TRIANGLE FIRE
ON THIS SITE WORKERS LOST THEIR LIVES IN THE
TRIANGLE SHIRTWAIST COMPANY FIRE ON
MARCH 25, 1911. OUT OF THEIR MARTYRDOM
CAME NEW CONCEPTS OF SOCIAL RESPONSIBILITY
AND LABOR LEGISLATION THAT HAVE HELPED
MAKE AMERICAN WORKING CONDITIONS THE
FINEST IN THE WORLD.
ILGWU

TRIANGLE SHIRTWAIST FIRE
(ASCH BUILDING)
HAS BEEN DESIGNATED A NATIONAL
HISTORIC LANDMARK.
The building possesses national significance in commemorating the
history of the United States of America
1991
National Park Service
United States Dept. of the Interior

The big union's discourse draws attention away from the martyrdom of the fire's victims, and the government's discourse minimizes it. Moreover, the union's opportunistic characterization of American working conditions as the best in the world is surely debatable. The government's assertion that the Brown building is merely a piece of "American history," another in a series of national monuments like the Lincoln Memorial and the Brooklyn Bridge, is equally outrageous.

THE GHOST OF Triangle will not be laid to rest so easily. There are UNITE retirees who still recall the "classic" shop. Miriam Baratz recalled that her great-uncle had a parlor that "looked like a little factory" and "employed" his two (under-age) children on the turn-of-the-century Lower East Side.[26] Yankee girls and Protestant tailors had labored in attic rooms to meet piecework quotas well before the sweatshop of the Jewish social protest writers, but the latter remains a template for later realities and descriptions: "[P]rimitive little shops [were] run by *landsleit* [countrymen] [and were] equipped with stove-heated pressing irons and foot-powered, or, if extraordinarily advanced, bicycle-powered sewing machines; a Torah in one corner where boss and worker prayed, played cards together, and deliberated over domestic intimacies; a workaday world riven by a thousand petty rivalries, competitions, jealousies, ingenious little rackets, and recurring cycles of submission, abuse, and sudden, rage-filled work stoppages."[27]

For 150 years, at times with great forcefulness and popular notice, the argument has continued between those who believe in the transient, the defunct, and the nonexistent shop and those who speak of the returning, unchanged, and thoroughly unwholesome shop. All of these observers—sociologists, paid or unpaid philanthropists, paternalists, eugenicists, socialists, and Social Realist artists—have brought their particular assumptions and reform impulses to the working-class site. In spite or because of the many mythologies surrounding it, the historical shop has been interpreted as a place of solitary antebellum urban suffering; a late-nineteenth-century tenement teeming with ethnic filth and disease; an immigrant escapee's rite of passage; a Progressive-era catchall for the unambitious; a dead end for those lacking skills; a throwback that challenges industrial progress as it variously invokes 1920s denial, erasure, sentimentality, nostalgia, and rage; a New Deal venue of visual memory and re-creation; a phenomenon to be represented by postindustrial artists of conscience; and a venue of either corporate shame or collegiate enlightenment.

After considering all of the discourses that have arisen over the last century and a half to represent the sweatshop experience, this study cannot point to any one of them as the prevailing narrative strain. Perhaps that is just the point. For as one historian of the 1911 Triangle fire remarked of the sweatshop narrative in general, "How people put events together depends a great deal on who they are and what they are trying to explain."[28] In the case of the surveyors, artists, and cultural or business managers who were the subject of this study, the sweatshop was a metaphor for belief in or criticism of the American Dream of economic mobility and freedom. If their myriad representations are any guide, the only certainty is that a host of observers will continue to debate how, whether, and to what extent the sweatshop has been, and remains, an American worksite. As, inevitably, the argument continues, it is to be hoped that laboring people themselves will bear witness and finally be heard.

NOTES

CHAPTER 1   NARRATING THE SHOP

1. Andrew Ross, "Introduction" and "After the Year of the Sweatshop: Post-script," in *No Sweat: Fashion, Free Trade, and the Rights of Garment Workers,* edited by Andrew Ross (New York: Verso, 1997), 9–38, 291–296; Edna Bonacich and Richard P. Applebaum, *Behind the Label: Exploitation in the Los Angeles Apparel Industry* (Berkeley: University of California Press, 2000), esp. 1–27; Nancy Green, *Ready-to-Wear and Ready-to-Work: A Century of Industry and Immigrants in Paris and New York* (Durham: Duke University Press, 1997), 137–160; Janet Zandy, *Hands: Working-Class Bodies Speak* (New Brunswick: Rutgers University Press, 2004); Daniel E. Bender, *From Sweatshop to Model Shop; Anti-Sweatshop Campaigns and Languages of Labor and Organizing, 1880–1934* (New Brunswick: Rutgers University Press, 2004). Whereas Bender's approach to the language of and crusades against sweated labor is through the sweatshop as a site of male workers' enfeebled bodies, I view the shop as a site of cultural anxiety about ethnicity, gender, and the flaws in the American Dream.
2. Rebekah Levin and Robert Ginsburg, *Sweatshops in Chicago: A Survey of Working Conditions in Low-Income and Immigrant Communities* (Chicago: Sweatshop Working Group of Chicago, 2000), 7–9.
3. Ibid., 8.
4. Ross, *No Sweat,* 296.
5. Linda Gail Becker, "Invisible Threads: Skill and the Discursive Marginalization of the Garment Industry Workforce," Ph.D. dissertation, University of Washington, 1997, 95.
6. Peter Liebhold and Harry R. Rubenstein, eds., *Between a Rock and a Hard Place: A History of American Sweatshops, 1820 to the Present* (Los Angeles: UCLA Asian American Studies Center, 1999), 7.
7. Quoted in *The Johns Hopkins Guide to Literary Criticism,* edited by Michael Groden and Martin Kreiswirth (Baltimore: Johns Hopkins University Press, 1994), 361.
8. An excellent documentary history on the founding of the garment trades and the subsequent formation of unions and strife is the collection *Out of the Sweatshop: The Struggle for Industrial Democracy,* edited by Leon Stein (New York: Quadrangle, 1977). It has been reissued in 2002 by ILR/Cornell University Press.
9. Beth S. Wenger, "Memory as Identity: The Invention of the Lower East Side," *American Jewish History* 85, no. 1 (1997): 4.
10. On the meaning of discourse outside the field of literary criticism, see Nancy Fraser, *Justice Interruptus: Critical Reflections* (New York: Routledge, 1997), 152.
11. Edna Bonacich, "Intense Challenges, Tentative Possibilities: Organizing Immi-

grant Garment Workers in Los Angeles," in *Organizing Immigrants: The Challenge for Unions in Contemporary California,* edited by Ruth Milkman (Ithaca: ILR Press, 2000), 130.

12. I take my definition of spectacle as public performance that attracts attention from Guy Debord, *The Society of the Spectacle* (New York: Zone, 1995).

13. It is not the province of this book to engage in a discussion of the political economy of the sweatshop except insofar as it surfaces in ideological pronouncements. Excellent discussions by other scholars continue to appear. I have also had to make some hard choices: largely excluded are modern strike photography, extensive references to film, and postindustrial trade union ephemera. All of these help form a tradition, and it is hoped that future studies will contextualize them.

14. On the new field of labor geography, in which the physical location and its effect on workers become a map of labor relations, see Andrew Herod, "The Spatiality of Labor Unionism," in *Organizing the Landscape: Geographical Perspectives on Labor Unionism,* edited by Andrew Herod (Minneapolis: University of Minnesota Press, 1998), 1–36.

15. See Michel Foucault, "Panopticism," in *The Foucault Reader,* edited by Paul Rabinow (New York: Pantheon, 1984), 206–213.

16. Hutchins Hapgood, quoted in Norman Kleeblatt and Susan Chevlowe, eds., *Painting a Place in America: Jewish Artists in New York, 1900–1945* (New York: Jewish Museum, 1991), 30.

17. Alessandro Portelli, "Working-Class Studies: Memory, Community, and Activism," keynote speech at Youngstown State University, May 15, 2000. Portelli develops this concept in *The Death of Luigi Trastulli and Other Essays* (Albany: State University of New York Press, 1990).

18. Françoise Basch, "Introduction," in Theresa S. Malkiel, *Diary of a Shirtwaist Striker* ([1910] Ithaca, N.Y.: ILR Press, 1990), 62, 71. On gender-specific conceptions of sweated labor, see Eileen Boris, *Home to Work: Motherhood and the Politics of Industrial Homework in the United States* (Cambridge: Cambridge University Press, 1994), and Nan Enstad, *Ladies of Labor, Girls of Adventure: Working Women, Popular Culture, and Labor at the Turn of the Twentieth Century* (New York: Columbia University Press, 1999), chaps. 3 and 4.

19. Michael Denning, *The Cultural Front: The Laboring of American Culture in the Twentieth Century* (London: Verso, 1996), 202.

20. Harold Rosenberg, quoted in Patricia Hills, *Urban Concern and Social Realism* (Boston: Boston University Art Gallery, n.d.), 17.

21. Modern artistic rebellions against representational art as well as paradigm shifts in thinking about socialism made the tradition of figurative social protest art tenuous. Almost weekly references to the "clichés of Social Realism" appear in the *New York Times,* a newspaper of record; see, for example, Ken Johnson, *New York Times,* June 13, 2003, E37.

22. The most recent Smithsonian exhibit Web address is: www.americanhistory. si.edu/sweatshops. By this book's publication date, this Web site, as well as any one of the others discussed, may well have changed.

23. Maurine W. Greenwald, "Visualizing Pittsburgh in the 1900s: Art and Photography in the Service of Social Reform," in *Pittsburgh Surveyed: Social Science and Social Reform in the Early Twentieth Century,* edited by Maurine W. Greenwald and Margo Anderson (Pittsburgh: University of Pittsburgh Press, 1996), 151.

24. Ibid.
25. A logical further development is retrofitting—building, say, a water park called Sandcastle, where people pay to slide in the water all afternoon, on the site of a mammoth machine shop, whose existence as a Homestead tributary is thus erased. See Judith Modell, *A Town without Steel: Revisioning Homestead* (Pittsburgh: University of Pittsburgh Press, 1998), 26.
26. Laurie Graham, *Singing the City* (Pittsburgh: University of Pittsburgh Press, 1998), 10.
27. Wenger, "Memory as Identity," 11.
28. Ibid.
29. Quoted in Ross, *No Sweat,* 10.

CHAPTER 2   A SHOP IS NOT A HOME

Corinne Brown was founder of the Illinois Women's Alliance, and was speaking of a typical Chicago sweatshop in 1891.
 1. See U.S. House of Representatives, Committee of Manufactures, 52nd Congress, 2nd Session, "Report on the Sweating System under House Resolution" (February 13, 1892). I am grateful to Daniel Bender for this citation.
 2. Todd Pugatch, "Historical Development of the Sweatshop," available at www.unc.edu/courses/ints092/sweat.html.
 3. William F. Buckley, Jr., "The Meaning of Everything," *New York Times Book Review*, October 12, 2003, 13. Its (and Buckley's) elitism notwithstanding, the *OED* is the most helpful source for the genesis of the word *sweatshop*.
 4. Observers at home and abroad, including the distinguished editor of *The Nation,* E. L. Godkin, as late as 1890 retained the conviction that the tenement conditions under the sweating system were worse in America than in Britain. The British conviction was that the sweatshop was more an American than a European phenomenon, although white slavery (oddly, the more damning term) was shared by both countries.
 5. Leon Stein, "Introduction," in *Out of the Sweatshop: The Struggle for Industrial Democracy,* edited by Leon Stein ([1977] Ithaca: ILR/Cornell University Press, 2002), xvi.
 6. A "workroom" was essentially a rented space managed by an independent seamstress and her few employees. Often malodorous sites of downward mobility for daughters of Civil War soldiers, these venues were staffed by exploited victims of the sewing trades. But also employed here were journeymen tailors and piece masters—skilled men and women, whether as managers or as tailors.
 7. Jeanne Boydston, *Home and Work: Housework, Wages, and the Ideology of Labor in the Early Republic* (New York: Oxford University Press, 1994), 59. See also Thomas Dublin, *Women at Work: The Transformation of Work and Community in Lowell, Massachusetts, 1826–1860* (New York: Columbia University Press, 1979), 1–14. See also Boydston's bibliographical note 4 on page 191.
 8. These truths found eloquent representation in stirring though officially promanagement fiction and narratives of factory operatives collected in Benita Eisler, ed., *The Lowell Offering (1840–1845)* (Philadelphia: J. B. Lippincott, 1975). For a recent argument on excessive industrial abuse at Lowell, see Julie Husband, "'The White Slave of the North': Lowell Mill Women and the Reproduction of 'Free' Labor," *Legacy* 16, no. 1 (1999): 11–21.

9. Thomas Hood, "The Song of the Shirt," in *Strong-Minded Women and Other Lost Voices from Nineteenth-Century England,* edited by Janet Horowitz Murray (New York: Pantheon, 1982), 351.

10. Christine Stansell, *City of Women: Sex and Class in New York* (New York: Alfred A. Knopf, 1986), 152.

11. Not all literature was so sanguine about the passions of textile factory girls. See Catharine Williams, *Fall River: An Authentic Narrative,* edited by Patricia Caldwell (New York: Oxford University Press, 1993), 5.

12. Cornelius Mathews, *The Career of Puffer Hopkins* ([1842] New York: Garrett, 1970), 95.

13. George Lippard, *The Nazarene* (Philadelphia: n.p., 1846), 167. Mark Lause, a scholar researching the Brotherhood of America, has found recently that Brotherhood papers in Philadelphia included a pamphlet by the "Industrial Association," a utopian socialist effort to establish a cooperative in the needle trades around 1850–1851 (Mark Lause, letter to the author, May 30, 2001). This represented a direct effort to improve the lot of women workers, particularly in Philadelphia in the Civil War period. Participants included a number of people like I. Rehm, a spiritualist who turned up later in the First International. Also, of course, the local needle trades gave rise to the Knights of Labor. See also Roger Butterfield, "George Lippard and His Secret Brotherhood," *Pennsylvania Magazine of History and Biography* 79 (1955): 285–301.

14. Lippard, *The Nazarene,* 167.

15. Florence Kelley, "The Sweating-System," in *Hull-House Maps and Papers* ([1895] New York: Arno Press/New York Times, 1970), 34. See also Vicki Goldberg, "Introduction," in *Lewis W. Hine: Children at Work,* edited by Vicki Goldberg (Munich: Prestel, 1999), 9.

16. Elizabeth Stuart Phelps, "Opening Address by Miss Phelps," *Workingman's Journal* 6 (May 1869): 1.

17. This homeless laborer anticipates today's trope of the low-wage worker compelled to sleep in a shelter or live in her car.

18. Louisa May Alcott, *Work: A Story of Experience* ([1873] New York: Schocken Books, 1977), 129. Despite the purity rhetoric, a "returned" seamstress is a former prostitute. The novel, a strange one, shifts from sunny to dour in its depictions of noncommunal sewing women's work spaces. In his "Sweatshop—Native Style," in *Out of the Sweatshop,* 3–19, Stein assumes that these early-nineteenth-century rooms were sweatshops—Alcott does not. Phelps seems to take a middle ground in her 1869 *Workingman's Journal* piece. It could be argued that antebellum reformers implied the term without using it, and that the inquiry into actual sites made the term possible.

19. For an analysis of Lowell women's sexuality and a summary of labor-historical and literary-critical controversies, see Laura Hapke, *Labor's Text: The Worker in American Fiction* (New Brunswick: Rutgers University Press, 2001), 69–76.

20. Stansell, *City of Women,* 105, 107, 118–119.

21. Such women's situations are described thus retrospectively by John R. Commons in 1901 and Helen L. Sumner in 1905 (who also pointed to her own time). See Stein, *Out of the Sweatshop,* 5–6 and 44–45, as well as modern historians like Stansell, *City of Women.*

22. Ava Baron and Susan E. Klepp, "'If I Didn't Have My Sewing Machine . . .': Women and Sewing Machine Technology," in *A Needle, a Bobbin, a Strike:*

Women Needleworkers in America, edited by Joan M. Jensen and Sue Davidson (Philadelphia:Temple University Press, 1984), 41.

23. See Jacob A. Riis, "Jewtown," in *How the Other Half Lives: Studies among the Tenements of New York* ([1890; revised 1902]; New York: Dover, 1971), 85–96. The famous photographs, though the subject of Riis's lantern-slide lectures, were not available in print form until 1900.

24. Thomas Kessner, *The Golden Door: Italian and Jewish Immigrant Mobility in New York City, 1880–1915* (New York: Oxford University Press, 1977), 136. See also Allen F. Davis, *Spearheads for Reform: The Social Settlements and the Progressive Movement, 1890–1914* (New York: Oxford University Press, 1967), 43.

25. Irving Howe, *World of Our Fathers* (New York: Simon & Schuster, 1976), 288. See also Arthur Mann, "Samuel Gompers and the Irony of Racism," *Antioch Review* 13 (June 1953): 206.

26. Bernard Mergen, "'Another Great Prize':The Jewish Labor Movement in the Context of American Labor History," *YIVO Annual of Jewish Social Science* 16 (1975–1976): 401.

27. David Montgomery, *The Fall of the House of Labor:The Workplace, the State, and American Labor Activism, 1865–1925* (Cambridge: Cambridge University Press, 1983), 83; see also Kessner, *The Golden Door,* chap. 7.

28. Kessner, *The Golden Door,* ix.

29. Walter A. Wyckoff, *The Workers:An Experiment in Reality,* vol. 1, *The West* (New York: Charles Scribner's Sons, 1898), 200.

30. *Seventh Biennial Report of the Bureau of Labor Statistics of Illinois, 1892* (Springfield: Bureau of Labor Statistics, 1893).

31. Eileen Boris, letter to the author, June 27, 2000; "The Evils of the Sweat-Shop," *Outlook* 51 (May 4, 1895): 734.

32. Scholars disagree. Although Eileen Boris finds "the simultaneous use of sweating, sweating system, and sweat shop or sweatshop in the late 1880s and certainly in the 1890s" (letter to the author, June 27, 2000), Daniel Bender writes: "The term sweatshop . . . originates in 1892 during a moment when there is peak interest in the contracting system of labor" (letter to the author, June 26, 2000). See also the exchange of views on H-labor@H.Net.Msu.Edu for June 20–26, 2000.

33. Mark Seltzer, in *Bodies and Machines* (New York: Routledge, 1992), speaks of "generic models and . . . concrete individuals" as "statistical persons" (113) that joined the "surveillance mode" (106).

34. Jacob A. Riis, *The Making of an American* ([1901] New York: Macmillan, 1903), esp. 153, 174.

35. Allon Schoener, ed., *Portal to America:The Lower East Side, 1870–1925* (New York: Holt, Rinehart, and Winston, 1967), 159.

36. Carroll D. Wright, *The Slums of Baltimore, Chicago, New York, and Philadelphia* ([1894] New York: Arno Press/New York Times, 1970). It was as if the term "sweatshop" was too graphic a label to place on work done by the "working girls" of major cities.

37. Katherine Kish Sklar, *Florence Kelley and the Nation's Work* (New Haven:Yale University Press, 1995), 209–210, 229. The quotation is from Kelley, "The Sweating-System," 34.

38. Paul S. Boyer, *Urban Masses and Moral Order in America, 1820–1920* (Cambridge: Harvard University Press, 1967), remains one of the best accounts of moral regulation in late-Victorian America.

39. Maren Stange, in *Symbols of Ideal Life: Social Documentary Photography in America, 1890–1950* (Cambridge: Cambridge University Press, 1989), has an excellent account of this discourse of social investigation on p. 34.
40. Ibid., 35.
41. Joan W. Scott, in a review of Alain Corbin, *The Foul and the Fragrant*, November 2, 1986, available at: web.lexis-nexis.com/universe.
42. Quoted ibid.
43. Marilyn T. Williams, *Washing "the Great Unwashed": Public Baths in Urban America, 1840–1920* (Columbus: Ohio State University Press, 1991), 1, 26.
44. Ibid., 1.
45. Kelley, "The Sweating-System," 30; see also Steven Fraser, *Labor Will Rule: Sidney Hillman and the Rise of American Labor* (Ithaca: Cornell University Press, 1999), 129; and Alan M. Kraut, *Silent Travelers: Germs, Genes, and the "Immigrant Menace"* (New York: Basic Books, 1994).
46. See also Jacob A. Riis, "How the Other Half Lives: Studies among the Tenements," *Scribner's Magazine* 6, no. 6 (December 1889): 646.
47. Joseph A. Amato, *Dust: A History of the Small and the Invisible* (Berkeley: University of California Press, 2000).
48. On Riis's lectures and lantern slide shows, see Stange, *Symbols of Ideal Life*. For biographical information on Riis, see *American Reformers*, edited by Alden Whitman (New York: H. W. Wilson, 1985), 689–690.
49. Bennard B. Perlman, *Painters of the Ashcan School: The Immortal Eight* (New York: Dover, 1988), 53, 54, 56.
50. Stange, *Symbols of Ideal Life*, 8; James B. Lane, *Jacob A. Riis and the American City* (Port Washington, N.Y.: Kennikat, 1974), 35, 48.
51. Perlman, *Painters of the Ashcan School*, 53.
52. Quoted in Williams, *Washing "the Great Unwashed,"* 15. The antebellum American Medical Association was the same organization that later promulgated the notion that Jews and Italians had different immigrant germs (Daniel Bender, letter to the author, June 26, 2000).
53. David Dubinsky and A. H. Raskin, *David Dubinsky: A Life with Labor* (New York: Simon & Schuster, 1977), 44, 49, 51, 52.
54. Susan A. Glenn, *Daughters of the Shtetl: Life and Labor in the Immigrant Generation* (Ithaca: Cornell University Press, 1990), 93–94.
55. Quoted in Sklar, *Florence Kelley and the Nation's Work*, 232.
56. In a modern reminiscence about the oldtime "moveable shop," Miriam Baratz recalled that her great-uncle paid a boy five cents to carry his machine to someone else's "shop." Miriam Baratz, interview with the author, New York City, June 22, 2000. For a discussion of Cahan's spirited sweatshop workers, see Hapke, *Labor's Text*, 109–112.
57. Kelley, "The Sweating-System."
58. Riis, *How the Other Half Lives*, 98, 106, 102, 104.
59. "Sweatshop Girl Tailors," *New York Herald Tribune*, June 18, 1897.
60. This is not to suggest that women's strikes were an early-twentieth-century invention. See Mary H. Blewett, *Men, Women, and Work: Class, Gender, and Protest in the New England Shoe Industry, 1780–1910* (Urbana: University of Illinois Press, 1988), chap. 9; Susan Levine, *Labor's True Woman: Carpet Weavers, Industrialization, and Labor Reform in the Gilded Age* (Philadelphia: Temple University Press, 1984), chap. 6; and Philip Foner, *Women and the American Labor*

Movement from Colonial Times to the Eve of World War I (New York: Free Press, 1979), chap. 14.

61. Nan Enstad even extends the resistant culture to working-girls' consumerism. See her *Ladies of Labor, Girls of Adventure: Working Women, Popular Culture, and Labor Politics at the Turn of the Twentieth Century* (New York: Columbia University Press, 1999), chaps.1 and 2.

62. On manual labor in general and women's reproductive systems, see William Sanger, *The History of Prostitution* (New York: Medical Publishing Company, 1898). Written in 1858, it was still in print, suggesting the longevity of the prejudices it inscribes.

63. Grant Allen, "Woman's Place in Nature," *Forum* 7 (June 1889): 223. See also Azel Ames, *Sex in Industry: A Plea for the Working Girl* (Boston: James R. Osgood, 1875), esp. 44–47.

64. Daniel Bender, "From Sweatshop to Model Shop: Anti-Sweatshop Campaigns and Languages of Labor and Organizing" (Ph.D. diss., New York University, 2001), chap. 5.

65. James W. Sullivan, "Cohen's Figure," in *Tenement Tales of New York* (New York: Henry Holt, 1895), 83.

66. Clare de Graffenreid, "The Condition of Wage-Earning Women," *Forum* (March 1893): 80. A full discussion of these essayists and novelists is in Laura Hapke, *Tales of the Working Girl: Wage-Earning Women in American Literature, 1890–1925* (New York: Twayne/Macmillan, 1992), chap. 2.

67. Sullivan, "Minnie Kelcey's Wedding," in *Tenement Tales of New York,* 81.

68. Ibid., and note 63 above. For Rose Baruch, see Jacob Riis, "The Cat Took the Kosher Meat," in *Out of Mulberry Street* ([1898] Upper Saddle River, N.J.: Gregg Press, 1970).

69. On British women writers who helped define the seamstress-seduction novel, see Sally Mitchell, *The Fallen Angel: Chastity, Class and Women's Reading, 1835–1880* (Bowling Green: Bowling Green University Press, 1981); on their American sisters, see Cathy N. Davidson, *Revolution and the Word: The Rise of the Novel in America* (New York: Oxford University Press, 1988).

70. Hutchins Hapgood, *The Spirit of the Ghetto: Studies of the Jewish Quarter of New York* ([1902] Cambridge: Belknap Press of Harvard University Press, 1967). Elizabeth Wilson, *The Sphinx in the City: Urban Life, the Control of Disorder, and Women* (Berkeley: University of California Press, 1991), 49–50. A representative period essay on saving the working girl, particularly the seamstress, from the sinful workplace is Edgar Fawcett, "The Woes of the New York Working-Girl," *Arena* 4 (1891): 26–35.

71. A particularly good discussion is Alain Corbin, *The Foul and the Fragrant: Odor and the French Social Imagination* (Cambridge, Mass.: Harvard University Press, 1986).

72. Although it appeared prior to the 1890s, still timely was the exposé by Helen Campbell, *Prisoners of Poverty* ([1887] Westport, Conn.: Greenwood, 1970), 23–24. See also Riis, "The Cat Took the Kosher Meat," and Sullivan, "Cohen's Figure."

73. E. L. Godkin, "Our Sweating System," *Nation,* June 19, 1890.

74. Quoted in Bender, "'A hero for the weak': Work, Consumption, and the Enfeebled Jewish Worker, 1881–1924," *International Labor and Working-Class History* 56 (Fall 1999): 5. Leonard Cassuto's grandmother, he noted, "wanted just

to be a good Jew after having to work in sweatshops on Saturdays." Interview with the author, Philadelphia, November 11, 2000.

75. Leonard Cassuto, interview with the author, Philadelphia, November 11, 2000.
76. Glenn, *Daughters of the Shtetl,* 106.
77. "The Life Story of a Polish Sweatshop Girl," *Life Stories of Undistinguished Americans,* edited by Hamilton Holt, introduction by Werner Sollors, 2nd ed. (New York: Routledge, 1990), 21–28.
78. Ronald Sanders, *The Downtown Jews: Portraits of an Immigrant Generation* (New York: Dover, 1987), 205; Howe, *World of Our Fathers,* 538.
79. Cahan's stories are not as "political" as his essays. His stories suggest a vibrant life in the shop, while his essays inveigh against conditions there.
80. Morris Rosenfeld, *Songs from the Ghetto* ([1898] Upper Saddle River, N.J.: Gregg Press, 1970), 3. For biographical information on Rosenfeld, see *Later National Literature,* part 3, available at: www.bartleby.org/228/0841.html.
81. Bender, "A hero for the weak," 8, quotes Wald on "tailors' disease."
82. Sanders, *The Downtown Jews,* 136.
83. Rosenfeld, *Songs from the Ghetto,* 7.
84. Fraser, *Labor Will Rule,* 33.
85. Christopher Prendergast, *Paris and the Nineteenth Century* (Oxford: Blackwell, 1992), 85.
86. Fraser, *Labor Will Rule,* 28.

CHAPTER 3   SURVIVING SITES

1. Carroll D. Wright, *The Working Girls of Boston* (Washington, D.C.: U.S. Government Printing Office, 1884); Wright, *Working Women in Large Cities* (Washington, D.C.: U.S. Government Printing Office, 1889).
2. Daniel E. Bender, "From Sweatshop to Model Shop: Anti-Sweatshop Campaigns and Languages of Labor and Organizing, 1880–1934" (Ph.D. dissertation, New York University, 2001), 13.
3. Maren Stange, *Symbols of Ideal Life: Social Documentary Photography in America, 1890–1950* (Cambridge: Cambridge University Press, 1989), 1–87. This focus persisted into the 1920s, with unions themselves supporting the politics of industrial engineering.
4. Theodore Dreiser, "The Transmigration of the Sweatshop," *Puritan* 7 (July 1898): 498.
5. Eileen Boris, reader's report for Rutgers University Press.
6. Excellent studies of the social survey movement are in Allen Davis, *Spearheads for Reform: The Social Settlements and the Progressive Movement, 1980–1914* (New York: Oxford University Press, 1967); John F. McClymer, *War and Welfare: Social Engineering in America, 1890–1925* (Westport, Conn.: Greenwood, 1980); and the essays by various hands in *The Social Survey in Historical Perspective, 1880–1940,* edited by Martin Bulmer, Kevin Bales, and Katherine Kish Sklar (Cambridge: Cambridge University Press, 1991).
7. Paul Kellogg, ed., *Wage-Earning Pittsburgh* (New York: Russell Sage Foundation, 1914), 27.
8. John F. McClymer, "The Pittsburgh Survey, 1907–1908: Forging an Ideology in the Steel District," *Pennsylvania History* 41 (April 1974): 169.
9. Stange, *Symbols of Ideal Life,* 49.

10. Mary Van Kleeck, "Women and Children Who Make Men's Clothes," *Survey* (April 1, 1911): 65–69. Modern historians accept the division, too: "cigar and garment manufacturing enterprises, small ones that could be classified as sweatshops and larger ones that became the factories of the neighborhood," are mentioned in Hasia R. Diner's excellent study, *Lower East Side Memories: A Jewish Place in America* (Princeton: Princeton University Press, 2000), 45 and 190, nn. 70–76.

11. Morris Hillquit, *Loose Leaves from a Busy Life* ([1936] New York: Da Capo Press, 1971), 1.

12. Jo Ann E. Argersinger, *Making the Amalgamated: Gender, Ethnicity, and Class in the Baltimore Clothing Industry* (Baltimore: Johns Hopkins University Press, 1999), 12.

13. Henry White, "Conditions Transformed by Label," *ILGWU Fourth Annual Convention*, commemorative/souvenir booklet, Cleveland, Ohio, June 1, 1903.

14. See, for instance, *The Common Welfare* (March 16, 1912): 1921.

15. Elizabeth Butler, "Sweated Work in Hudson County, New Jersey," *Charities and the Commons*, December 21, 1907, 1,257.

16. Paul Kellogg, "Editor's Foreword," in Crystal Eastman, *Work Accidents and the Law* (New York: Russell Sage Foundation, 1910), v.

17. Margo Anderson and Maurine Greenwald, "The Pittsburgh Survey in Historical Perspective," in *Pittsburgh Surveyed: Social Science and Social Reform in the Early Twentieth Century*, ed. Maurine W. Greenwald and Margo Anderson (Pittsburgh: University of Pittsburgh Press, 1996), 1.

18. Mario Maffi, *Gateway to Ethnicity: Ethnic Cultures on New York's Lower East Side* (New York: New York University Press, 1995), 144.

19. John Fitch, *The Steel Workers, 1907–1908* (New York: Russell Sage Foundation, 1910), chap. 1, esp. 9–17. Elizabeth Butler makes a similar distinction between ethnics and whites in *Women and the Trades: Pittsburgh, 1907–1908* ([1909] Pittsburgh: University of Pittsburgh Press, 1984), 104.

20. Eastman, *Work Accidents and the Law,* 91.

21. Ibid., 5.

22. See *Census of Manufactures, 1914,* vol. 2 (Washington, D.C.: U.S. Government Printing Office, 1916), 184. Wheelbarrows, whips, windmills, and window screens, to cite some other exotic examples, received thorough scrutiny as well (5). Whether bypassing conditions, as in census data, or investigating manifold abuses, as in reports of appointed commissions of inquiry, by 1910 the official line was impatience at the existence of sweatshops.

23. Louise C. Odencrantz, *Italian Women in Industry: A Study of Conditions in New York City* (New York: Russell Sage Foundation, 1919), 32.

24. Mary Van Kleeck, *The Artificial Flower Makers* (New York: Russell Sage Foundation, 1913), 23–24.

25. Odencrantz, *Italian Women in Industry,* 31–32. See also Annie Marion MacLean, "The Sweat-Shop in Summer," *American Journal of Sociology* 9, no. 3 (November 1903): 289.

26. Butler, *Women and the Trades,* 103 (emphasis added).

27. Butler's only nod to unassimilated workers is a reference to "tense women" (ibid., 103). She then reverts to her discussion of the success ethic.

28. MacLean, for instance, alludes vaguely to "a region where many sweat-shops flourish . . . near the [Monongahela] river" ("The Sweat-Shop in Summer," 293).

29. By 1910 there were many pockets of garment manufacturing in every major

eastern seaboard city and in the midwestern and Rust Belt population centers. Framing garment production within the larger rhetoric of the steel mill observer John Fitch, Elizabeth Butler, when she toured Pittsburgh's many small garment factories in lofts and basements, found that the sites were "industrially indefensible." They "divide themselves into factories and workshops. As a working definition . . . the establishments which occupy buildings used only for business purposes and in which power machinery is installed will be called factories; when the shop occupies a building used also as a residence, or when although in a business building, it makes use of foot power *and hand work*, it will be called a workshop" (10, emphasis added). In "the small shops . . . the prevailing type of garment workroom" (128) she invoked the old contractors' workroom where jobs done by outworkers were delivered for "inside" work.

30. Thomas K. Urdahl, "The Normal Labor Day in Coal Mines," *American Economic Association Quarterly* (April 1908): 157.
31. Butler, "Sweated Work in Hudson County," 1,264.
32. Hine's photos appear in Sue Ainslie Clark and Edith Wyatt, "Working-Girls' Budgets: The Shirtwaist-Makers and Their Strike," *McClure's* 36 (November 1910): 70–86.
33. *The Survey* 27 (January 27, 1912): 1656–1657. See also *Factory Investigating Report, State of New York*, no. 20, March 1, 1912 (Albany: J. B. Lyons, 1912).
34. The classic account is her own. See Alice Hamilton, *Exploring the Dangerous Trades* (Boston : Little, Brown, 1943).
35. Frances Perkins, "The Reminiscences of Frances Perkins," Columbia University Oral History Collection, 132–141; George Martin, *Madam Secretary: Frances Perkins* (Boston: Houghton Mifflin, 1976), chap. 8, gives background on Perkins's involvement in the Triangle fire investigation. A fine film in this regard is *You May Call Her Madam Secretary*, directed by Marjory Potts, produced and written by Marjory and Robert Potts (Vineyard Video Production, 1987). Perkins wrote the *Fire Safety Report of the 1914 Factory Investigating Committee of New York State*, no. 28 (February 1914).
36. Quoted in Leon Stein, ed., *Out of the Sweatshop: The Struggle for Industrial Democracy* ([1977] Ithaca: ILR/Cornell University Press, 2002), 189.
37. Leon Stein, *The Triangle Fire* (New York: Carroll and Graf, 1962), 14–16. Of the legion sources on the fire, especially good is Arthur F. McEvoy, "The Triangle Shirtwaist Factory Fire of 1911: Social Change, Industrial Accidents, and the Evolution of Common-Sense Causality," *Law and Social Inquiry* 20, no. 2 (Spring 1995): 621–651.
38. MacLean, "The Sweat-Shop in Summer," 295.
39. Stein, *Out of the Sweatshop*, 51–52.
40. *New York State, Factory Investigating Commission, Fourth Report*, Senate doc. 43, vols. 1 and 2 (Albany: J. B. Lyons, 1915).
41. The rule of silence was well known. See Susan A. Glenn, *Daughters of the Shtetl: Life and Labor in the Immigrant Generation* (Ithaca: Cornell University Press, 1990), 153, n. 91. A firsthand account is in Agnes Smedley, *Daughter of Earth* ([1929] New York: Feminist Press, 1973), 80–85.
42. Although almost every garment industry observer comments on the overcrowded conditions, exact measurements are hard to come by. On overall conditions, see, among others, Alice Kessler-Harris, *Out to Work: A History of Wage-Earning Women in the United States* (New York: Oxford University Press, 1982), 108–217; the novels of Meredith Tax, *Rivington Street* (New York: Mor-

row, 1982) and *Union Square* (New York: Avon, 1988); Anne Marion MacLean, *Wage-Earning Women* (New York: Macmillan, 1910), 31–54; Theresa S. Malkiel, *The Diary of a Shirtwaist Striker* ([1910] Ithaca, N.Y.: ILR Press, 1990; and Meredith Tax, *The Rising of the Women: Feminist Solidarity and Class Conflict, 1880–1917* (New York: Monthly Review Press, 1980).

43. *New York Call,* March 27, 1911, 1.
44. *Jewish Daily Forward,* March 29, 1911. For his signature laments, see Morris Rosenfeld, *Songs from the Ghetto* ([1898]; Upper Saddle River, N.J.: Gregg Press, 1970), 2–32.
45. Quoted in Stein, *The Triangle Fire,* 144.
46. Joseph Brandes, "From Sweatshop to Stability: Jewish Labor between Two World Wars," *YIVO Annual* 16 (1976): 19.
47. To this day few women are on the podium for the annual commemoration in front of the Brown Building.
48. Quoted in Stein, *Out of the Sweatshop,* 122.
49. Brandes, "From Sweatshop to Stability," 19–20.
50. Hillquit, *Loose Leaves from a Busy Life,* 15–30. The ACW from the beginning had multilingual newspapers. See also Kellogg, *Wage-Earning Pittsburgh,* 201. See pages 273–274 for praise of the ILGWU's 1913 Chicago protocols.
51. Stein, *Out of the Sweatshops,* sects. 6 and 7, esp. p. 149. Provision for sympathy strikes, wildcat strikes, and other protests in aid of workers in other garment trades were nowhere to be found in the protocols.
52. Glenn, *Daughters of the Shtetl,* 108.
53. Ibid., 116.
54. Local 89 of the ILGWU was staffed by women and men, but pay scales were unequal. Annelise Orleck, *Common Sense and a Little Fire: Women and Working-Class Politics in the United States, 1900–1965* (Chapel Hill: University of North Carolina Press, 1995), 4. For a good discussion of "unwritten laws that kept women out of certain jobs," see Glenn, *Daughters of the Shtetl,* chap. 3.
55. Walter Lippman, "The Campaign against Sweating," *New Republic* 2 (March 27, 1915): 1.
56. Orleck, *Common Sense and a Little Fire,* 66.
57. Elizabeth Dutcher, "Budgets of the Triangle Fire Victims," *Life and Labor* (September 11, 1912): 265.
58. A good summary of opposing schools is in the introduction to Orleck, *Common Sense and a Little Fire.*
59. Louis Wirth, "Urbanism as a Way of Life," in Louis Wirth, *On Cities and Social Life,* edited by Albert J. Reiss, Jr. (Chicago: University of Chicago Press, 1964), 74.
60. Ibid., 95.
61. See "The Life Story of a Polish Sweatshop Girl," in *Life Stories of Undistinguished Americans,* edited by Hamilton Holt ([1906]; New York: Routledge, 1990), 21–28.
62. Louis Wirth, *On Cities and Social Life,* 95. See also Hasia R. Diner, "Introduction" to Louis Wirth, *The Ghetto* ([1928] Chicago: University of Chicago Press, 1957), xi–xiii, who provides a succinct account of Park's accommodation and assimilation thinking.
63. Carla Cappetti, *Writing Chicago: Modernism, Ethnography, and the Novel* (New York: Columbia University Press, 1993), chap. 2, esp. 42–45.
64. See Wirth, *The Ghetto,* 188.

65. I am indebted to Roger Salerno for alerting me to the phrase "sociology noir."

66. W. I. Thomas, *The Unadjusted Girl* ([1923]; Montclair: Paterson Smith, 1969), 172–173.

67. New revisionist studies of Italian seamstresses' activism by Jennifer Guglielmo have just appeared. See also Donna Gabaccia and Franca Iovetta, *Women, Gender, and Transnational Lives: Italian Workers of the World* (Toronto: University of Toronto Press, 2000). See my discussion of Ginevra Fasanella in chapter 4 below.

68. Nan Enstad, *Ladies of Labor, Girls of Adventure: Working Women, Popular Culture, and Labor Politics at the Turn of the Twentieth Century* (New York: Columbia University Press, 1999), 123.

69. Robert E. Park, "Life History," *American Journal of Sociology* 79, no. 2 (September 1973), 254.

70. Anzia Yezierska, "Hunger," in Anzia Yezierska, *Hungry Hearts* (1920; reprint, New York: Signet, 1996), 34.

71. Yezierska also writes of seamstresses ("America and I," 1923, and *Salome of the Tenements*, 1923), shopgirls (*Arrogant Beggar*, 1927), and, as secondary characters, prostitutes ("Wild Winter Love," 1923).

72. Wirth wrote approvingly of the study ("Urbanism as a Way of Life," 238). See W. I. Thomas and Florian Znaniecki, *The Polish Peasant in Europe and America* (New York: Octagon House, 1974).

73. Anzia Yezierska, *All I Could Never Be* (New York: Brewer, Warren & Putnam, 1932), features Yezierska as Fanya Ivanowa and John Dewey as Henry Scott.

74. Ellen Golub, "Eat Your Heart Out: The Fiction of Anzia Yezierska," *Studies in American Jewish Literature* 3 (1983): 58.

75. Bella Spewack, *Streets: A Memoir of the Lower East Side* (New York: Feminist Press, 1995). She became a celebrity for her upbeat musical comedy collaborations with her husband, Sam Spewack.

76. Anzia Yezierska, "Bread and Wine in the Wilderness," in *The Open Cage: An Anzia Yezierska Collection* (New York: Persea Books, 1979), 191. The Great Depression provided some interesting postscripts for the two women. Spewack's show business writing career was then in full swing. Yezierska's postimmigrant interactions with Yiddish workers had also ceased. But she scrambled for a living in the lean years of the early Depression, which found her doing guidebooks of New York that did not include sweatshop retrospection. She was too busy considering herself in a sweated situation at the WPA Writers' Project.

77. Hutchins Hapgood, "A Singer of Labor," in his *The Spirit of the Ghetto* ([1902] Cambridge: Belknap Press of Harvard University Press, 1967), 103.

78. For biographical material on Asch and Schwartz, see Nahma Sandrow, *Vagabond Stars: A World History of Yiddish Theater* (New York: Harper & Row, 1977), 183–184, 271–272.

79. Samuel L. Leiter, "*Uncle Moses*," in *The Encyclopedia of the New York Stage, 1930–1940* (New York: Greenwood, 1989), 1,057. Schwartz had founded the Yiddish Art Theater in 1921.

80. Sholem Asch, *Uncle Moses*, translated by Isaac Goldberg ([1917] New York: E. P. Dutton, 1920), 154. The very durability of the work in its various forms suggests the ethnic need to position the shop in American labor history.

81. J. Hoberman, "Der Ershter Talkies: 'Uncle Moses' and the Coming of the Yiddish Sound Film," *Film Comment* 27, no. 6 (November–December 1991), 37. I

disagree with Hoberman's view that the film "makes no attempt to date its action to an earlier era."

82. A kinder, gentler Moses inhabits the film version, which has union sympathies.

83. One of the best collections of Hine photographs, complete with a critical biography and extensive photographic inventory of his oeuvre is Walter Rosenblum and Naomi Rosenblum, *America and Lewis Hine,* introduction by Alan Trachtenberg (New York: Aperture, 1997). I am also indebted to *Photo Story: Selected Letters and Photographs of Lewis W. Hine,* edited by Daile Kaplan (Washington: Smithsonian Institution Press, 1992), and Robert Westbrook, "Lewis Hine and the Ethics of Progressive Camerawork," *Tikkun* 2, no. 2 (May/June 1987): 15–42.

84. Rosenblum and Rosenblum, *America and Lewis Hine,* 20–21.

85. Lewis Hine, "Tasks in the Tenements," *Child Labor Bulletin* (published by National Child Labor Committee) 3 (1914–1915): 97.

86. Ironically, Hine's career would continue to decline in the very New Deal decade that revivified scrutiny of sweated garment trades.

CHAPTER 4 NEWSREEL OF MEMORY

1. Interview with Walter Srebnick, August 1, 2002, New York City, about his mother, Antoinette Susana Rita Caruso (b. 1901), who, after doing home piecework in the South Bronx from the age of ten, began at the shop in the early 1920s and became an organizer for the garment unions.

2. Steven Fraser, *Labor Will Rule: Sidney Hillman and the Rise of American Labor* (New York: Basic Books, 1991), 316.

3. Quoted ibid., 324.

4. In a limited way that didn't include sweatshops, abstract and surrealist painters also participated in creating this landscape. See Patricia Hills, *Social Concern and Urban Realism* (Boston: Boston University Art Gallery, n.d.).

5. The WPA/FAP imprimatur graced many period catalogs. See, for example, the exhibition catalog *Recent Fine Prints: Federal Art Gallery* (New York: FAP/WPA, 1937).

6. An excellent book in this regard is Marlene Park and Gerald Markowitz, *Democratic Vistas: Post Offices and Public Art in the New Deal* (Philadelphia: Temple University Press, 1984).

7. "Interview," *Ilya Bolotowsky* (New York: Guggenheim Museum, 1977), n.p.

8. Quoted in Andrew Hemingway, *Artists on the Left: American Artists and the Communist Movement, 1926–1956* (New Haven: Yale University Press, 2002), 115.

9. A good chronology is in Louis Lozowick, *William Gropper* (Philadelphia: Art Alliance Press, 1983), 70–73. I am indebted to him for pertinent biographical facts about Gropper.

10. Reprinted in Lozowick, *William Gropper,* 29.

11. *Federal Support for the Visual Arts: The New Deal and Now,* edited by Francis V. O'Connor (New York: New York Graphic Society, 1969), 32.

12. Quoted in Wahneta T. Robinson, "Introduction," in *William Gropper* (Long Beach, Calif.: Long Beach Museum of Art, n.d.), n.p.

13. August L. Freundlich, "William Gropper: A Critique," in *William Gropper: Retrospective* (Coral Gables, Fla.: University of Miami, 1968), 11–12.

14. Quoted in Lozowick, *William Gropper,* 19.
15. Ibid.
16. *Seamstress* (1938), ACA Galleries, New York City.
17. "Steady Employment" and "Dishwasher" (both 1932) are *New Masses* cartoons, reprinted in Milton W. Brown, *American Painting from the Armory Show to the Great Depression* (Princeton: Princeton University Press, 1955), 189.
18. Lozowick, *William Gropper,* 90.
19. *Women Carrying Faggots* (1858), Lehman Collection, Metropolitan Museum, New York. See also Georges Seurat's *Men Hammering Stakes: Lumberjacks* (1882–1883), Metropolitan Museum, New York.
20. "They work like oxen," writes Charlie LeDuff. Remarks a Fulton Fish Market worker, "Every man on these slips works himself into a hump"; "Bending Elbows," *New York Times,* August 13, 2000.
21. Linda Gail Becker, "Invisible Threads: Skill and the Discursive Marginalization of the Garment Industry's Workforce," Ph.D. dissertation, University of Washington, 1997.
22. Marc Chagall, *Remembrance* (c. 1918), Guggenheim Museum, New York.
23. O'Connor, *Federal Support for the Visual Arts,* 18.
24. Ibid., 238n.
25. A fine example is Francis Bonn, *Woman Spinning* (1861), Metropolitan Museum, New York.
26. On Degas's laundresses, some owned by New York's Metropolitan Museum, "depicted as a dark, curved form in silhouette," see Theodore Reff, "Degas: A Master among Masters," *Metropolitan Museum of Art Bulletin* 34, no. 4 (Spring 1977): 56. See also Mary Cassatt, *Sewing by Lamplight* (1891), Morgan Library Thaw Collection, New York.
27. Ellen Wiley Todd, *The "New Woman" Revisited: Painting and Gender Politics on Fourteenth Street* (Berkeley: University of California Press, 1993), has excellent discussions of shopgirls and office girls as proletarians (chaps. 6 and 7) but does not identify seamstresses as such.
28. Quoted in Norman L. Kleeblatt and Susan Chevlowe, eds., *Painting a Place in America: Jewish Artists in New York, 1900–1945* (New York: Jewish Museum, 1991), 57, 59.
29. Linda Nochlin, *Representing Women* (New York: Thames and Hudson, 1999), 91.
30. "The Intimate Interiors of Edouard Vuillard," exhibition pamphlet, May 1990, Brooklyn Museum, Brooklyn, N.Y.
31. Edward Hopper, *New York Interior* (1921), Whitney Museum, New York, Josephine Hopper bequest.
32. Quoted in "Moses Soyer, 74, Dead; Traditional U.S. Painter," *New York Times,* September 3, 1974. See also Moses Soyer and Robert W. Gill, *Painting the Human Figure* (New York: Watson/Gaptill, 1964).
33. *Girl at Sewing Machine* (c. 1939), Whitney Museum, New York.
34. Biographical information on Biddle is in Frances K. Pohl, *In the Eye of the Storm: An Art of Conscience, 1930–1970* (San Francisco: Pomegranate Art Books, 1995), 39–40.
35. Reprints and solid discussions of these and other Biddle works appear in Hemingway, *Artists on the Left,* 60, 136, and in Bram Dijkstra, *American Expressionism: Art and Social Change, 1920–1950* (New York: Harry N. Abrams, 2003), 163.

36. "This panel was part of a five-panel series depicting Society Freed Through Justice—The Tenement and Sweatshop of Yesterday Can Be the Life Planned with Justice of Tomorrow. . . . It was executed in 1935–36, as a tempera on board 39 × 30½ inches . . . and [was] a transfer from the General Services Administration." Unsigned letter from National Museum of American Art archivist, to author, May 16, 2003. The Archives of American Art has the Biddle papers.
37. Park and Markowitz, *Democratic Vistas,* 95.
38. "A Mural Draws Big Interest in a Small-Town Elementary School," *New York Times,* July 5, 1998.
39. There were ironies aplenty in this attempt to understand the sweatshop in New Deal terms. Dubinsky labeled Roosevelt a runaway shop and said it would throw garment workers in New York City out of work; the community folded soon.
40. I am indebted to the Susan Noyes Platt article for identifying the Triangle reference. I have relied as well on her meticulous analysis of the murals' content, her information about Shahn's *Art Front* and radical days, and her fine comparison of this to Shahn's more radical Bronx Post Office piece; Susan Noyes Platt, "The Jersey Homesteads Mural: Ben Shahn, Bernarda Bryson, and History Painting in the 1930s," in *Redefining American History Painting,* edited by Patricia Mullan Burnham and Lucretia H. Giese (Cambridge: Cambridge University Press, 1995), 294–309.
41. Diana L. Linden, "The New Deal Murals of Ben Shahn," *Antiques Magazine* 150, no. 5 (November 1996): 711.
42. Ernest Fiene, *History of the Needlecraft Industry,* reprinted in *Adopt-A-Mural* (New York: Municipal Art Society, 1991), 30–31.
43. Eli Jacobi, "The WPA," in O'Connor, *Federal Support for the Visual Arts,* 102.
44. There were returns to the old sweatshop as well; see his 1949 ink drawing *Man at Loom,* reprinted in Lozowick, *William Gropper,* 126.
45. Roger Keeran, personal communication to the author, September 4, 2002.
46. Eugene Salamin, letter to the author, October 20, 2002.
47. Salamin started working in a factory in April 1929, earning sixteen dollars a week for five twelve-hour days, "which was very good for that time, for me. Two years later I was lucky to get work for twelve dollars a week"; ibid.
48. Roger Keeran, "Marxist Center Art Sale to Feature Work of Eugene Salamin," *People's Weekly World,* March 25, 2000, 16.
49. Eugene Salamin, letter to the author, September 26, 2002.
50. Quoted in Keeran, "Marxist Center," 16.
51. I am indebted to Roger Keeran for the phrase "underground artist." Professor Keeran knew and has interviewed Salamin a number of times and owns the largest collection of his works outside of the artist's own.
52. Metropolitan Museum, New York. See also in the museum collection Jan Van Eyck, *Medici St. Jerome.*
53. For a fine discussion of the HUAC crackdown on artists, writers, and other creative people, see Jane De Hart Matthews, "Art and Politics in Cold War America," *American Historical Review* 81 (October 1976): 762–787. The widest context is provided in Ellen Schrecker, *Many Are the Crimes: McCarthyism in America* (Boston: Little, Brown, 1998).
54. Lozowick, *William Gropper,* 71.
55. Gropper, plate 187, reprinted ibid., 90.

CHAPTER 5   THE SWEATSHOP RETURNS

1. On blacks in the ILGWU (Local 22), see Jack Salzman and Adina Back, *Bridges and Boundaries: African-Americans and Jews* (New York: George Braziller, 1992).
2. A good general discussion is Herbert Hill, "Black Protest and the Struggle for Union Democracy," *Issues in Industrial Society* 1 (January 1969): 23–25.
3. William H. Harris, *The Harder We Run: Black Workers since the Civil War* (New York: Oxford University Press, 1982), is still one of the best surveys. See pp. 141, 166.
4. As early as 1934, the ILGWU had sent Rose Pesotta to Seattle, San Francisco, and Los Angeles to rally sweated Chinese and Hispanic female labor. In a telling move, she later resigned from organizing activity, citing the union's inattention to women's issues. The black and Hispanic women joined and surpassed in numbers the Italian and Jewish seamstresses. The trade's lower reaches had always been woman-fueled, and by 1958, 80 percent of the ILGWU workers were women—low paid at $2.10 per hour. Rose Pesotta, *Bread upon the Waters* ([1944]; Ithaca, N.Y.: ILR Press, 1987), chaps. 2–4.
5. Altagracia Ortiz, "Puerto Ricans in the Garment Industry of New York City, 1920–1960," in *Labor Divided: Race and Ethnicity in United States Labor Struggles,* edited by Robert Asher and Charles Stephenson (Albany: State University of New York Press, 1990), 106–108.
6. "Between a Rock and a Hard Place," *Labor's Heritage* 4, no. 4 (Spring 1998): 17. On Asians in pre-1970s California, see Don T. Nakamishi, "A Bright Light of Revelation," in *Between a Rock and a Hard Place,* edited by Peter Liebhold and Harry Rubenstein (Los Angeles: UCLA Asian American Studies Center, 1999), vii.
7. *Nightsongs,* NF Films/American Playhouse, produced by Thomas A. Fucci, directed by Marva Nabili (1984).
8. Steven High, *Industrial Sunset: The Making of North America's Rust Belt* (Toronto: University of Toronto Press, 2003), anchors the term in the fifteen years between 1969 and 1984. A classic study of the crucial Homestead, Pennsylvania, shutdown, sees the 1986 closing as a postindustrial death knell. See William Serrin, *Homestead: The Triumph and Tragedy of an American Steel Town* (New York: Vintage Books, 1993). See also Ruth Milkman, *Farewell to the Factory: Auto Workers in the Late Twentieth Century* (Berkeley: University of California Press, 1997).
9. Quoted in Tracy Sugarman, "Echoes on Paper," *Labor's Heritage* (Winter 1994): 22.
10. Debra E. Bernhardt and Rachel Bernstein, *Ordinary People, Extraordinary Lives* (New York: New York University Press, 2000), 71–72.
11. For information on Ginevra Fasanella, I am indebted to Paul S. D'Ambrosio, "Preface," in *Ralph Fasanella's America* (Cooperstown, N.Y.: Fenimore Art Museum, 2001), 18–23.
12. A good article on Italian garment trade unionism and the role of locals 48 and 89 is Rudolf Vecoli, "Pane e Guistizia," *La Parola del Popolo* 26 (September–October 1976): 55–61.
13. John Berger, *About Looking* (New York: Vintage International, 1980), 106–107.
14. By the 1970s, Fasanella had been in political exile and out of touch with the Jewish-Italian unionists of the old ILGWU for decades. His own experience was the blacklist rather than the ethnic socialist cadre.

15. For an article that rewrites his radicalism, see Peter Carroll, "Ralph Fasanella Limns the Story of the Workingman," *Smithsonian,* August 1993, 58–69.

16. D'Ambrosio, *Ralph Fasanella's America,* 13.

17. Alfred Kazin, *A Walker in the City* ([1946] New York: Harvest, 1979), 6.

18. Eva Fasanella, "Preface," in D'Ambrosio, *Ralph Fasanella's America,* n.p; the phrase "complex dialogue" is on page 13.

19. *The Young Savages,* United Artists, produced by Harold Hecht, directed by John Frankenheimer (1960). Burt Lancaster added cachet to this "socially concerned" film about East Harlem's Thunderbird gang.

20. Patrick Watson, *Fasanella's City* (New York: Ballantine Books, 1973), 51.

21. Ruth Milkman, "Organizing Immigrant Women in New York's Chinatown: An Interview with Katie Quan," in *Women and Unions: Forging a Partnership,* edited by Dorothy Sue Cobble (Ithaca, N.Y.: ILR Press, 1993), 281–298; Prof. Jeri Reed, University of Oklahoma, letter to the author regarding her Chicago ILGWU organizing in the 1970s and 1980s, June 15, 2001.

22. Watson, *Fasanella's City,* 99.

23. Quoted ibid., 102.

24. Quoted ibid., 51.

25. On Fasanella's anti-unionism, see ibid., 93.

26. Frank Gettings, "Introduction," in *Sue Coe: Directions* (gallery catalog for exhibition held March 17–June 19, 1994), Washington, D.C.: Smithsonian Institution, Hirshhorn Museum and Sculpture Garden, 1994), n.p.

27. Ibid.

28. Sue Coe, "Porkopolis Series," *New Yorker,* November 7, 1994, 229–233.

29. Lois E. Nesbitt, "Sue Coe," *Artforum,* January 1990, 136–137; Sue Geer, "Porkopolis: The Nightmare Vision of Sue Coe," *Los Angeles Times,* July 23, 1991. See pquasb.pqarchiver.com/latimes/doc.

30. Ibid.

31. Sue Coe, e-mail to the author, March 3, 2003.

32. Ida Torres, Central Labor Council member, conversation with the author, New York City, June 4, 2000.

33. Laura Ho, Catherine Powell, and Leti Volpp, "(Dis)Assembling Rights of Women Workers . . . ," *Harvard Civil Rights–Civil Liberties Law Review* (Summer 1996): 383.

34. David Riker, interview with the author, New York City, July 24, 2000.

35. Camilo Jose Vergara, *The New American Ghetto* (New Brunswick: Rutgers University Press, 1995), 77, 99.

36. Sebastiao Salgado, *Workers: An Archaeology of the Industrial Age* (New York: Aperture, 1995). See, in this regard, Raleigh Trevelyan, "Mud, Sweat, and Tears: Strange and Mighty Are the Labors of Humanity in Sebastiao Salgado's Photographs," *New York Times Book Review,* February 26, 1995, 13.

37. David Riker, letter to the author, March 15, 2003.

38. Alan Trachtenberg, *Reading American Photographs: Images as History, Mathew Brady to Walker Evans* (New York: Hill and Wang, 1989), 124.

39. Riker, interview with the author, July 24, 2000.

40. Kazin, *A Walker in the City,* 38.

41. Charles Hagen, "The Changeless Poor: Images a Century Apart," *New York Times,* February 6, 1995, C23.

42. For people's murals with Hispanic labor themes in the 1970s, see Paul Buhle

and Edmund B. Sullivan, *Images of American Radicalism* (Hanover, Mass.: Christopher Publishing House, 1998), 63, 400; see also "San Francisco Artist Martin Wong," *San Francisco Examiner,* August 22, 1999, reprinted at: www. sfgate.com/cgi.

43. Common Threads Artist Group Project, *Hidden Labor: Uncovering L.A.'s Garment Industry,* www.usc.edu/isd/archives/la/pubart/Downtown/HiddenLabor. Regarding the dates of the original show, the Web site only informs the reader that the exhibit was "taken down on May 15, 1998."

44. Only at this writing is it available online.

CHAPTER 6   EL MONTE AND THE SMITHSONIAN FUROR

1. Michael Krikorian, "Two Brothers Sentenced to Six Years in Thai Slavery Case," *Los Angeles Times,* April 30, 1996, 3.

2. Alan Sekula, "Dismantling Modernism: Reinventing Documentary," *Massachusetts Review* 19 (Winter 1978): 866.

3. Robert Stuart Nathan and Edward Pomerance, "Wedded Bliss," episode of *Law and Order,* directed by Vern Gillum (1992).

4. Visit the Smithsonian's website at www.si.edu/nmah/ve/sweatshops; see also americanhistory.si.edu/sweatshops/index.htm.

5. Joanna Ramey, "Smithsonian Readies Sweatshop Exhibit," *Women's Wear Daily* 174, no. 4 (July 7, 1997): 4.

6. Spencer Crew, opening label for "Between a Rock and a Hard Place: A History of Sweatshops, 1820 to the Present," exhibit at the Smithsonian Institution, April 22–October 30, 1998. See Web site for full text.

7. Julie Su, quoted in *No Sweat: Fashion, Free Trade, and the Rights of Garment Workers,* edited by Andrew Ross (New York: Verso, 1997), 146.

8. "INS Deserves No Credit," *Los Angeles Daily News,* reprinted in *Los Angeles Daily Journal,* August 16, 1995, 5.

9. K. Connie Kang, "Once Virtual Slaves, 71 Thai Workers Win U.S. Residency," *Los Angeles Times,* November 18, 2002, B1.

10. For a good account of the case and future possibilities of suing manufacturers, see Samantha C. Halem, "Slaves to Fashion: A Thirteenth Amendment Litigation Strategy to Abolish Sweatshops in the Garment Industry," *San Diego Law Review* 36 (1999), 397–453.

11. Representative coverage includes David Finnigan, "Our Cheap Clothes Are Their Horror Stories," *National Catholic Review* (Kansas City), December 29, 1995, 6; Duane Noriyuki, "Milestones: Surviving Injustice to Cradle New Beginnings," *Los Angeles Times,* April 25, 2001, E1; David E. Rovella, "Sweatshop Settlement Draws Others: Four Nonparties Agree to Terms of the $1.25 Million Pact," *New York Law Journal* 222, n. 83 (October 27, 1999), available at: web4.infotrac.galegroup.com/itw.

12. "INS Deserves No Credit," 5.

13. Patrick J. McDonnell, "Retailers Assailed in Sweatshop Protest," *Los Angeles Times,* February 24, 1996, 9. Far from southern California, one exception was Finnigan, "Our Cheap Clothes Are Their Horror Stories," 6.

14. George White, "'Good Guy' Labor List Gets a Bad Rap," *Los Angeles Times,* December 6, 1995, 1.

15. *Malee Bureerong et al., Plaintiffs, v. Tavee Uvawas, et al., Defendants,* no. CV95-5958 ABC, U.S. District Court, C.D. California, January 8, 1996. See

westlaw@westgroup.com.

16. Tom Mrozek, "Defendants Plead Guilty in Sweatshop Case," *Los Angeles Daily Journal,* February 12, 1996, 3; Kang, "Once Virtual Slaves," B1.

17. Krikorian, "Two Brothers Sentenced to Six Years in Thai Slavery Case," 3.

18. Sekula, "Dismantling Modernism," 866.

19. Krikorian, "Two Brothers Sentenced to Six Years in Thai Slavery Case," 3.

20. "Inside the Sweatshop," *Tacoma News Tribune,* reprinted in *Los Angeles Daily Journal,* August 16, 1995, 5.

21. *New York Times,* August 4, 1995, A1; August 15, 1995, A14; August 16, 1995, A22; August 20, 1995, A28; September 7, 1995, A28; September 9, 1995, A28; February 11, 1996, A39; March 9, 1996, A11.

22. Richard Stott, "Between a Rock and a Hard Place" (review), *Journal of American History* 86, no. 1 (June 1999): 186.

23. Spencer R. Crew, " 'Balanced' Sweatshop Exhibit" (letter to the editor), *Los Angeles Times,* reprinted in *Washington Post,* October 7, 1997, A16. The letter was frequently reprinted.

24. Irvin Molotosky, "Furor Builds over Sweatshop Exhibition," *New York Times,* September 20, 1995, B12.

25. Jason Zengerle, "Exhibiting Bias," *New Republic* 217, no. 16 (October 16, 1997): 18. See also Ramey, "Smithsonian Readies Sweatshop Exhibit," 4, and www.democracynow. org/archive.

26. Molotosky, "Furor Builds over Sweatshop Exhibition."

27. Quoted in Jacqueline Trescott, "In 'Sweatshops,' Smithsonian Holds Back the Outrage," *Washington Post,* April 22, 1998, D1.

28. Eric H. Roth, "Third Thoughts on a Museum of Tolerance Exhibit," *Santa Monica Mirror* 29, no. 1 (January 5–11, 2000).

29. Clarice Stasz, "The Early History of Visual Sociology," in *Images of Information: Still Photography in the Social Sciences,* edited by Jon Wagner (Beverly Hills, Calif.: Sage Publications, 1979).

30. K. Connie Kang, "Museum Hosts Controversial Factory Exhibit," *Los Angeles Times,* November 15, 1999, 1.

31. The terms "logistical problem" and "affective drama" appear in Adrian Rifkin, *Street Noises: Parisian Pleasure, 1900–1940* (Manchester: Manchester University Press, 1993), 98.

32. Mary Alexander, "Exhibit Review," *Technology and Culture* 40, no. 4 (1999): 863.

33. Ibid., 862. Contrast this with a visit to the United States Holocaust Museum in Washington, D.C., where each visitor must take the passport of a camp victim.

34. Roth, "Third Thoughts on a Museum of Tolerance Exhibit."

35. Ibid. A review of the show in its only other venue, the Los Angeles Museum of Tolerance, Roth's article contains the best summary of the exhibit.

36. Kang, "Museum Hosts Controversial Factory Exhibit," 1. Compare this article with Zengerle, "Exhibiting Bias," 4, and Stott, "Between a Rock and a Hard Place," 186.

37. Quoted in George White, "Rejected Sweatshop Exhibit Won't Go on Road," *Houston Chronicle,* July 15, 1998, 10.

38. Phillip Matier and Andrew Ross, "Smithsonian's Sweatshop Exhibit Comes Apart at the Seams," *San Francisco Chronicle,* July 17, 1998, A17.

39. Michael Kilian, "Garment Makers Decry Exhibit on Sweatshops," *Chicago Tri-*

bune, April 22, 1998, 17. See also White, "Rejected Sweatshop Exhibit Won't Go on Road."

40. "Smithsonian Exhibit," *Los Angeles Weekly,* May 12–18, 2000, available at: www.sweatshopwatch.org/swatch/headlines/2000exhbiit_may.html.

41. Peter Blumberg, "Making the Industry Sweat," *Los Angeles Daily Journal,* March 23, 1999, 1.

42. Leonard I. Beerman, "Sweatshops Continue but Nobody Is to Blame," *Los Angeles Times,* October 24, 1999, 6. Notably, however, the piece gives no manufacturers' names.

43. Edwin J. Boyer, "Sweatshop Exhibit Revives Painful Memories," *Los Angeles Times,* January 24, 2000, B1.

44. Peter Liebhold and Harry Rubenstein, "Introduction," in *Between a Rock and a Hard Place* (Los Angeles: Asian American Justice Center, 1999), 3, 10, 11.

45. Ibid., 11.

46. Ibid.

47. Quoted in Molotosky, "Furor Builds over Sweatshop Exhibition," B12.

48. Boyer, "Sweatshop Exhibit Revives Painful Memories," B1.

49. Ivan Karp, "Culture and Representation," in *Exhibiting Cultures: The Poetics and Politics of Museum Displays,* edited by Ivan Karp and Steven D. Lavine (Washington, D.C.: Smithsonian Institution Press, 1991), 11–12.

50. Ibid.

51. Laura Ho, Catherine Powell, and Leti Volpp, "(Dis)Assembling Rights of Women Workers along the Global Assembly Line: Human Rights and the Garment Industry," *Harvard Civil Rights–Civil Liberties Review* 31 (Summer 1996): 385.

CHAPTER 7   NIKE'S SWEATSHOP QUANDARY
AND THE INDUSTRIAL SUBLIME

1. U.S. Department of Labor, *Garment Enforcement Report, October 1996–December 1996* (Washington, D.C.: U.S. Government Printing Office, 1997).

2. For information on Global, see Larry Rohter, "Hondurans in 'Sweatshops' See Opportunity," *New York Times,* July 18, 1996, A1.

3. Steven Greenhouse, "Live with Kathie Lee and Apparel Workers," *New York Times,* May 31, 1996, B3; "Donna Karan," *New York Times,* June 8, 2000.

4. Steven Greenhouse, "Sweatshop Raids Cast Doubt on Ability of Garment Makers to Police Factories," *New York Times,* July 18, 1997, A10.

5. Bob Herbert, "Nike's Boot Camps," *New York Times,* March 31, 1997, A15.

6. "Introduction," *The Sweatshop Quandary: Corporate Responsibility on the Global Frontier,* edited by Pamela Varney (Washington, D.C.: Investor Responsibility Research Center, 1998), 15.

7. Ibid., 17.

8. Bill Richards, "Nike to Increase Minimum Age in Asia for New Hirings, Improve Air Quality," *Wall Street Journal,* May 13, 1998, B10; "Nike's Knight Agrees to Disclose Factories Overseas if Rivals Do," *Wall Street Journal,* March 12, 1999, B2.

9. Aaron Bernstein and Kelley Holland, "Nike Finally Does It," *Business Week,* May 25, 1998, 46.

10. Kit Lively, "Nike Chief Ends Giving to Protest University of Oregon's Tie to Anti-Sweatshop Group," *Chronicle of Higher Education,* May 5, 2000, A43.

11. David Moberg, "Monitoring Nike," *In These Times,* 15, no. 22 (June 28, 1998): 20.

12. "Phillips–Van Heusen's Treachery," [news item], *Sweatshop Watch Newsletter,* Fall 2001, n.p.

13. William McCall, "Nike Battles Backlash from Overseas Sweatshops," *Marketing News,* November 9, 1998, 14.

14. See an interesting exchange on this question in the letters to the editor, *New York Times,* May 15, 2000, A20.

15. Martha Banta, *Taylored Lives: Narrative Productions in the Age of Taylor, Veblen, and Ford* (Chicago: University of Chicago Press, 1993), 15. See also Michael W. Munley, "Stories of Work for the American Century: *Taylored Lives,*" *American Quarterly* 46 (September 1994): 462–469.

16. Anil Nayar [manager of a garment wholesale operation], "How to Help Third World Garment Workers" (letter to the editor), *New York Times,* October 21, 1995, A20.

17. Varney, ed., *Sweatshop Quandary,* 46.

18. Ibid., 48.

19. "In Defense of Sweatshops," ibid., 45.

20. *Bobbin Magazine* cover page, and "Mission Statement," *Bobbin* 41, no. 5 (January 2000): 3.

21. Ibid., 2.

22. Olga G. West, "Mexican Firms Concentrate on Capital Investment," ibid., 18.

23. Ibid., 21.

24. George Vairnanktarakis and Janice Kim Winch, "Probability in the Engineering and Information Sciences," *Bobbin* 9 no. 3 (September 1998): 457–473.

25. Ibid., 457. See also "Keeping New York in Fashion: A Strategic Plan for the Future of the New York Fashion Industry" (New York: Kurt Salmon Associates, 1992).

26. Scott Greathead, "Making It Right: Sweatshops, Ethics, and Retailer Responsibility," *Chain Store Executive* 78, no. 5 (May 2002): 195.

27. Maurine W. Greenwald, "Visualizing Pittsburgh in the 1900s: Art and Photography in the Service of Social Reform," in *Pittsburgh Surveyed: Social Science and Social Reform in the Early Twentieth Century,* edited by Maurine W. Greenwald and Margo Anderson (Pittsburgh: University of Pittsburgh Press, 1996), 146.

28. See "An Online Look: Inside Nike's Contract Factories" at the Nike Web site: www.nikebiz.com, from which all subsequent quotes are taken unless otherwise indicated. (There may well be a series of new versions in the offing.) As of March 2003, the Web site informs readers that the reforms of outside evaluators recommended two years ago are still in "remediation."

29. Andrew Ross, "Introduction," in *No Sweat: Fashion, Free Trade, and the Rights of Garment Workers,* edited by Andrew Ross (New York: Verso, 1997), 25.

30. Nike Corporation press release, on current Web site, www.nikebiz.com.

31. "Comprehensive Factory Evaluation Report prepared on Kukdong International Mexico," *Verite,* March 2001.

32. Kristi Ellis, "Global Labor Pains: Advocates Worry Abuse Will Rise as Factories Relocate," *Business and Industry,* October 14, 2002, available at: RDS.Database@rdsinc.com

33. "Comprehensive Evaluation Report," p. 10, available at: www.nikebiz.com.

Julia Preston, "Mexico's May Day March Shows Worker Anger at Official Unions," *New York Times,* May 2, 1996, A14.

34. "Nike Case before U.S. High Court," *Los Angeles Times,* April 21, 2003, sect. 3, p. 2; David G. Savage, "Justices Urged to Reject Suit against Nike," *Los Angeles Times,* April 24, 2003, sect.1, p. 20; "Supreme Court Won't Hear Nike Speech Case," *The Quill* [Chicago], 91, no. 6 (August 2003): 6; Harris Diamond, "Court's Decision a Blow to Free Speech," *Brandweek* 44 (July 2003): 21.

35. Lyle Denniston, "Justices Grapple with Nike Case," *Boston Globe*, April 24, 2003, E3.

36. Savage, "Justices Urged to Reject Suit against Nike."

37. Stanley Holmes, "Free Speech or False Advertising?" *Business Week,* April 28, 2003, 69. The odd coalition that defended Nike included the AFL-CIO and the American Civil Liberties Union. See the *Los Angeles Times,* April 24, 2003.

38. Guy Debord, *Society of the Spectacle*, translated by Donald Nicholson-Smith (New York: Zone Books, 1995). He remarks that such a society was "a world that made itself" (49).

39. Jenn Nichols, "Keeping up with the Joadses: Working-Class Culture, Anti-Globalization, and Romantic Anthropology," paper presented at the Working-Class Studies Conference, Youngstown State University, May 16, 2001.

40. Slates, clothing ad, *New York Times Magazine,* September 12, 1999.

41. Alan Sekula, "Dismantling Modernism: Reinventing Documentary," *Massachusetts Review* 19 (Winter 1978): 712.

42. Ross, *No Sweat,* 257.

43. Phillips Petroleum, ad, *New York Times,* March 3, 2001, A19.

44. Ross, *No Sweat,* 9.

45. H-labor e-mail from John Logan, November 11, 2000, H-labor@ H-Net.Msu.edu.

46. Ellis, "Global Labor Pains: Advocates Worry Abuse Will Rise as Factories Relocate."

47. Quoted in Greenwald, "Visualizing Pittsburgh," 246.

48. Ellis, "Global Labor Pains."

49. Albert Z. Carr, "Can an Executive Afford a Conscience?" *Harvard Business Review* (July–August 1970): 58.

CHAPTER 8   WATCHING OUT FOR THE SHOP

1. Global Sweatshop Coalition, flier, 2000.

2. See the Boycott Nike website at: www.geocities.com/Athens/Acropolis/ 5232.

3. "Conference Plenaries" at the conference "Labor's Next Century: New Alliances, Sweatshops, and the Global South," New York University, April 7–8, 2000.

4. Thomas Friedman, "The New Human Rights," *New York Times,* July 30, 1999, 2.

5. Miriam Ching Yoon Louie, *Sweatshop Warriors: Immigrant Women Workers Take on the Global Factory* (Boston: South End Press, 2001).

6. Martin Van Der Were, "The Worker Rights Consortium Makes Strides toward Legitimacy," *Chronicle of Higher Education*, April 21, 2000, A41.
7. Tim Waters, address at conference on "Labor's Next Century," New York University, April 7, 2000. For an example of scholar/activist attention to the symbolism of sweatshops in venues such as home clerical computer work, for instance, see Eileen Boris and Nelson Lichtenstein, "Home Clerical Work Isn't New," *Los Angeles Times*, January 9, 2000, 2. For a highly provocative essay on the sweatshop as the chief symbol of lower-tier academic labor, see Bruce Robbins, "The Sweatshop Sublime," in *The Public Intellectual*, edited by Helen Small (London: Blackwell, 2002), chap. 8.
8. David Gonzalez, "Latin Sweatshops Pressed by U.S. Campus Power: Dominican Plant Signs Labor Pact," *New York Times*, April 4, 2003, A3.
9. Louise Lee and Aaron Bernstein, "Who Says Student Protests Don't Matter?" *Business Week*, June 12, 2000, 94–95.
10. See the Sweatshop Watch Web site at: www.sweatshopwatch.org.
11. See the Garment Worker Center Web site at: www.garmentworkercenter.org.
12. Interview with Mayra Mendoza, Garment Workers' Justice Center, New York City, May 2000.
13. Rebekah Levin and Robert Ginsburg, *Sweatshops in Chicago: Conditions in Low-Income and Immigrant Communities, A Survey, February 16, 2000* (Chicago: Sweatshop Working Group of Chicago, 2000), 48.
14. See the Web site for the Union Semester Program through the Queens College Office of Worker Education: www.qc.edu/unionsemester.
15. See the Triangle Web site at: www.ilr.cornell.edu/trianglefire; see also the LaborNet Web site at: www.igc.org/igc/ln/resources/unions.html, or igc.apc.org/swatch.
16. See also the Web site of the AFL-CIO (www.aflcio.org). Cyberspace is by far the largest arena yet for discussion of the American sweatshop; it constitutes a veritable education of its own. Each site is conscious of the need to involve students and offers assignments and resources. See, for example, the Web site of the Maquila Solidarity Network of Canada's Ethical Trading Action Network (www.maquilasolidarity.org), a branch of the Campaign for Labor Rights (www.campaignforlaborrights.org). For a menu of causes, see www.sweatshops.org, www.sweatshopwatch.org, and www.uniteunion.orgmembers/members/html.
17. "Lessons in Labor: A Summer Course," *New York Times*, August 9, 1996, B2.
18. Ibid.
19. Sherry Linkon and John Russo, "The Directors' Report," *Working-Class Notes* (Youngstown Center for Working-Class Studies) (Fall 2001), 1.
20. Center for Inter-American Policy call for students to research the poultry industry, H-labor@H-Net.msu.edu, May 2003.
21. See "Labor History Service-Learning Course" emails on H-labor, September 9, 2000, available at H-labor@h-net.msu.edu.
22. Elvis Mitchell, "Sweatshop or College?: Guess Which One Mom's Pushing," *New York Times*, October 18, 2002, E13.
23. Flier announcing the program "The New Sweatshops," New York, March 27, 1995, sponsored by the ILGWU and the Wagner Archives.
24. "The Triangle Fire," *NYC Call*, March 28, 1911, 1.

25. "Shame on You, NYU" (handbill), Tamiment Library, New York University, New York City.
26. Interview with Miriam Baratz, UNITE Retirees Center, New York City, June 28, 2001.
27. Steven Fraser, *Labor Will Rule: Sidney Hillman and the Rise of American Labor* (Ithaca, N.Y.: Cornell University Press, 1991), 199–200.
28. Arthur F. McEvoy, "The Triangle Shirtwaist Fire of 1911: Social Change, Industrial Accidents, and the Evolution of Common-Sense Causality," *Law and Social Inquiry* 20, no. 2 (Spring 1995): 625.

SELECTED BIBLIOGRAPHY

Abbott, Edith. *Women in Industry*. [1910] New York: Arno Press, 1969.

Adopt-a-Mural. New York: Municipal Art Society, 1991.

Alcott, Louisa May. *Work: A Story of Experience*. [1873] New York: Schocken Books, 1977.

Alexander, Mary. "Exhibit Review." *Technology and Culture* 40, no. 4 (October 1999): 861–865.

Amato, Joseph A. *Dust: A History of the Small and the Invisible*. Berkeley: University of California Press, 2000.

Ames, Azel. *Sex in Industry: A Plea for the Working Girl*. Boston: James R. Osgood, 1875.

Anderson, Margo, and Maurine Greenwald. "The Pittsburgh Survey in Historical Perspective." In *Pittsburgh Surveyed: Social Science and Social Reform in the Early Twentieth Century*, edited by Maurine W. Greenwald and Margo Anderson. Pittsburgh: University of Pittsburgh Press, 1996, 1–14.

Anderson, Nels. *The Hobo: The Sociology of the Homeless Man*. [1923] Chicago: University of Chicago Press, 1965.

Argersinger, Jo Ann E. *Making the Amalgamated: Gender, Ethnicity, and Class in the Baltimore Clothing Industry*. Baltimore: Johns Hopkins University Press, 1999.

Arthur, T. S. *The Seamstress: A Tale of the Times*. Philadelphia: R. G. Berford, 1843.

Asch, Sholem. *Uncle Moses*. Translated by Isaac Goldberg. [1917] New York: E. P. Dutton, 1920.

Banta, Martha. *Taylored Lives: Narrative Productions in the Age of Taylor, Veblen, and Ford*. Chicago: University of Chicago Press, 1993.

Baron, Ava, and Susan E. Klepp. "'If I Didn't Have My Sewing Machine . . .': Women and Sewing Machine Technology." In *A Needle, a Bobbin, a Strike: Women Needleworkers in America*, edited by Joan M. Jensen and Sue Davidson. Philadelphia: Temple University Press, 1984, 20–59.

Barret, Michelle. *The Politics of Truth from Marx to Foucault*. Stanford: Stanford University Press, 1991.

Becker, Linda Gail. "Invisible Threads: Skill and the Discursive Marginalization of the Garment Industry Workforce." Ph.D. dissertation, University of Washington, 1997.

Bender, Daniel. "From Sweatshop to Model Shop: Anti-Sweatshop Campaigns and Languages of Labor and Organizing, 1880–1934." Ph.D. dissertation, New York University, 2001.

Bender, Daniel, and Richard Greenwald, eds. *Sweatshop U.S.A.: Essays in Social History* New York: Routledge, 2004.

Biddle, George. *An American Artist's Story*. Boston: Little, Brown, 1939.

Bonacich, Edna, and Richard P. Appelbaum. *Behind the Label: Exploitation in the Los Angeles Apparel Industry*. Berkeley: University of California Press, 2000.

Boris, Eileen. *Home to Work: Motherhood and the Politics of Industrial Homework in the United States*. Cambridge: Cambridge University Press, 1994.

Boydston, Jeanne. *Home and Work: Housework, Wages, and the Ideology of Labor in the Early Republic*. New York: Oxford University Press, 1994.

Boyer, Paul S. *Urban Masses and Moral Order in America, 1820–1920*. Cambridge: Harvard University Press, 1967.

Brandes, Joseph. "From Sweatshop to Stability: Jewish Labor between Two World Wars." *YIVO Annual* 16 (1976): 1–149.

Bremner, Robert H. *From the Depths: The Discovery of Poverty in the United States*. New York: New York University Press, 1956.

Buhle, Mari Jo. *Women and American Socialism, 1870–1920*. Urbana: University of Illinois Press, 1981.

Buhle, Paul, and Edmund Sullivan. *Images of American Radicalism*. Hanover, Mass.: Christopher Publishing House, 1998.

Bulmer, Martin. "The Social Survey Movement." In *Pittsburgh Surveyed, Social Science and Social Reform in the Early Twentieth Century*, edited by Maurine W. Greenwald and Margo Anderson. Pittsburgh: University of Pittsburgh Press, 1996, 15–43.

Butler, Elizabeth Beardsley. *Women and the Trades: Pittsburgh, 1907–1908*. [1909] Pittsburgh: University of Pittsburgh Press, 1984.

Butterfield, Roger. "George Lippard and His Secret Brotherhood." *Pennsylvania Magazine of History and Biography* 79 (1955): 285–301.

Cahan, Abraham. *The Imported Bridegroom and Other Stories of the New York Ghetto*. [1898] New York: Dover, 1960.

Campbell, Helen. *Prisoners of Poverty*. [1887] Westport, Conn.: Greenwood, 1970.

Cappetti, Carla. *Writing Chicago: Modernism, Ethnography, and the Novel*. New York: Columbia University Press, 1993.

Carr, Albert Z. "Can an Executive Afford a Conscience?" *Harvard Business Review* (July–August 1970): 58–64.

Carroll, Peter. "Ralph Fasanella Limns the Story of the Workingman." *Smithsonian*, August 1993, 58–69.

Census of Manufactures, 1914. Vol. 2. Washington, D.C.: U.S. Government Printing Office, 1916.

Clark, Sue Ainslie, and Elizabeth Wyatt. *Making Both Ends Meet: The Income and Outlay of New York Working Girls*. New York: Macmillan, 1911.

———. "Working Girls' Budgets: The Shirtwaist Makers and Their Strike." *McClure's* 36 (November 1910): 70–86.

Cobble, Dorothy Sue. *Women and Unions: Forging a Partnership*. Ithaca, N.Y.: ILR Press, 1993.

Coe, Sue. "Porkopolis Series." *New Yorker*, November 7, 1994, 229–233.

"Comprehensive Factory Evaluation Report Prepared on Kukdong International Mexico."Verite, Inc., March 2001 (independent auditor's report).

Comstock, Sarah. "The Uprising of the Girls." *Collier's* (December 25, 1909): 14–16.

Corbin, Alain. *The Foul and the Fragrant: Odor and the French Social Imagination.* Cambridge: Harvard University Press, 1986.

Crane, Stephen. *Maggie: A Girl of the Streets.* Edited by Thomas Gullason. [1893] New York: W. W. Norton, 1974.

Davis, Allen F. *Spearheads for Reform: The Social Settlements and the Progressive Movement, 1890–1914.* New York: Oxford University Press, 1967.

Debord, Guy. *The Society of the Spectacle.* Translated by Donald Nicholson-Smith. New York: Zone Books, 1995.

Diner, Hasia R. *Lower East Side Memories: A Jewish Place in America.* Princeton: Princeton University Press, 2000.

Dreiser, Theodore. "The Transmigration of the Sweatshop." Puritan 7 (July 1898): 498–502.

Dubinsky, David, and A. H. Raskin. *David Dubinsky: A Life with Labor.* New York: Simon & Schuster, 1977.

Dublin, Thomas. *Women at Work: The Transformation of Work and Community in Lowell, Massachusetts, 1826–1860.* New York: Columbia University Press, 1979.

Dutcher, Elizabeth. "Budgets of the Triangle Fire Victims." *Life and Labor* (September 11, 1912): 265–267.

Eastman, Crystal. *Work Accidents and the Law.* New York: Russell Sage Foundation, 1910.

Eisler, Benita, ed. *The Lowell Offering: Writings by New England Mill Women, 1840–1845.* Philadelphia: J. B. Lippincott, 1975.

Enstad, Nan. *Ladies of Labor, Girls of Adventure: Working Women, Popular Culture, and Labor Politics at the Turn of the Twentieth Century.* New York: Columbia University Press, 1999.

"The Evils of the Sweat-Shop." *Outlook* 51 (May 4, 1895): 734–735.

Factory Investigating Report, State of New York. No. 20, March 1, 1912. Albany: J. B. Lyons, 1912.

Fawcett, Edgar. "The Woes of the New York Working-Girl." *Arena* 4 (1891): 26–35.

Federal Support for the Visual Arts: The New Deal and Now. Edited by Francis V. O'Connor. New York: New York Graphic Society, 1969.

Finnigan, David. "Our Cheap Clothes Are Their Horror Stories." *National Catholic Review* (Kansas City), December 29, 1995, 6.

Fitch, John. *The Steel Workers, 1907–1908.* New York: Russell Sage Foundation, 1910.

Foner, Philip S. *Women and the American Labor Movement from Colonial Times to the Eve of World War I.* New York: Free Press, 1979.

Fraser, Steven. *Labor Will Rule: Sidney Hillman and the Rise of American Labor.* New York: Basic Books, 1991.

Gandal, Keith. *The Virtues of the Vicious: Jacob Riis, Stephen Crane, and the Spectacle of the Slum.* New York: Oxford University Press, 1997.

Garment Industry Efforts to Address the Prevalence and Conditions of Sweatshops. Report to the Chairman, Subcommittee on Commerce, Consumer and Monetary

Affairs, Committee on Government Operations, House of Representatives. Washington, D.C.: United States General Accounting Office, 1994.

Glenn, Susan A. *Daughters of the Shtetl: Life and Labor in the Immigrant Generation.* Ithaca: Cornell University Press, 1990.

Godkin, E. L. "Our Sweating System." *Nation* 50 (June 19, 1890): 482.

Gold, Michael. *Jews without Money.* [1935] New York: Carroll and Graf, 1996.

Goldberg, Vicki, ed. *Lewis W. Hine: Children at Work.* Munich: Prestel, 1999.

Goldstein, Bruce, et al. "Enforcing Fair Labor Standards in the Modern American Sweatshop: Rediscovering the Statutory Definition of Employment." 46 *UCLA Law Review* 983 (April 1999): 1078–1102.

Greathead, Scott. "Making It Right: Sweatshops, Ethics, and Retailer Responsibility." *Chain Store Executive* 78, no. 5 (May 2002): 195.

Green, Nancy. *Ready-to-Wear and Ready-to-Work: A Century of Industry and Immigrants in Paris and New York.* Durham: Duke University Press, 1997.

Halem, Samantha C. "Slaves to Fashion: A Thirteenth Amendment Litigation Strategy to Abolish Sweatshops in the Garment Industry." *San Diego Law Review* 36 (1999): 397–453.

Hales, Peter Bacon. *Silver Cities: The Photography of American Urbanization, 1839–1915.* Philadelphia: Temple University Press, 1984.

Hamilton, Alice. *Exploring the Dangerous Trades.* Boston: Little, Brown, 1943.

Hapgood, Hutchins. *The Spirit of the Ghetto: Studies of the Jewish Quarter of New York.* [1902] Cambridge: Belknap Press of Harvard University Press, 1967.

Hapke, Laura. *Labor's Text: The Worker in American Fiction.* New Brunswick: Rutgers University Press, 2001.

Herod, Andrew. "The Spatiality of Labor Unionism." In *Organizing the Landscape: Geographical Perspectives on Labor Unionism,* edited by Andrew Herod. Minneapolis: University of Minnesota Press, 1998.

Hill, Herbert. "Guardians of the Sweatshops: The Trade Unions, Racism, and the Garment Industry." In *Puerto Rico and Puerto Ricans: Studies in History and Society,* edited by Adalberto Lopez and James Petra. New York: John Wiley and Sons, 1974, 353–416.

Hill, Joseph A. *Women in Gainful Occupations, 1870–1920.* Washington, D.C.: Government Printing Office, 1929.

Hillquit, Morris. *Loose Leaves from a Busy Life.* [1936] New York: Da Capo Press, 1971.

Hills, Patricia. *Urban Concern and Social Realism.* Boston: Boston University Art Gallery, n.d.

Ho, Laura, Catherine Powell, and Leti Volpp. "(Dis)Assembling Rights of Women Workers along the Global Assembly Line: Human Rights and the Garment Industry." *Harvard Civil Rights–Civil Liberties Review* 31 (Summer 1996): 384–414.

Hoberman, J. "Der Ershter Talkies: 'Uncle Moses' and the Coming of the Yiddish Sound Film." *Film Comment* 27, no. 6 (November–December 1991), 32–40.

Holmes, Stanley. "Free Speech or False Advertising?" *Business Week,* April 28, 2003, 69.

Hood, Thomas. "The Song of the Shirt." In *Strong-Minded Women and Other Lost Voices from Nineteenth-Century England,* edited by Janet Horowitz Murray. New York: Pantheon, 1982, 351.

Howe, Irving: *World of Our Fathers.* New York: Simon & Schuster, 1976.

Husband, Julie. "'The White Slave of the North': Lowell Mill Women and the Re-production of 'Free' Labor." *Legacy* 16, no. 1 (1999): 11–21.

Joselit, Jenna Weissman. "Telling Tales: Or, How a Slum Became a Shrine." *Jewish Social Studies* 2, no. 2 (Winter 1996): 54–63.

Kahle, Lynn R., David M. Boush, and Mark Phelps. "Good Morning, Vietnam: An Ethical Analysis of Nike Activities in Southeast Asia." *Sport Marketing Quarterly* 9, no. 1 (2000): 43–52.

Karp, Ivan. "Culture and Representation." In *Exhibiting Cultures: The Poetics and Politics of Museum Displays,* edited by Ivan Karp and Steven D. Lavine. Washington, D.C.: Smithsonian Institution Press, 1991.

Katz, Daniel. "A Union of Many Cultures: Yiddish Socialism and Industrial Organization in the ILGWU, 1913–1941." Ph.D. dissertation, Rutgers University, 2003.

Kazin, Alfred. *A Walker in the City.* [1946] New York: Harvest Press, 1979.

Keeping New York in Fashion: A Strategic Plan for the Future of the New York Fashion Industry. New York: Kurt Salmon Associates/Garment Industry Development Corporation, 1992.

Kelley, Florence. "The Sweating-System." In *Hull-House Maps and Papers.* [1895] New York: Arno Press/New York Times, 1970, 27–45.

Kellogg, Paul. "Monongah." *Charities and the Commons* 19 (January 1908): 1,313–1,328.

———. *Wage-Earning Pittsburgh.* New York: Russell Sage Foundation, 1914.

Kessler-Harris, Alice. *Out to Work: A History of Wage-Earning Women in the United States.* New York: Oxford University Press, 1982.

Kessner, Thomas. *The Golden Door: Italian and Jewish Immigrant Mobility in New York City, 1880–1915.* New York: Oxford University Press, 1977.

Kleeblatt, Norman, and Susan Chevlowe, eds. *Painting a Place in America: Jewish Artists in New York, 1900–1945.* New York: Jewish Museum, 1991.

Kleinberg, S. J. *The Shadow of the Mills: Working-Class Families in Pittsburgh, 1870–1907.* Pittsburgh: University of Pittsburgh Press, 1989.

Kraut, Alan M. *Silent Travelers: Germs, Genes, and the "Immigrant Menace."* New York: Basic Books, 1994.

Lee, Louise, and Aaron Bernstein. "Who Says Student Protests Don't Matter?" *Business Week,* June 12, 2000, 94–95.

Levin, Rebekah, and Robert Ginsburg. *Sweatshops in Chicago: Conditions in Low-Income and Immigrant Communities, A Survey, February 16, 2000.* Chicago: Sweatshop Working Group of Chicago, 2000.

Levine, Louis. *The Women's Garment Workers: A History of the International Ladies' Garment Workers Union.* New York: B.W. Huebsch, 1924.

Liebhold, Peter, and Harry R. Rubenstein, eds. *Between a Rock and a Hard Place: A History of American Sweatshops, 1820 to the Present.* Los Angeles: UCLA Asian American Studies Center, 1999.

———. "History of Sweatshops." In *Between a Rock and a Hard Place.* Los Angeles: UCLA Asian American Studies Center, 1999, 1–15.

"The Life Story of a Polish Sweatshop Girl." In *Life Stories of Undistinguished Americans.* Edited by Hamilton Holt, introduction by Werner Sollors. 2nd ed. New York: Routledge, 1990, 21–28.

Lippard, George. *The Nazarene*. Philadelphia: n.p., 1846.

Louie, Miriam Ching Yoon. *Sweatshop Warriors: Immigrant Women Workers Take on the Global Factory*. Boston: South End Press, 2001.

Lozowick, Louis. *William Gropper*. Philadelphia: Art Alliance Press, 1983.

MacLean, Annie Marion. "The Sweat-Shop in Summer." *American Journal of Sociology* 9, no. 3 (November 1903): 289–309.

———. *Wage-Earning Women*. New York: Macmillan, 1910.

Maffi, Mario. *Gateway to Ethnicity: Ethnic Cultures on New York's Lower East Side*. New York: New York University Press, 1995.

Malkiel, Theresa S. *The Diary of a Shirtwaist Striker*. [1910] Ithaca, N.Y.: ILR Press, 1990.

Mathews, Cornelius. *The Career of Puffer Hopkins*. [1842] New York: Garrett, 1970.

McClymer, John F. "The Pittsburgh Survey, 1907–1908: Forging an Ideology in the Steel District." *Pennsylvania History* 41 (April 1974): 169–188.

McEvoy, Arthur F. "The Triangle Shirtwaist Factory Fire of 1911: Social Change, Industrial Accidents, and the Evolution of Common-Sense Causality." *Law and Social Inquiry* 20, no. 2 (Spring 1995): 625–651.

Mergen, Bernard. "'Another Great Prize': The Jewish Labor Movement in the Context of American Labor History." *YIVO Annual of Jewish Social Science* 16 (1975–1976): 394–423.

Montgomery, David. *The Fall of the House of Labor: The Workplace, the State, and American Labor Activism, 1865–1925*. Cambridge: Cambridge University Press, 1983.

Naduris-Weissman, Eli. "Confronting the Sweatshop Industry: Student-Labor Activism Advances." *Against the Current* n.s. 14, no. 5 (1999): 11–13.

Nesbitt, Lois E. "Sue Coe." *Artforum* (January 1990): 136–137.

New York in Fashion: A Strategic Plan for the Future of the New York Fashion Industry. New York: Kurt Salmon Associates, 1992.

New York State, Factory Investigating Commission, Fourth Report, Senate doc. 43, vols., 1 and 2. Albany: J. B. Lyons, 1915.

Nochlin, Linda. *Representing Women*. New York: Thames and Hudson, 1999.

Odencrantz, Louise C. *Italian Women in Industry: A Study of Conditions in New York City*. New York: Russell Sage Foundation, 1913.

Orleck, Annelise. *Common Sense and a Little Fire: Women and Working-Class Politics in the United States, 1900–1965*. Chapel Hill: University of North Carolina Press, 1995.

Park, Marlene, and Gerald Markowitz. *Democratic Vistas: Post Offices and Public Art in the New Deal*. Philadelphia: Temple University Press, 1984.

Park, Robert E. "The City as a Social Laboratory." In *Chicago: An Experiment in Social Science Research*, edited by T. V. White and L. D. Smith. Chicago: University of Chicago Press, 1929, 1–19.

———. "Life History." *American Journal of Sociology* 79, no. 2 (September 1973): 243–260.

Peiss, Kathy. *Cheap Amusements: Working Women and Leisure in Turn-of-the-Century New York*. Philadelphia: Temple University Press, 1986.

Perlman, Bennard B. *Painters of the Ashcan School: The Immortal Eight*. New York: Dover, 1988.

Petras, Elizabeth McLean. "The Shirt on Your Back: Immigrant Workers and the Reorganization of the Garment Industry." *Social Justice* 19 (1992): 76–114.

Phelps, Elizabeth Stuart. "Opening Address by Miss Phelps." *Workingman's Journal* 6 (May 1869): 1.

Platt, Susan Noyes. "The Jersey Homesteads Mural: Ben Shahn, Bernarda Bryson, and History Painting in the 1930s." In *Redefining American History Painting,* edited by Patricia Mullan Burnham and Lucretia H. Giese (Cambridge: Cambridge University Press, 1995, 294–309.

Pohl, Frances K. *In the Eye of the Storm: An Art of Conscience, 1930–1970.* San Francisco: Pomegranate Art Books, 1995.

Portelli, Alessandro. *The Death of Luigi Trastulli and Other Essays.* Albany: State University of New York Press, 1990.

Prendergast, Christopher. *Paris and the Nineteenth Century.* Oxford: Blackwell, 1992.

Recent Fine Prints: Federal Art Gallery. New York: FAP/WPA, 1937.

Reports of the Industrial Commission on Immigration and on Education. Vol. 15. Washington: Government Printing Office, 1901.

Rifkin, Adrian. *Street Noises: Parisian Pleasure, 1900–1940.* Manchester: Manchester University Press, 1993.

Riis, Jacob. *How the Other Half Lives: Studies among the Tenements of New York.* [1890; revised 1902]. New York: Dover, 1971.

———. *Out of Mulberry Street.* [1898] Upper Saddle River, N.J.: Gregg Press, 1970.

Rosenfeld, Morris. *Songs from the Ghetto.* [1898] Upper Saddle River, N.J.: Gregg Press, 1970.

Ross, Andrew, ed. *No Sweat: Fashion, Free Trade, and the Rights of Garment Workers.* New York: Verso, 1997.

Salgado, Sebastiao. *Workers: An Archaeology of the Industrial Age.* New York: Aperture, 1995.

Sanders, Ronald. *The Downtown Jews: Portraits of an Immigrant Generation.* New York: Dover, 1987.

Sanger, William. *The History of Prostitution.* [1858] New York: Medical Publishing Company, 1898.

Schneiderman, Rose. "A Capmaker's Story." *Independent* 58 (April 27, 1905): 935–938.

Scott, Miriam. "The Spirit of the Girl Strikers." *Outlook* 94 (February 19, 1909): 394–395.

Second Report of the Factory Investigating Commission. State of New York. Vol. 2. Albany: J. B. Lyons, 1913.

Seidman, Joel. *The Needle Trades.* New York: Farrar and Rinehart, 1942.

Sekula, Alan. "Dismantling Modernism: Reinventing Documentary (Notes on the Politics of Representation)." *Massachusetts Review* 19 (Winter 1978): 859–883.

Seller, Maxine Schwartz. "The Uprising of the Twenty Thousand: Sex, Class, and Ethnicity in the Shirtwaist Makers' Strike of 1909." In *"Struggle a Hard Battle": Essays on Working-Class Immigrants,* edited by Dirk Hoerder. DeKalb: Northern Illinois University Press, 1986, 254–279.

Seltzer, Mark. *Bodies and Machines.* New York: Routledge, 1992.

Soyer, Moses, and Robert W. Gill. *Painting the Human Figure.* New York: Watson/Gaptill, 1964.

Spewack, Bella Cohen. *Streets: A Memoir of the Lower East Side.* New York: Feminist Press, 1995.

Stange, Maren. *Symbols of Ideal Life: Social Documentary Photography in America, 1890–1950.* Cambridge: Cambridge University Press, 1989.

Stansell, Christine. *City of Women: Sex and Class in New York.* New York: Alfred A. Knopf, 1986.

Stein, Leon, ed. *Out of the Sweatshop: The Struggle for Industrial Democracy.* [1977] Ithaca: ILR/Cornell University Press, 2002.

Sugarman, Tracy. "Echoes on Paper: Reflections on My Garment Workers Sketchbook, 1950." *Labor's Heritage* (Winter 1994): 22–25.

Sullivan, James W. *Tenement Tales of New York.* New York: Henry Holt, 1895.

Sumner, Helen L. *Report on the Condition of Women and Child Wage-Earners in the United States.* Vol. 9. Washington, D.C.: Government Printing Office, 1910.

Tax, Meredith. *The Rising of the Women: Feminist Solidarity and Class Conflict, 1890–1917.* New York: Monthly Review Press, 1980.

Taylor, R. B. *Sweatshops in the Sun: Child Labor on the Farm.* Boston: Beacon, 1973.

Thomas, William Isaac. *The Unadjusted Girl.* [1923] Montclair, N.J.: Paterson Smith, 1969.

Todd, Ellen Wiley. *The "New Woman" Revisited: Painting and Gender Politics on Fourteenth Street.* Berkeley: University of California Press, 1993.

Trachtenberg, Alan. *Reading American Photographs: Images as History, Mathew Brady to Walker Evans.* New York: Hill and Wang, 1989.

United States Department of Labor, *Garment Enforcement Report, October 1996–December 1996.* Washington, D.C.: U.S. Government Printing Office, 1997.

Vairnanktarakis, George, and Janice Kim Winch. "Probability in the Engineering and Information Sciences." *Bobbin* 9, no. 3 (September 1998): 457–473.

Van Kleeck, Mary. *The Artificial Flower Makers.* New York: Russell Sage Foundation, 1913.

———. "Women and Children Who Make Men's Clothes." *Survey* (April 1, 1911): 65–69.

Varney, Pamela, ed. *The Sweatshop Quandary: Corporate Responsibility on the Global Frontier.* Washington, D.C.: Investor Responsibility Research Center, 1998.

Vecoli, Rudolph. "Pane e Giustizia." *La Parola del Popolo* 26 (September/October 1976): 55–61.

Veiller, Lawrence. "The Tenement House Exhibition." *Charities and the Commons* 4 (February 17, 1900): 1–11.

Vergara, Camilo Jose. *The New American Ghetto.* New Brunswick: Rutgers University Press, 1995.

Wagner-Martin, Linda. *Telling Women's Lives: The New Biography.* New Brunswick: Rutgers University Press, 1994.

Watson, Patrick. *Fasanella's City: The Paintings of Ralph Fasanella, with the Story of His Life and Art.* New York: Ballantine Books, 1973.

White, Henry. "Conditions Transformed by Label." *ILGWU Fourth Annual Convention,* commemorative/souvenir booklet, Cleveland, Ohio, June 1, 1903.

Willet, Mabel Hurd. *The Employment of Women in the Clothing Trade.* New York: Columbia University Press, 1902.

Williams, Catharine. *Fall River: An Authentic Narrative.* Edited by Patricia Caldwell. New York: Oxford University Press, 1993.

Williams, Marilyn T. *Washing "the Great Unwashed": Public Baths in Urban America, 1840–1920.* Columbus: Ohio State University Press, 1991.

Wilson, Elizabeth. *The Sphinx in the City: Urban Life, the Control of Disorder, and Women.* Berkeley: University of California Press, 1991.

Wirth, Louis. *The Ghetto.* [1928] Chicago: University of Chicago Press, 1997.

———. *Urbanism as a Way of Life.* Indianapolis: Bobbs-Merrill, 1969.

Working Women in Large Cities. Washington, D.C.: Government Printing Office, 1889.

Wright, Carroll D. *The Slums of Baltimore, Chicago, New York, and Philadelphia.* [1894] New York: Arno Press/New York Times, 1970.

Wyckoff, Walter A. *The Workers: An Experiment in Reality.* Vol. 1, *The West.* New York: Charles Scribner's Sons, 1898.

Yew, Elizabeth. "Medical Inspection of Immigrants at Ellis Island, 1891–1924." *Bulletin of the New York Academy of Medicine* 56 (June 1980): 488–510.

Yezierska, Anzia. *All I Could Never Be.* New York: Brewer, Warren, & Putnam, 1932.

———. *Hungry Hearts and Other Stories.* [1920] New York: Persea Books, 1985.

Zengerle, Jason. "Exhibiting Bias." *New Republic* 217, no. 16 (October 16, 1997): 18–20.

Index

U.S. firms abroad, 137; and global industry, 126, 133

U.S. history, and sweatshop history, 126–127

U.S. Holocaust Museum, Washington, DC, 84, 175n33

U.S. Supreme Court, 139

United Steelworkers of America (USW), 146

United Students Against Sweatshops (USAS), 144, 148, 152

University of California at Berkeley, 146; Institute of Industrial Relations, 151

University of California at Los Angeles, Asian American Studies Center, 125

University of Chicago, 143

University of Texas, Lozano Long Institute of Latin American Studies, 152

"Uprising of the 20,000," 55

upward mobility, 6–7, 11, 81

USW. *See* United Steelworkers of America

Van Eyck, Jan, *Medici St. Jerome,* 171n52

Van Kleeck, Mary, 164n10; *The Artificial Flower Makers,* 47

Vecoli, Rudolf, 172n12

Vergara, Camilo Jose, *New American Ghetto,* 103

Verite Evaluators, 137

Vietnam, 138

Vietnam War, 91

visual arts, 71, 90. *See also* films; paintings; photographs

Vuillard, Edouard, 78

Wage-Earning Pittsburgh, 43, 44

Wallace, Mike, 12

Waters, Tim, 146, 147

Web sites, 130, 142, 144, 148, 151, 179n16

Wenger, Beth, 4, 12

White, George, 111

white slavery, 159n4

Williams, Catharine, 160n11

Wirth, Louis, 56, 168n72; *The Ghetto,* 58

women: health of, in the workplace, 31; images of, 77–79; organizing, 172n4; and resistance, 31; roles of, 37, 39; and sewing work, 19–20; in strikes, 50, 162–163n60; in sweatshops, 31–33; as workers, 49–56, 59, 89, 160n13, 163n62, 167n54; writers, 32, 163n69

Women's Trade Union League, 148

Wong, Martin, 106

Worker Rights Consortium (WRC), 135, 144, 146

workers, 21; as authors, 34; bodies of, 28; erased, 134; in factories, 132; in fiction, 35; homeless, 22, 160n17; and machines, 49; management of, 132; public image, 137; as service providers, 142; voices of 121, 149–150

Workers' Alliance, 93

Workers for Freedom, 140

working class, 95–97; and art, 90–108; and popular culture, 140–143; portraits of, 73–87; solidarity, 7–8

"working-class chic," 11

working conditions, 50, 123, 149

working poor, 104, 107

workplace accidents. *See* accidents in the workplace

workshops, academic, 146

Works Progress Administration. *See* WPA

World Trade Organization (WTO), 133

WPA, 9, 66, 71, 76, 169n5; artists, 10, 70–72, 83, 87, 106; mural art, 79, 81

WRC. *See* Worker Rights
   Consortium
Wright, Carroll D., 26, 40

Yale University, 152
Yezierska, Anzia, 59–61, 168nn71, 76;
   All I Could Never Be, 9, 60–61;
   "Hunger," 60; "Soap and Water," 60

Yiddish Art Theater, 63
Yiddish literature, 62; theater and film,
   63
The Young Savages [film], 95

Znaniecki, Florian, 56; and W. I.
   Thomas, *The Polish Peasant in
   Europe and America,* 60

About the Author

Laura Hapke has taught at Queens College, Hunter College, and Pace University in New York. She is the author of numerous books and articles on labor, class, and culture. Her most recent works include *Labor's Text: The Worker in American Fiction* and *Daughters of the Great Depression: Women, Work, and Fiction in the American 1930s.*